Ethnographies of Collaborative Economies across Europe

Understanding Sharing and Caring

Edited by
Penny Travlou and Luigina Ciolfi

]u[

cost
EUROPEAN COOPERATION
IN SCIENCE & TECHNOLOGY

Funded by the Horizon 2020 Framework Programme
of the European Union

Published by
Ubiquity Press Ltd.
Unit 322–323
Whitechapel Technology Centre
75 Whitechapel Road
London E1 1DU
www.ubiquitypress.com

Text © the authors 2022

First published 2022

Cover design by Amber Dalgleish
Cover image by Penny Travlou

Print and digital versions typeset by Siliconchips Services Ltd.

ISBN (Paperback): 978-1-914481-24-6
ISBN (PDF): 978-1-914481-25-3
ISBN (EPUB): 978-1-914481-26-0
ISBN (Mobi): 978-1-914481-27-7

DOI: https://doi.org/10.5334/bct

The full text of this book has been peer-reviewed to ensure high academic
standards. For full review policies, see http://www.ubiquitypress.com/

Suggested citation:
Travlou, P. and Ciolfi, L. (eds.) 2022. *Ethnographies of Collaborative Economies
across Europe: Understanding Sharing and Caring.* London: Ubiquity Press.
DOI: https://doi.org/10.5334/bct. License: CC BY-NC-ND

To read the free, open access version of this book
online, visit https://doi.org/10.5334/bct or scan
this QR code with your mobile device:

Contents

Acknowledgements

This publication is based upon work from the COST Action *"From Sharing to Caring: Examining Socio-Technical of the Collaborative Economy"* (sharingandcaring.eu), supported by COST (European Cooperation in Science and Technology). COST is a funding agency for research and innovation networks. COST Actions help connect research initiatives across Europe and enable scientists to grow their ideas by sharing them with their peers. This boosts their research, career and innovation. www.cost.eu

Contributors

Chiara Bassetti is Senior Assistant Professor of Qualitative Methods at the Department of Sociology and Social Research of the University of Trento, and a researcher at the Institute of Cognitive Sciences and Technologies of the Italian National Research Council (CNR). An ethnographer and ethnomethodologist, her main research focus rests on social interaction, cultural phenomena and collaborative practices. The body and performing arts are areas of special interest. Further research concerns grassroots initiatives and socio-economic innovation across the online and the offline dimensions. Dr. Bassetti is Co-Editor in Chief of Etnografia e Ricerca Qualitativa – the Italian journal of Ethnography and Qualitative Research.

Anikó Bernát is a researcher at TARKI Social Research Institute since 2002 in Hungary. She has specialized in migration and social inclusion and areas related to the development of the situation of vulnerable groups (such as the Roma, migrants and refugees, disabled people and homeless people) and solidarity movements and civil philanthropic actions targeting these groups. She has contributed to EU research targeting various vulnerable groups and working currently as the Senior Roma Expert of the cross-country survey project "*FRA Roma 2020 Survey*" of the Fundamental Rights Agency of the EU (2020–2021). She is a working group leader of the research project: "*R-HOME: Roma: Housing, Opportunities, Mobilisation and Empowerment*", funded by the Rights Equality and Citizenship Programme (REC), DG Justice (EC). She is a working group co-leader in the COST Action '*International Ethnic and*

Immigrant Minorities' Survey Data Network' (ETHMIGSURVEYDATA, CA16111). Recently she led the cross-country research project "*Migration patterns and attitudes towards migratory movements: The case of Hungary, Poland, Lithuania and Bulgaria*" funded by Friedrich Ebert Stiftung (2018–2020) and the evaluation of *Asia-Europe Migration Project* commissioned by the Asia-Europe Foundation (Singapore, 2016).

Anita Čeh Časni is Associate Professor and the Vice Head of the Department of Statistics, Faculty of Economics and Business, University of Zagreb and a Secretary of the Croatian Statistical Association. Her research interests include applied statistical methods in tourism and macroeconomics, panel data analysis, housing economics, sustainability and educational statistics. She has been awarded for both her scientific and teaching work. Additionally, she is a researcher on 3 COST actions, one ERASMUS+ project and one scientific project financed by the Croatian Scientific Foundation. She recently became a Vice director of the Institute for Euro-Asian Studies thus promoting international cooperation between Faculty of Economics and Business and Euro-Asian countries.

Samantha Cenere is an urban geographer and holds a PhD in Urban and Regional Development. She is currently Postdoctoral researcher in the Inter-university Department of Regional and Urban Studies and Planning at the Polytechnic University of Turin, Italy, working on the Horizon 2020 project SMARTDEST. Her PhD research investigated the rising of Makers and Fablabs as examples of the socio-spatial reconfiguration of work and production brought about in urban contexts by the spreading of collaborative practices and innovative digital technologies.

Luigina Ciolfi is Professor of Human-Computer Interaction in the School of Applied Psychology at University College Cork (Ireland). She holds a Ph.D. from the University of Limerick and a Laurea (summa cum laude), from the University of Siena, both specialising in Human-Computer Interaction. Professor Ciolfi researches human practices and experiences of digital technologies in everyday settings, with a focus on collaboration, participation and placemaking. Her work connects computing, social sciences and design, and aims to understand and design digital technologies in a thoughtful and participatory way. Professor Ciolfi has published extensively in HCI, CSCW (Computer-Supported Cooperative Work) and Interaction Design. She has authored over 100 publications, including two monographs, and has edited several books and collections. She is an Associate Editor of the CSCW Journal, as well as a scientific referee for many conferences and journals in her field.

Kosjenka Dumančić is Associate Professor of Commercial Law, Vice-Dean for international relations and projects, and the Head of Institute for Euro-Asian Studies at the University of Zagreb, Faculty of Economics and Business. Her research interests are in the fields of European company law, European internal market law, and collaborative economy. Currently, she is actively involved in an EU-funded Erasmus+ COLECO Project which aims to examine the impacts of the collaborative economy in Europe, focusing on peer-to-peer accommodation platforms and participating in the EU project UNIC – an alliance of eight European universities educating trough teaching, research and community engagement, towards inclusive societies.

Dicte Frost is exploring the parallel trajectories of ethnographic research and on-ground sustainability activism through project and event coordination. Holding a BA in European Studies from University of Southern Denmark, she has been conducting fieldwork in the area of ecovilllages, economics and legal structures. She is interested in allowing fluidity between the world of academia and that of practice and immersion. She is especially occupied with exploring various formats to communicate her research and facilitate a sustainable transition. She has been speaking at various conferences, creating infographics and teaching material, arranging a festival, shaping video content, publishing academic articles and recently informing a podcast.

Justin Larner is an interdisciplinary researcher and consultant, whose work spans the domains of management, computing and design. Specialising in the design of networked organisational and business models to achieve more than economic gain, his approach involves listening to and facilitating sensemaking with entrepreneurs and their stakeholders. Justin's current research builds on a varied career, including community development, management consultancy and voluntary sector development.

Ann Light is Professor of Design and Creative Technology, University of Sussex, UK, and Professor of Interaction Design, Social Change and Sustainability, Malmo University, Sweden. She is a qualitative researcher and interaction theorist, specializing in participatory design, human-computer interaction and collaborative future-making. She leads a research node on the European Union *Creative Practices for Transformational Futures* project and her next book is called 'Designs to Reshape Humanity: Integrity and Cunning in the Anthropocene'.

Catherine Lyons is a freelance consultant and business developer to the third sector, with emphasis on social justice in the circular economy. She has a specialist interest in digital supply chains, following a career in international publishing and data services. Catherine is currently undertaking a Masters in Public Administration at Queen Margaret University and holds a BA from Wadham College, Oxford.

Cristina Miguel is Senior Lecturer in Digital Communication at the University of Gothenburg, Sweden. She received her PhD in Media and Communications from the University of Leeds, UK. Her research interests include digital culture (networked intimacy, online communities, dating apps, and online privacy) and digital economy (sharing economy, the political economy of social media, and influencer marketing). She has published her research in high-ranked peer-reviewed academic journals, including the *International Journal of Hospitality Management, Social Media+ Society,* and *Convergence.*

Olga Orlić is an anthropologist (University of Zagreb). As a curator at the Ethnographic Museum of Istria (2001–2006) she received the annual award of the Croatian Ethnological Society for the best ethnographic exhibition "Weavers in Istria" (2004). Since 2006 she has been employed at the Institute for Anthropological Research in Zagreb. She has collaborated on several national and international projects. She participated in the COST action "From Sharing to Caring: Examining Socio-Technical Aspects of the Collaborative Economy" and was the Principal Investigator in two national programs of popularization of science. Since 2020 she is leading the research project "Solidarity Economy in Croatia: An Anthropological Perspective" (SOLIDARan), funded by the Croatian Science Foundation. She is a member of the editorial boards of the Ethnological Forum and Ethnological Researches journals.

Dimitris Pettas is a Marie Skłodowska-Curie Postdoctoral Fellow at the Institute of Urban and Regional Planning, Technical University of Berlin (TUB). He holds a PhD from the National Technical University of Athens (School of Architecture). He has worked as a postdoctoral researcher at the Regional Development Institute (Panteion University), the National Technical University of Athens and the Research Centre for the Humanities. He has also been a lecturer in the Social and Solidarity Economy postgraduate programme at the Hellenic Open University. His research interests include the study of: the social production of public space, the development of platform economy and its impact on urban environment, the role of power relations and agency in modes of urban governance, the emergence and broader transformative potentialities of grassroots collaborative and social/ solidarity economy initiatives, the exploration and comparative analysis of epistemological and ontological approaches concerning the production of urban environment and urban life.

Alena Rýparová is a PhD candidate in Social Geography and Regional Development at the Faculty of Science, Masaryk University. She is also part of the research project "Spaces of Quiet Sustainability: Self-provisioning and Sharing". Her doctoral and project research are both focused on non-profit sharing among people unrelated by kinship or friendship. She is interested in how sharing networks emerge and work from the point of view of relational spatiality.

Maria Cristina Sciannamblo is research fellow at Sapienza University of Rome, Department of Communication and Social Research. In the past four years, she has been working in two H2020 projects – PIE News/Commonfare and Grassroot Wavelenghts – aimed at addressing social challenges through the participatory design of digital technologies. Her research sits at the intersection of Science and Technology Studies, Communication Studies, and Participatory Design.

Maurizio Teli is Associate Professor in the Department of Planning at the University of Aalborg, Denmark. He holds a PhD in Sociology and Social Research and has always worked in interdisciplinary contexts focusing on the political dimensions of the production and use of digital technologies. He has developed an ethnographic sensibility, now extended to include digital methods, for the study of software development and for the participatory design of digital technologies. He has worked in or coordinated a few EU funded projects. He is now focusing on the design of digital technologies nurturing the common, in particular as Research and Innovation Coordinator of the PIE News/Commonfare H2020 project and as part of the Grassroots Radio project.

Penny Travlou is Senior Lecturer in Cultural Geography and Theory (Edinburgh School of Architecture & Landscape Architecture, University of Edinburgh). Her research focuses on spatial justice, the commons, collaborative practices, emerging networks and ethnography. She has been involved in international research projects funded by the EU and UK Research Councils. Since 2011, she has been doing ethnographic research on collaborative practices in emerging networks (e.g. digital art practitioners, collaborative economy initiatives, translocal migrants and refugees). Alongside her academic work, Penny is an activist on social justice and the commons. She has been actively involved in a number of grassroots and self-organised initiatives on housing and refugees' rights. She is Co-Director of the *Feminist Autonomous Centre for Research* in Athens, a non-profit independent research organisation that focuses on feminist and queer studies, participatory education and activism.

Rodrigo Perez-Vega is Senior Lecturer in Digital Marketing and Analytics at Kent Business School at the University of Kent, UK. His research interests are in digital marketing, social media and consumer behaviour in online environments, the sharing economy, and applications of AI in Marketing. He has published his work in *Tourism Management, The Journal of Business Research, The Service Industries Journal and Marketing Review*. He is also the co-author of the book "Essentials of Digital Marketing". Rodrigo has also been invited to speak at practitioners' conferences such as the SME Summit and Social Media Summit.

Vera Vidal is a Ph.D. candidate in the Dimmons-Internet Interdisciplinary Institute research group, at the Open University of Catalonia (Spain). She researches the commons-oriented sharing economy and platform cooperatives in Catalonia.

Competing interests

'The editors declare that they have no competing interests in publishing this book.'

Introduction: Ethnographies of Collaborative Economies across Europe

Penny Travlou
University of Edinburgh, UK
Luigina Ciolfi
University College Cork, Ireland

Introduction

The terms "sharing economy" and "collaborative economy" have been commonly used in recent years to refer to a proliferation of initiatives, business models and forms of work: from the far-reaching corporate digital platforms that facilitate the organisation of cooperative practices, to local, regional and community-led collaborative initiatives in housing, tourism, transport, social enterprise, culture, the arts, etc. (European Commission 2016; Avram et al. 2017). As its name implies, the collaborative economy is considered as "a new socio-economic model based on collaboration, access to, and the socialization of, value production, facilitated by digital technologies" (Arcidiacono, Gardini and Pais 2018: 276). The concept is used to refer to a wide variety of very diverse practices from time banks and urban gardens, to global digital platforms and co-working spaces (Avram et al. 2017). At the same time, the

How to cite this book chapter:
Travlou, P. and Ciolfi, L. 2022. Introduction: Ethnographies of Collaborative Economies across Europe. In: Travlou, P. and Ciolfi, L. (eds.) *Ethnographies of Collaborative Economies across Europe: Understanding Sharing and Caring.* Pp. 1–9. London: Ubiquity Press. DOI: https://doi.org/10.5334/bct.a. License: CC BY-NC-ND

controversial nature of the "collaborative economy" and its applications has triggered many debates (see Schor 2015; Slee 2016). Some authors embrace the collaborative economy as a practice that opens the possibility for a "more just and equitable society based on the logic of peer-to-peer collaboration" (del Moral-Espin and Fernandez-Garcia 2018: 401). Others take a much more critical view, arguing that the collaborative economy should be understood as capitalism's last stand" (del Moral-Espin and Fernandez-Garcia 2018: 401; see also Martin 2016). This controversy reveals the complex, changing and multifaceted nature of the collaborative economy and of its multiple impacts on local and regional economies and societies (Cheng, 2016), and raises questions regarding its governance (Teli and Bassetti 2021). As a subject of academic research, the collaborative economy has received much attention in recent years by scholars from diverse disciplines who have explored its practices, cultures, lived experiences, and socio-technical systems. Empirical investigations, including case studies and related data sets, document the realities, impacts and implications of the collaborative economy, and develop methodological and epistemological insights into its context. This book is a further contribution to the in-depth qualitative understanding of the collaborative economy phenomenon. It stems from a unique effort to capture the complexities of the collaborative economy in Europe through ethnographic research. The collaborative economy includes a broad range of economic practices, subjectable to the full gamut of epistemological and empirical approaches, including large-scale and/or quantitative studies (see, for example, Akande et al. 2020, and Sanna and Michelini 2021). This notwithstanding, we argue for the need for, and relevance of, adopting a qualitative stance to document and understand experiences, practices, and models of collaborative economy that involve individuals, groups, and communities. As the phenomena that can be identified as instances of collaborative economy diversify and span various platforms, media, organisations, and communities, the ethnographic approaches that explore these complex phenomena must unavoidably evolve. At the same time, it is crucial to document, share, and reflect upon the practices of ethnographic inquiry that examine collaborative economies, and the practices of finding dissemination. The ethnographies of collaborative economies provide rich accounts that contribute to the painting of a complex landscape that spans several countries and regions, and diverse political, cultural, and organisational backdrops. Due to this diversity, the reflection on the role of ethnographic researchers, and on their stance and outlook, are of paramount interest across the disciplines involved in collaborative economy research.

This book emerges from a long-term, multinational, cross-European collaboration between researchers from various disciplines (e.g., sociology, anthropology, geography, business studies, law, computing, information systems), career stages, and epistemological backgrounds, brought together by a shared research interest in the collaborative economy. The material and intellectual context of the book was provided by the COST Action "*From Sharing to Caring: Examining the Socio-Technical Aspects of the Collaborative Economy*" (CA16121, 2016), a European initiative supported by COST – European Cooperation in Science and Technology, which lasted for four years (2017–2021). This COST Action (henceforth referred to as "*Sharing & Caring*") aimed at building and growing

> a network of actors (including scholars, practitioners, communities and policy makers) focusing on the development of collaborative economy models and platforms and on social and technological implications of the collaborative economy through a practice-focused approach (See https://sharingandcaring.eu).

Sharing & Caring was joined by researchers and practitioners from various academic and non-profit institutions based in over thirty countries. The research collaborators studied the sociotechnical systems and human practices involved in the complex landscape of the collaborative economy in Europe, and compared between, and reflected upon, local, regional, national, and international initiatives. In regular meetings and workshops, the participating researchers discussed elements of the current discourse on the collaborative economy, worked together on the deliverables of the Action (reports, white papers, case studies, and toolkits), and formulated a European agenda of research on the socio-technical aspects of the collaborative economy, including the design of future technological platforms, the technical infrastructure, and the legal, ethical, and financial implications. The Action participants thus articulated a European research perspective on the collaborative economy, based on the EU values of social innovation and in line with the Europe 2020 strategic objective of achieving a smart, sustainable, and inclusive economy. One of the four *Sharing & Caring* working groups, WG1, aimed to systematically analyse practices of digitally-mediated collaborative economy through a series of in-depth ethnographic studies that contributed "*insights on the practices involved and on the forms community aggregates around these practices*" (see https://sharingandcaring.eu/). This research underpinned the development of a multifaceted perspective on sharing and caring practices, and informed the conceptual framework for interpreting and classifying different instances of collaborative economy.

The WG1 produced an online repository of ethnographic case studies and initiated a directory of people involved in various aspects of the European collaborative economy. The goal was to provide a systematic and comprehensive theoretical perspective that aligns the collected findings and can serve as a taxonomy and guide for further research. Within *Sharing & Caring*, ethnographic research was recognised as pivotal for understanding and unpacking the complexity of models and patterns of the collaborative economy. For this purpose, the WG1 team also developed an ethnographic methodological toolkit that can be used by researchers within and beyond the COST Action to provide a descriptive mapping of the collaborative economy landscape. In addition, this toolkit provides a broad set of research directions and thematic categories that could inform future empirical research. The themes included in the toolkit are not meant to be exhaustive; they merely outline prospective research directions and offer a snapshot of the *Sharing & Caring* members' research interests. More specifically, the toolkit concentrates on two distinct, and, arguably, mutually incompatible, types of collaborative economy: transglobal digital platforms (such as, for example, the short-term rental service Airbnb and its alternatives) and local bottom-up initiatives (Fedosov, Lampinen and Travlou 2020).

To further capture the breadth of ethnographic research on the collaborative economy in Europe, the editors of this book and WG1 participants organised an international conference at the University of Edinburgh (*EthnoCol 2019*, held on October 25th 2019 and supported by the Action). The origins of this book can be traced back to that event: the presentations of current research and the lively discussions between attendees from several countries and disciplines, provided fertile ground for developing the chapters that make up this book.

For *EthnoCol 2019*, we solicited short papers contributing ethnographic accounts and understandings of collaborative economy practices and communities. We also welcomed contributions focusing on the methodological aspects of collaborative economy research, such as collaborative ethnography, participatory action research, co-design, etc. To document the complexity and richness of ethnographic research on the collaborative economy we sought ethnographic accounts of practices and/or of forms of community aggregation in collaborative economy settings; ethnographic case studies of collaborative economy initiatives, frameworks and platforms; instances of ethnographically-informed design of collaborative systems in support of collaborative economy practices; reflections on the theoretical, epistemological, and methodological challenges of studying the collaborative economy ethnographically. Post-conference, some authors were invited to extend their short papers into the chapters that make up this volume. This book, the first publication on the ethnography of the collaborative economy in Europe, covers a trans-national range of European projects analysed through a cross-disciplinary perspective.

Themes and Open Issues in This Book

Each chapter represents a timely contribution to the current state of the art in the identification and analysis of the broad range of phenomena that constitute the collaborative economy. Together, the book chapters reflect the variegated character of the collaborative economy and the diversity of its themes and practices. The chapters fall within four main themes (as represented in the four parts of the book): a) ethnographies of sharing economy practices; b) ethnographies of grassroots local initiatives; c) ethnographies of co-designing collaborative economies; and, d) ethnographies of spaces for collaborative economy.

Part one starts with Ann Light's discussion on the concept of trust within local initiatives (Chapter 1). Ann Light interrogates how transitions in trust between strangers may affect engagement, looking specifically at the growth of 'relational assets' (Light and Miskelly 2015). Her chapter draws material from neighbourhood-level case studies, proposing a range of ethnographic forms to deepen our reading of these social aspects of transaction, including a place for our own response to new types of transaction. In Chapter 2, Dicte Frost examines sharing and collaborative practices in ecovillages across five European countries (Spain, Slovenia, Ukraine, Germany, and Denmark). In this cross-European, multi-sited study, Dicte Frost carried out in-depth interviews with different stakeholders to document the practices of sharing in ecovillages: the experiences and methodologies of sharing, its enablers, and the limitations to sharing practices in the communities. She found that, in contrast to settlement arrangements that push their members towards competition, ecovillages incentivise collaboration and sharing: ecovillage communities thus merge collaborative and market-based economies, and function as intermediate, or transitioning, spaces. Dicte Frost's research stresses the importance of aligning the individual values of sharing and collaboration with those of the communities. Using a single local case study in Scotland, in Chapter 3, Catherine Lyons and Morgan Currie describe *Easy Sharing*, a pilot service from the Edinburgh Tool Library (ETL). *Easy Sharing* introduces an alternative economic infrastructure, a Library of Things, that can engender sharing over time. Through ethnography and surveys, Catherine Lyons and Morgan Currie investigate the drivers and barriers to participation in the sharing economy, and interrogate the receptiveness, capacity, and barriers of those who use the Library of Things over retail consumption. The authors conclude that a platform-mediated sharing economy would be not so much an innovation as in fact a restoration of historic social bonding, mitigating the pressures of current deprivation by introducing infrastructure to strengthen community. In Chapter 4, Samantha Cenere investigates collaborative workplaces through her ethnography of the situated practices of organising a Fablab in Turin, Italy. Fablabs (short for Fabrication Labs) are workshops for digital fabrication, where members can use a variety of shared tools and resources to construct smart devices on a small scale or just for themselves. The author argues that collaborative economies could be understood as the emergent outcome of the interaction between economic theories and heterogeneous socio-technical arrangements: it is through this interaction that collaborative economies are brought into being, demonstrating how economics performs the economy. In her chapter, Samantha Cenere also highlights how this process of actualization is never stable, and can sometimes fail.

The second part of the book comprises three chapters on ethnographies of local grassroots initiatives. In Chapter 5, Anikó Bernat looks at solidarity as it was manifested within grassroots groups in Hungary during the 2015 'migration crisis'. Through her ethnographic study, Bernat explores the model of 'going online to acting offline': she investigates how the efficient use of social media platforms fueled, and interacted with, the offline activity of solidarity-driven humanitarian aid movements during the aforementioned 'crisis'. One of her key findings is that the use of social media platforms (predominantly Facebook) enabled volunteer grassroots groups to form very rapidly, operate with extraordinary effectiveness, and exercise wide influence, at a level that has never been experienced before in a humanitarian crisis in Hungary. In Chapter 6, Vera Vidal presents her ethnographic fieldwork with *La Comunicadora*: a training programme for socio-economic innovation and technological sovereignty for collaborative economy projects in Barcelona. The author reflects on how, in the context of municipalism, the State is attempting to channel sharing economy initiatives to promote alternative social economies. From a similar perspective, in Chapter 7, Olga Orlíc, Anita Čeh Časni, and Kosjenka Dumančic discuss community as a focal point in the solidarity economy. Their exploration is grounded on their interdisciplinary study of community-supported agriculture, food citizenship, and solidarity economy in Croatia.

In the three chapters that constitute the third part of the book, the focus shifts onto ethnographies of co-designing collaborative economies. Chiara Bassetti (Chapter 8) presents the case study of Santacoin (SC), a digital complementary currency co-designed, implemented, and deployed at a 10-day performance art festival in Italy. The author provides an ethnographic account of this collaborative intervention and its main results, and reflects on two key dimensions of the SC project: the intersection of 'moneywork' and caring practices as explicitly thematised in the public space, and the role social interaction, relationships, and communities in collective imagination experimentations. In Chapter 9, Justin Larner discusses the methodological challenges of studying the collaborative economy ethnographically in order to develop new business models and platforms. His discussion focuses on annotated portfolios, a human-computer interaction technique that enables worker experience to inform business model design. Larner demonstrates how annotated portfolios can also be used by researchers to articulate designs latent in ethnographic data gathered from engagement with workers, and how this application can inform the design of new business models in the collaborative economy. The last chapter (10) in this part of the book, written collaboratively by five authors from three different institutions and countries (Italy, Portugal, and Denmark), Maria Cristina Sciannamblo, Roberto Cibin, Petra Žišt, Chris Csíkszentmíhalyi, and Maurizio Teli explore the concept of care within the ethnographically-informed design of collaborative systems in two European projects and uncovers how this design can support care-based practices of social collaboration in different contexts.

In the fourth and final part of the book, the focus turns to the spatiality of the collaborative economy, with three chapters dedicated to its urban dimension. In Chapter 11, Alena Rýparová looks at sharing practices as manifested in social and/or environmental initiatives in Brno, Czech Republic. She examines the organisation of these initiatives into communities or networks, their access to resources within these networks, and the motivation of people to participate – a motivation that does not include that of financial profit. This examination offers an insight into the fundamental question of what makes us share services, goods, knowledge, etc. with others, even with strangers. In Chapter 12, a two-city case study of Airbnb, Cristina Miguel and Rodrigo Perez-Vega examine the experiences and views of relevant stakeholders in the Airbnb sphere in London and Barcelona: hosts, guests, Airbnb public policy managers, rental apartment companies, council representatives, and other local authorities. In this study, the authors unpack questions pertaining to Airbnb as a sharing economy platform and the barriers to, and opportunities for, ethical practice that this platform generates. Miguel and Perez-Vega identify the challenges stemming from their comparative research in two different urban settings and the controversial nature of the Airbnb phenomenon, and articulate research strategies for overcoming some of these challenges. In Chapter 13, the discussion moves to the struggles against Airbnb by grassroots housing activist groups in Athens, Greece. Dimitris Pettas and Penny Travlou explore a conflict between two distinct actors at the different ends of the collaborative economy spectrum: Airbnb, a sharing economy platform with a global reach and economic impact, and housing activists inspired by the principles and values of solidarity and care economy. The authors argue that, despite their common framing as parts of the collaborative economy, 'platform capitalism' and grassroots collaborative practices are the materialisation of different – and contrasting – visions concerning the organisation of production, consumption, and social reproduction, affording fundamentally different capacities and possibilities of empowerment.

The chapters that make up this edited book follow, respond, and expand upon the literature and debates on the collaborative economy. They offer novel insights into the open questions of collaborative economic practice, substantiated by original ethnographic research across several European countries. By examining the collaborative economy through the common lens of ethnographic methods, this book sheds new light on the complexities of both the collaborative economy and of its ethnographic exploration. Along these lines, "collaboration" becomes problematised as a phenomenon of varying reach, actors involved, and values aspired. Hence we refer to "economies" and "ethnographies" also in the plural to acknowledge such diversity of thrust. Collaboration is also manifested in the authorship of the chapters and in the nature of the research: a coming together of disciplines and of multiple actors including researchers, activists, community representatives, policymakers, and/or local authorities.

Furthermore, the book demonstrates how inter- and trans-disciplinary perspectives, informed by transnational collaborative research in geography, sociology, economics and management, computer-supported cooperative work, and collaborative computing (among other scholarly fields), can enrich the current debates on the collaborative economy.

This book can be read through different keys: not only disciplinary ones, but also in terms of positionality. We envision a varied readership (such as policymakers, members of communities, activists, and students and researchers) that can take away insights from it. From the various disciplines coming together we can learn of the importance of 'joined-up', multi-faceted and in-depth examination of contemporary phenomena. Ethnography becomes common epistemological ground for such rich exploration reflecting on the fact that situated knowledge can help view and learn from case studies over time. The different ethnographic studies the chapters discuss offer a unique opportunity to look holistically at the theme of the collaborative economy, from various perspectives, voices and narratives.

Finally, we acknowledge that this book has been written during the life of the *Sharing and Caring* COST Action (2017–2021), with work documented in the chapters having been conducted before the COVID-19 pandemic hit the world. Much has changed since. The landscape of the collaborative economy, at the level of both global networked platforms and locally-driven sharing initiatives, has been significantly impacted by the pandemic. At the time of completing this Introduction in May 2022, Europe is also affected by the Russian invasion of Ukraine and ongoing conflict, with new movements of people and aid, and collaborative solidarity initiatives, as well as profound changes in the economies of many European countries.

While we acknowledge that these events have changed the landscape of the collaborative economy in Europe, we believe that this volume's contributions are still useful to lead to impact to readers approaching this in the future: they represent a model for the thoughtful and rich examination of other multi-faceted phenomena involving communities, digital platforms, and collaborative processes that may emerge going forward. Furthermore, they represent the potential of local collaborative economy initiatives to create more sustainable and 'slow' futures, as well as the risks and challenges of large scale platform-based economies. They can inspire future scenarios when it comes to facing and tackling other crises such as the climate and humanitarian crises.

Acknowledgments

We acknowledge all the colleagues who gave their time to review early abstracts and paper submissions towards the production of this book: Gabriela Avram, Chiara Bassetti, Vida Česnuityté, Richard Coyne, Morgan Currie, Dimitris Dalakoglou, Anna Farmaki, Alessandro Gandini, Karen Gregory, Cindy Kohtala, Airi Lampinen, Cristina Miguel, Maria Partalidou, Chiara Rossitto, Mariacristina Sciannamblo, Chris Speed, James Stewart, and Özge Subaşi.

We thank the proofreader Brendan O'Brien for his excellent work.

We also acknowledge the support of the COST Action *"From Sharing to Caring: Examining the Socio-Technical Aspects of the Collaborative Economy"* (CA16121, 2017–2021), and of the Chair Dr Gabriela Avram.

References

Akande, A., Cabral, P. and Casteleyn, S. 2020 Understanding the sharing economy and its implication on sustainability in smart cities. *Journal of Cleaner Production*, Vol. 277, 2020, 1240–77. https://doi.org/10.1016/j.jclepro.2020.124077.

Arcidiacono, D., Gandini, A. and Pais, I. 2018 Sharing what? The 'sharing economy' in the sociological debate. *The Sociological Review Monographs*, vol. 66(2): 275–288.

Avram, G., Choi, J. H., De Paoli, S., Light, A., Lyle P., and Teli, M. 2017 Collaborative Economies: From Sharing to Caring. *Proceedings of the 8th International Conference on Communities and Technologies*, 305–307. https://doi.org/10.1145/3083671.3083712

CA 16121 (COST Action "From Sharing to Caring"). 2016 *Memorandum of Understanding.* https://e-services.cost.eu/files/domain_files/CA/Action _CA1 6121/mou/CA16121-e.pdf

Cheng, M. 2016 Sharing economy: A review and agenda for future research. *International Journal of Hospitality Management*, vol. 57: 60–70.

del Moral-Espin, L. and Fernandez-Garcia, M. 2018 Moving beyond dichotomies? The Collaborative Economy scene in Andalusia and the role of public actors in shaping it. *The Sociological Review Monographs*, vol. 66(2): 401–424.

European Commission. 2016 *Communication From the Commission to the European Parliament, the Council, the European Economic and Social Committee and the Committee of the Regions: A European Agenda for the Collaborative Economy.* COM(2016) 356.

Fedosov, A., Lampinen, A. and Travlou, P. 2020 *From Global to Local Sharing Initiatives: Devising an Ethnographic Research Toolkit for the Collaborative Economy.* https://sharingandcaring.eu/news/global-local-sharing-initiatives -devising-ethnographic-research-toolkit-collaborative-economy

Martin, C.J. 2016 The sharing economy: A pathway to sustainability or a nightmarish form of neoliberal capitalism? *Ecological Economics*, vol. 121: 149–159.

Sanna, V.S. and Michelini, L. (2020), *White Paper on Impact Methods. WG3 Deliverable: Impacts of the Collaborative Economy.* Available at: https://sharingandcaring.eu/sites/default/files/files/WhitePapersDeliverables /D3.1_WhitePaperonImpactMeasuringMethods.pdf

Schor, J. 2015 *Interview. The sharing economy: hyper-capitalism or a sustainable alterna-tive?* Retrieved from https://www.youtube.com/watch?v=-Qq7Gy F3smc (accessed on 20 September 2016).

Slee, T. 2016 *What's yours is mine: Against the sharing economy.* New York, NY: Or Books

Teli, M. and Bassetti, C. (Eds) 2021 *Becoming a Platform in Europe. On the Governance of the Collaborative Economy.* Boston-Delft: now publishers

PART I

Ethnographies of Sharing Economi(es) Practices

Trust in Collaborative Economies and How to Study It: Relational Assets and the Making of More-than-Strangers

Ann Light

University of Sussex, UK and Malmö University, Sweden

Abstract

This chapter explores the nature of trust in collaborative economies: how we might see the work that trust is doing and know that it is the phenomenon of trust that we are looking at. It contrasts the work that neighbourhoods and locally focused enterprises undertake – to build trust as a valued interpersonal quality – with the legal mechanisms of the digital sharing economy, which resituate trust, shifting the focus from partners in a transaction to dependence on technology. In doing so, it identifies different roles that trust is playing and poses the question as to whether our reading of trust is subtle enough for the purposes of our designing. Along the way, it proposes a range of ethnographic forms to deepen our reading of these social aspects of transaction, including a place for our own response to new types of transaction. In doing so, it seeks to inform on the transition of groups of strangers into economies and collaborators: the 'more-than-strangers' of the title.

How to cite this book chapter:
Light, A. 2022. Trust in Collaborative Economies and How to Study It: Relational Assets and the Making of More-than-Strangers. In: Travlou, P. and Ciolfi, L. (eds.) *Ethnographies of Collaborative Economies across Europe: Understanding Sharing and Caring.* Pp. 13–29. London: Ubiquity Press. DOI: https://doi.org/10.5334/bct.b. License: CC BY-NC-ND

Introduction

Trust is a major part of shopping, sharing, lending and renting. As soon as any exchange of resources is proposed, inter-actor concerns arise and a judgement must be made each way as to whether the other partner(s) will offer the benefits implied and how far we can make ourselves vulnerable to potential damage. There is no certainty, ahead of venturing one's assets, whether contracts will hold up or people will be honourable in their promises. In one way or another, economies run on trust.

This has meant that, over millennia, outside cultures where all property is held in common, various mechanisms for exchange have been designed to minimize risk in exchanges, with consequent shifts in how trust is sited and managed. If trust in a transaction is low, then there are trustable safeguards put in place round the transaction to give confidence that mechanisms for recouping any loss are in place.

How one trusts is affected by the intimacy with which one knows other parties. It is not given as a blanket approval for all exchanges. For instance, if I know you well, I might trust that you would pay back a loan, while not trusting you with garden tools. (In fact, the better I know you, the more I know how I can trust you.) In the latest incarnation of shifting relations – of global networked economies run on phones and internet browsers – what used to rely on people's knowledge of each other or the circles of trust round individuals, communities and companies has been replaced by systems that run on a scale where even national legal systems of recompense are dwarfed and superseded. Their very scale is impressive when it comes to building trust, yet as these new monopolies develop to connect buyers and sellers, they must rely on something other than personal knowledge, bringing new concerns.

In this chapter, I look at trust in both intimate and scaled contexts, how it develops and even how we might know that it is *trust* we are looking at.

Transactions and trust

In collaborations, trust is both a desirable quality for building sense of belonging and a vulnerability that leaves people open to exploitation. A transaction is a particular case in point. As noted, there is some subtlety to how trust plays out in transacting. Nonetheless, the role of trust in transactions has principally come to attention as technical mediation impacts willingness to buy, with 'numerous articles emanating from information systems and computing researchers and focusing on the link between online or systems security and trust' (Arnott 2007: 982). An example is Barbosa et al.'s (2020) analysis of trust behaviours using the Airbnb platform. Written with Airbnb employees, the study offers methodology to enable the measurement of users' propensity to trust other users on a sharing economy platform. For example, knowing that using an affordance on the interface signals low propensity to trust others, 'designers could implement the affordance in ways that better support these users in making their decisions, such as by providing additional information or by guiding them on how to use a feature more effectively' (Barbosa et al. 2020: 2141).

Relatedly, marketing researcher David C. Arnott comments that much analysis of trust in transactions has been undertaken using positivist methods: 'With the growth of the interpretivist approach to the study of marketing phenomena, it was surprising, and a little disappointing, that case study, grounded theory or ethnographic studies were not viewed as viable methods of studying what is, in essence, an unmeasurable entity,' he says of trust (Arnott 2007: 986). As other authors of this book do, I take a qualitative approach to analysis, situated in the first person (as author and commentator, but also as method). Further, I explore trust in longer-term relations and not merely as something needed sufficiently to make transaction possible.

With technology, rather than acquaintances vouching for others, the emphasis is on management of risk and there is a creep towards marketization of everyday life. This orientation is in contrast to trust in other everyday exchanges. Legal expert Yochai Benkler (2004) draws attention to the difference between social exchange and market transactions: A social exchange may defer reciprocation, build indebtedness (Benkler 2004), and use it to create social ties that are based on trusting the other, even if there is still an understanding that some exchange between partners is relevant. A market transaction removes indebtedness by opening and closing the exchange in one go, minimizing contact (Benkler 2004) and siting trust in the mechanism of exchange, not so much the partners doing the exchanging. In other words, in formal exchanges, the transactional quality creates an expectation of an immediate reciprocation of some kind to relieve both partners of the need to trust over time – what Benkler calls 'crispness'.

Russell Belk, an expert on the related theme of sharing, illustrates the combined social and economic motives of neighbourhood transaction and how it informs trust:

> We may pay a neighbour's child a fee for babysitting, but we also regard the family of babysitter as friends and neighbours. But a commercial babysitting service tends to be … less personal and relationships are more likely to end when the sitter leaves our home. Trust in relatives and the neighbourhood sitter is fostered by closeness and familiarity, whereas trust in the commercial sitter is fostered by the screening processes of their organization and its guarantees and liability insurance. (Belk, 2014: 12)

So, a question for this chapter is how far the collaborative economies around us are also solidarity economies in which people recognize their potential to support each other and others. Do people act for the pleasure and power such relations create? Or is all life to be understood as trading units? Ethnographic processes are better able to address such questions than quantitative studies.

Social aspects of formal exchange

Because of a focus on promoting commerce and using metrics to understand how, an overlooked aspect of transacting, in general, is the social aspect of formal exchange. Some years ago, I studied a farmers' market in southern England (Light et al., 2010). Watching people talk in the queue about the products at their chosen stall, one of the interesting features was the sociality of the outing. Connections were made with other shoppers and with the stallholders, which might be transitory, but which were part of the market. There was music. The mood was celebratory.

It brought to mind anthropology literature on shopping: for instance, sociologist John F. Sherry's work on a flea market, which challenged the prevalent view that shopping can be reduced to the analysis of purchasing and selling (1990). He describes markets as festive-informal, where social aspects of the interaction among shoppers and with stallholders form a significant reason for visiting such events. The use of narrative in such settings also differs from the marketing of big business. In Sherry's words, '[d]ealers impart meaning to their goods, providing cultural biographies for objects, which many consumers believe enhance their value' (1990: 22). Lawson (2010) offers a similar reading of artisan transactions: 'when I buy X, I'm giving [money] to artists in exchange for them being awesome. Awesomeness is something I'm willing to put a cash value on. As are lots of people.' My comment at the time was that transacting involves gaining the right to identify with a producer (Light et al. 2010: 209).

Even when these exchanges are now conducted with the help of digital mediation, many complex relations are involved if producers of goods are artisan (such as in the craft marketplace Etsy) or if the goods themselves have a history (such as selling rare items on eBay). Stories and certification come into play. Demonstrating authenticity brings further trust concerns (Gilmore & Pine 2007): are either the producers or the product what they are claim to be? Do they need to be, or is a good story enough? We do not always trust all aspects of an interaction equally.

Collaborative economies have an inherent social dynamic. An early corporate account gives a definition: 'Customers are not just using social technologies to share their activities, opinions, and media, but also to share goods and services. In this evolution, companies risk being disrupted as customers buy from each other.' (Owyang et al. 2013: 3). Owyang et al. do not explicitly consider it, but customers are not only buying from one another, but *with* one another.

The potential for complicated markets is established by producing the software to mediate them (e.g., Lampinen & Brown 2017). A definition for usage comes from Avram et al.'s (2019) analysis: 'digital platforms are in essence connective and collaborative, creating a digital action point where multiple networks meet. These qualities have been enhanced through the development of on-site collaborative features.'

Trust is a slippery creature in these contexts. Further, in looking at the work that trust does in economies, we must, as researchers, decide where we find it and how we will know it. The observing of trust is both a methodological and a definitional act. As Sherry (1990) demonstrates and Light (2010) follows, techniques of observation and engagement pay dividends in discovering social relations that constitute the *collaboration* of collaborative economies. A paradox prevails: if we look at how trust and judgement co-exist in exchange, we see that trust both stands in for judgement and also forms the basis on which it is made. Unless we study the social dimensions, collaborative economies are merely transplanted transactions, without a perspective on what else they enable. Trust gets reduced to a map of where people will and will not click.

Collaborative economies and connecting strangers

Trust is needed for communality to flourish, and that flourishing communality builds a form of trust, but as our understanding of relations changes (for instance, becomes more transactional), so does our expectation of the work that trust will do. When there are collectives involved in the transacting, this allows for inter-actor dynamics that, mediated by technology or not, influence how people are willing to commit and with/to whom.

There is a common wisdom in collaborative economy contexts (e.g., Botsman & Rogers 2010; Botsman 2017) that machine matching and vetting promotes the growth of exchange by supporting 'strangers trusting strangers' (Slee 2015).[1] It is true there has been fast growth in services that involve access, not ownership, from car rides (e.g., Uber) to room rental (e.g., Airbnb), and the development of concepts such as *Mobility as a Service*, where you order or lease a vehicle as you need it, rather than owning it outright. Against such simple attributions for this rise, Frenken & Schor (2017) observe that, as more people participate in platforms for economic reasons, social interaction declines. They suggest that the codification of trust into

---

[1] This is to ignore the degree to which society is composed of strangers trusting strangers already, such as the trust we have in the actions of train drivers, pilots, nurses, refuse collectors, even other road users, etc.

ratings and technical fixes, such as smart locks for home lets, mean less face-to-face contact, commenting that sharing platforms may instead be harmful to social cohesion. Looking at these shifts, growth in the collaborative economy can be seen to align with trusting the legalistic processes of verification and the technical mediation offered by corporations and their platforms (e.g., Lampinen & Brown 2017). Strangers are not so much trusting strangers as machines and contracts.

Addressing these concerns, Hawlitschek et al. (2016) point to three foci for trust in the sharing economy: peer, platform and product. Another category of trust, outside this definition, relates to the social impact of the organizations behind these platforms and their careful management of image (e.g., Airbnb 2014; Cox & Slee 2016). In these orientations, the sociality of the people creating and engaging in collaboration gets scarcely a look. Yet some collaborative economies are not using technology as mediator (i.e., managing trust through machine vetting), so how are they managing trust issues?

Method

Taking all these elements into consideration, we can ask how transitions in trust that affect engagement might be observed and what journey takes place over time for the groups involved. The answer inevitably points to more than one method. My examples reveal the difference between exploring transactions at scale, such as the global activities of the scaling sharing economy (Light & Miskelly 2019), and considering the growth of trust and social exchange in specific places. Both shape relations, affecting how people live alongside each other, but there is little in the way of parallel as to how. Being interested in the growth of 'relational assets' (Light & Miskelly 2015), of which, I would claim, neighbourhood trust is one, I discuss two local case studies where relations between neighbourhood members change. I also consider my own experience as a means of making the global local. To understand these particular contexts, I draw on multiple sources and the use of diverse qualitative methods – short- and long-term observation, interviews and auto-ethnography.

The Role of Trust in the Sharing Economy

Most writing on trust in the sharing economy focuses on applications for trust (see Räisänen et al. 2021, but also Möhlmann 2021), not trust itself or the body of analysis that considers trust as a social force. This ignores the relational and constructive nature of trust referred to above. It has the same tendency towards reductionism that Sherry observes in analysis of shopping as buying and selling – and for related reasons. There is a history of trying to optimize the transactional elements and thus devaluing the other work that trust performs.

Trust in society

Considerable sociological imagination has been applied to the work that trust does for/between people. For instance, Lewis & Weigert (1985) describe trust as a functional alternative to rational prediction. It is a relational quality that reduces complexity and allows people to make rapid judgments on situations (Lewis & Weigert 1985). Meanwhile Giddens addresses both trust and the reliability of structures, introducing the related idea of ontological security (1990), a feeling that you can trust in the integrity of people and reliability of things: 'the confidence that most human beings have in the continuity of their self-identity and in the constancy of their surrounding social and material environments of action' (Giddens 1990: 92). He argues that trust is precisely the link between faith and confidence that is neither one nor the other. Luhmann (1979) points to how the act of trusting relies on a belief that others trust – in other words, a trust in trust. Individuals are able to make the leap of trust on the assumption that others in the social world join in the leap. Above all, this body of work recognizes trust as a collective attribute, applicable to relations among people rather than psychological states taken individually (Lewis & Weigert 1985).

However, Cheshire, writing about the quality of trust in online contexts, points to its elusive nature from a design perspective (2013). He draws attention to the three key features of designing for what he calls *interpersonal* trust –

- repeated interactions between parties over time
- acts of risk-taking
- the presence of uncertainty

– leading him to the paradox of building assurance structures – such as those that guarantee risk-free interactions on sharing economy platforms – which decrease uncertainty and thus the potential for interpersonal trust. In other words, he shows that designing for 'trust' in a technical system can actually decrease the potential for trust. If we use Giddens' language, the emphasis on reliability comes at the expense of a need for integrity.

When Yoko Akama and I explored care, we noted that trust is an important part of collaborative work and alleviates the need to explain motives and describe what one is about to do. It is situated in the moment and in the relations of the encounter as well as the wider social and political frames of meeting. 'Arguably, trust is another kind of knowledge into which people develop insight over years of experience with social situations' and yet 'trust can be regarded as a "faulty" way of knowing because it cannot be publicly verifiable' (Light & Akama 2019). We observed that this kind of knowing is rarely credited. Trusting people is seen as a prerequisite for doing the 'real' work, not a kind of informed judgement (Light & Akama 2019). To see it as informed judgement is to destabilize the normal binaries of trust/knowledge and trust/distrust.

The scaling sharing economy

In sharing economy applications, we see trust in harness to reliability as a major factor in promoting the use of global services. Clearly, profit motives inform the giants – what Shareable refers to as *sharing economy deathstars* (Gorenflo 2015). I have drawn attention to the qualities that characterize a would-be monopoly at scale in describing Airbnb (Light & Miskelly 2019):

- *Crisp*: brokering homes (and 'experiences') using an automated search process, handling vetting and payment.
- *Scaling, homogenizing*: remote from the trade it brokers, using the internet to perform functions and collect data on users.
- *Individualizing, monetizing*: enabling financial transactions for individual renters and hosts and taking a cut.
- *Unscrupulous*: weakening social and legal protection to increase reach and profit. (It mobilizes users against regulators. It avoids tax where it can. Beyond its own market, it is driving up rents as people take properties out of rental – it takes no responsibility for this 'externality'.)

Reading this list gives the lie to any sense of benign motives for the business behind the platform, for we can see the claims it makes balanced with its erosion of social bonds. Some of the negative social actions are deliberate – such as campaigning to change legislation to reduce tax liabilities – and others are more incidental – such as bringing a financialized and individualized culture into places where more social forms of interdependence were in operation. Airbnb claims to build sociality and act environmentally (Airbnb 2014), but its actions are belied by its impacts. This is greenwashing (Weston, 2021) – designing the company's public environmental profile to maximize corporate gain. Common across these venture-funded companies using digital networks for reach is lack of regard for anything except profit, ignoring the impacts of disrupting existing patterns of sharing, consuming and coexisting. The wake of these 'deathstars' (Gorenflo 2015) is not just commercial contexts that site trust in vetting tools, but a global domestic context into which these financialized values have been imported, shoring up a sense of remoteness from others in the process.

Other Economies

In this section, I present two examples of more localized, collective and non-financial encounters to contrast with the 'deathstars'. Both are written up elsewhere (Light & Miskelly 2014, 2015, 2019), so I do not dwell on methodological or case details, but review how trust worked in these contexts and how we learnt about it.

A cross-section

The first example is a cross-sectional study of collective sharing initiatives in a small neighbourhood of London (see Light & Miskelly 2014, 2015, 2019). Exploring multiple sharing activities, this allowed us to compare contexts at one moment, i.e., something more than a single case study. Looking at the activities occurring in a neighbourhood, we were able not only to compare between enterprises, but also to look at the cumulative effect of multiple activities in one area, thus also forming a case study of their impact together. While some interviews and observations pointed to how trust was formed, this analysis was more able to inform on how trust was understood by the participants in the study and how it evidenced as part of daily life in the moment. Thus, the *Design for Sharing* study (Light & Miskelly 2014) drew attention to how trust supported sharing and how it had enabled new enterprises to start up, convinced that support would be available. A theme raised by multiple informants 'was how trust develops over time and how to scale that up' (Light & Miskelly 2019).

> We heard how trust grows in a neighbourhood as people engage together in small-scale collaborations and communal ownerships, which then lead to more ambitious projects as a group. Strangers are welcomed into creative association with others and so cease to be strangers. Leaders emerge and become known and trusted. Informal systems develop that suit those participating – and part of growing this trust in each other is evolving these systems together. People feel that they are contributing, area-wide, to the evolution of trust and systems of collaboration. (Light & Miskelly 2019).

Our informants could be articulate on the nature and siting of trust because it was apparent to them just how important a factor it is to promote social sustainability, sharing and wellbeing in a neighbourhood. Nonetheless, at no point did the research team ask for a definition of how trust was being understood and used, nor did we ask our informants to gather and compare notes about it. Both these approaches might have given us greater understanding of what was taking place. However, it was after data collection, when the material was analysed inductively, that the overarching significance of trust for building communality became apparent and so we made it a greater focus in the second study.

A longitudinal study

Significant longitudinal studies are less common than cross-sectional studies because funding and academic regimes do not support these well. However, in looking at the work of trust in collaborative economies, a longitudinal study has the merit of allowing for the observation of how economies emerge and how social structures form them and form around them. The second example I offer involved a longitudinal study of another South London initiative (Light 2019; Light & Miskelly 2019).

The Makerhood platform was set up in 2010 to connect local craft makers with purchasers and ceased in 2019. Makerhood (https://makerhood.home .blog/about/) ran as a social enterprise led by volunteers and overseen by a steering group, showcasing the work of local makers to encourage a buy-local ethos. At its outset, it was an ecommerce brokering platform, but that model gave way during its first years as it became obvious that the platform's value was not to manage money, but to connect and support makers, reflecting the founders' (environmental and social) goals of quality of life and reduced consumption.

The Makerhood model shifted from one-to-one meetings between makers and their customers to assembling people with an interest in craft and business. Bringing makers face to face to make craft and share concerns became as important as online marketing. Gradually this devolved too till club events were run by local makers instead of the core team. Over time, the platform primarily supported craft-people in making, selling and networking. Yet Makerhood had very local ambitions and a sense that scaling would not suit the project or benefit the neighbourhoods it might scale to; instead, it devolved leadership to share opportunities, skills, materials and platform ownership. In other words, it fostered the sharing economy that the networked economy giants only pay lip service to.

In this narrative, there is a clear point where interpersonal and organizational trust takes over from trust in technology as the service develops and becomes known. Unlike other services, it does not rely on third parties, such as Paypal, to inspire confidence, but uses ultra-local knowledge to win trust, so that measures taken to make the service safe and easy reflect 'a concern for people's wellbeing more related to the ethics of being intermediary than trust as understood in the scaling sharing economy' (Light & Miskelly 2019).

Makerhood addresses privacy and safety by proposing sensible hand-over spots. This is not electing a category of meeting place (such as supermarket or post office) as a scaling service might, but naming a particularly safe spot on a particular street, because everyone knows the same streets, including the platform founders (Light & Miskelly 2019). 'These gestures give people confidence in the founders in the same way that it develops with everyone else … trust is built between people through repeated encounter and mutual interest' (Light & Miskelly 2019). It turned out, at these close quarters, that this trust made the financial component of Makerhood's digital platform unnecessary. Trust lived in the concern of people engaging with others and responding to their handiwork, 'not the production of satisfactory items and smooth transactions' (Light & Miskelly 2019).

We go on to argue that trust is situated in the places and social relations of Makerhood, where makers in the maker clubs lend resources because they live close and can even reclaim items between sessions if needed. Mutual trust came from getting to know each other through Makerhood events (Light & Miskelly 2019).

I quote these sections in some detail because they point to a different under-standing of trust in sharing from that being advanced by sharing economy rhetoric. Trust in organisations and their values replaces trust in the vetting of the machines; sharing is not subject to the 'crisp' values of immediate exchange (Benkler 2004), but is used to drive the development of indebtedness, care and a trust centred in common places, touchpoints and values.

These insights were gathered by attending to the development of Makerhood over its whole 10-year journey from inception to transition to a less formal structure. Of course, I might have learnt almost as much from observing two critical points of transition: when the service went from being digitally medi-ated to abandoning the ecommerce element; and from a marketing and selling body to club-based member organization. However, there were more subtle developments that would have been lost to view without the end-to-end survey. And it is very difficult to know when to drop into the lives of busy social enter-prises, so, pragmatically, I could not have known when to focus. The act of stay-ing in touch, reading newsletters, chatting to the organizers regularly, attending the Christmas events, pop-up shops and fairs, and so on was pleasurable, but also an essential part of developing trust with the team and observing how it developed in their activities. Even watching the dissolution of the organization was informative: to see how carefully the founders passed things on to the com-munity that had grown round them.

Relational assets

These examples point to *relational assets*, 'the social benefits that emerge over time from local sharing initiatives, making further initiatives more likely to succeed' (Light & Miskelly, 2015). Relational assets are the emergent but immaterial capacities that come with the accumulation of multiple collabora-tive care initiatives within a locale. They are based in the place in which they aggregate, thus being collective rather than individual; linking communities within a neighbourhood and beneficial to everyone within that neighbourhood to some degree. They emerge through the accumulation of processes, initia-tives and tools for sharing resources, developed through local collaborations and the exercise of goodwill. They depend on proximity, existing relations and types of material resources to some degree, but even an emerging collective vision can be seen as a relational asset, changing imaginaries and aspirations for a locale, thus also changing the dynamics of an area. Trust is a significant part of these relational assets: and, like trust in trust (Luhmann 1979), these assets can embody a virtuous cycle – where the more you give, the more you get. Clearly some parts of a community and some communities can benefit more from developing this culture than others (awareness of this dynamic can help address inequalities). Yet the virtuous spiral promotes agency and pro-social values.

In both of my examples, we observed that trusting peers has a temporal quality: people engage in small-scale collaborations and communal ownerships, leading to more ambitious projects as a group. This evolution is established by thinking about scale and leadership and what is appropriate to ask of people in terms of distance, work and commitment. In recent work (Light & Miskelly 2019), I looked at how this extends into the sociotechnical infrastructuring of networks built by actions of collaboration, sharing and using each other's resources, defining this as 'meshing'. It is possible to design to increase trust in each other, rather than the technical mechanisms of exchange, even using technical means.

'Instead of removing the onerous task of growing trust, neighbourhoods could invest in visibility over time for judging others' actions and building confidence' (Light & Miskelly 2019). Social networks, where local groups post and discuss, are a resource for building off-line friendships. Giving access to one another in less demanding circumstances allows trust to develop. Tools that scaffold trust can become redundant as relationships grow and more people become involved in helping with local initiatives. It is in this way that people who were strangers become more-than-strangers to each other. And all of this can be observed using longitudinal means.

When not to trust

Trust has correlates in suspicion and scepticism. My instincts to investigate a different kind of trust from the mechanisms of vetting and brokering do not come from nowhere. A strong ecological sensibility informs my thinking and many years of researching to understand how neighbourhoods can become more than merely multiple individual households, but instead serve as vital units for preserving life and fostering more sustainable futures. It hurts me, as it hurts everyone, when we move further from the values of interdependence.

But people are inconsistent and contradictory. I know, in using Airbnb, I am using a company that I do not trust, even while I am safely picking homes to visit. I have a level of trust in the owners' descriptions and integrity (peers/product) because I read carefully and base my judgement on how things are said. I also trust that my payment will be handled correctly (platform), despite not trusting the uses my data will be put to or that the company can avoid accidental data breaches. I try to pick homes to rent, not properties bought to let out, yet I have been valuing convenience and novelty over my sense of how the world should be. As noted, I am not unaware of the wider impacts that Airbnb has on society and consider these undesirable. I have chosen not to adopt newer services, such as Uber, because of their ethics and impact (Goulden 2017), yet I tried Airbnb so early (and found its promise so exciting) that I have long been caught in an embodied personal recognition of how little *using* equates to *trusting*. A trust for the transactions has developed over time in tandem with distrust, dismay and resignation. I am not alone in this complex play of emotions and ethical conflict and, over time, it is changing my behaviour away from using the services. The Covid-19 pandemic, with its enforced break for all travel, has further changed the patterns that I once followed. And as I write more about the platform, my sense of what is acceptable and how my thoughts are affected by what I read becomes a source of data in its own right.

Discussion: Trusting Each Other?

The nature of trust, as indicated above, is that it emerges over time and evolves as confidence and familiarity increase. If, as I suggest, trust is, in fact, a contrasting kind of *knowledge* that people develop over years of experience with social situations (Light & Akama 2019), how does it form? By observing our responses and those of others, in situ, in contrast to more mechanical forms of analysis, we open the way to a richer and more satisfying account of life and its potentials. The following sections speak to this richness and can only be understood through embodied methods, not so much in terms of co-locating, but bringing all aspects of experience into sight.

It is possible to see that trusting may be risky, but it does not need to be random. Choosing to trust people – in the moment, for the task at hand – involves judgement. So, though trust is often dismissed as the absence of knowledge, it is knowledge based on different criteria. In organizational literature, it is considered a balance of cognition-based and affective response to others, which is then linked to action such as 'relying' on someone (e.g., McAllister 1995). It is an embodied way of knowing and frequently hard to articulate. The experience has close links with affect, captured perhaps in talk of 'feeling trust', even when we draw on knowledges and experiences to support it. Looked at as informed judgement, trust becomes important in constituting and maintaining collaborative economies: it is a full partner in collaboration.

It is possible to see that trust is not *consensus*, with all the flattening out and removal of difference that the concept of consensus carries. It is not recognition of likeness (indeed, McAllister (1995) shows that recognizing likeness is not directly correlated with trusting). Instead, it may be recognition, in difference, of shared steadfastness or a shared desire for steadfastness. Thus, it is an enabler of difference. It creates the affective space needed to hold the recognition of difference in relation with the act of coming together and collaborating. We might see this as beneficial impact of increasing ontological security (Giddens 1990). I suggest that, facing neoliberalism, by accepting difference and yet providing a means of coming together, we recharge *the political*, allowing critical and creative dynamics to shape economic relations. This acts to correct relying on and supporting the *transactional* to inform our economies.

In this way, a study of trust can also be the means to make a redefinition of trust – from a negligible precursor in the business of exchange (managed through software and delegated to third parties such as Paypal) to the prime enabling force in the development of neighbourhoods, greater socio-ecological wellbeing and relational assets. It is this kind of trust that allows strangers to become more-than-strangers, even if they stay more remote than kith or kin. It is challenging and important work.

This element of work is captured by Carr (2016), suggesting ownership may be a more attractive option than sharing resources in a neighbourhood with an account of the drawbacks of sharing an electric drill between neighbours: 'You have to hash out the financial and logistical arrangements, you have to figure out where the drill happens to be at the moment you need it, and you have to go out and pick it up and bring it home (burning gas, perhaps, as well as time). And if somebody else wants to use the drill at the same time you need it, then you're in for some negotiations and probably some aggravation. And if the drill breaks or gets lost (or a 'little screw head' gets misplaced), a whole new set of transaction costs kick in.' Carr does not say if he is speaking from personal experience, but we may recognize the phenomenon.

Yet, observing the growth of collective initiatives at a local level has enabled me to assemble a contrasting account from people (and enterprises) doing this work. As Philippe of a timebank in south London concludes: 'The value of sharing is people connecting. It's a social value. I think it goes beyond "I've got a spare drill, you can use that." In sharing my drill with you, I'm connecting with you and, if I'm connecting with you, I've got potentially a sense of identity with a community of people or a neighbourhood' (see Light & Miskelly 2014). There are diverse structures that work to enable collective sharing and manage the development of trust between parties, all of which can be observed if we have the patience. Further, we can see how the growth of trust supports the flourishing of these types of institution.

We can also use these insights to reduce the friction Carr (2016) refers to. A design agenda that fully embraces the complexities of trust and starts from a recognition of how the social good is balanced with the inconvenience to individuals gives us a chance to build more sensitive systems. That starts with good observational practices, from noting our personal inconsistencies to longitudinal engagement with the structures and relations appearing around us. It needs to be approached with care. Some emotional labour is necessary for trust to grow between more-than-strangers; it does damage to the work of cooperation to re-site trust rather than cultivate it (see also Sennett, 2013). Essential to creating well-conceived collaborative economies is a nuanced reading of trust and how it is formed. That requires qualitative contextual research and a commitment to encountering the many forms of trust that make our societies run. An infinite number of one-dimensional studies showing how technical features affect user behaviour cannot substitute for inductive research into the unfolding of collaboration. Understanding trust, of all things, requires a situated and multifaceted approach.

References

AirBnB. 2014. *New Study Reveals A Greener Way to Travel: Airbnb Community Shows Environmental Benefits of Home Sharing.* Airbnb: https://www.airbnb.co.uk/press/news/new-study-reveals-a-greener-way-to-travel-airbnb-community-shows-environmental-benefits-of-home-sharing.

Arnott, D.C. 2007 Trust: current thinking and future research. *European Journal of Marketing*, 41(9/10).

Avram, G., Hee-jeong Choi, J., De Paoli, S., Light, A., Lyle, P. and Teli, T. 2019 Introduction to the Special Issue on Repositioning CoDesign in the age of platform capitalism: from sharing to caring, *Co-Design*, pp185–191

Barbosa, N.M., Sun, E., Antin, J. and Parigi, P. 2020 Designing for Trust: A Behavioral Framework for Sharing Economy Platforms. *Proc. Web Conference 2020* (WWW '20). ACM, New York, NY. https://doi.org/10.1145/3366423.3380279

Benkler, Y. 2004 Sharing Nicely: On Shareable Goods and the Emergence of Sharing as a Modality of Economic Production, *Yale Law Journal*, 114(November), pp273–358

Botsman, R. 2017 *Who Can You Trust?: How Technology Brought Us Together and Why It Might Drive Us Apart*, New York, NY: Public Affairs

Botsman, R. and Rogers, R. 2010 *What's Mine is Yours: The rise of collaborative consumption*, New York: Harper Business

Carr, N. 2015 *Of drills and holes and Ronald Coase: the limits of sharing*: http://www.roughtype.com/?p=6527

Cheshire, C. 2013 Online Trust, Trustworthiness, or Assurance? *Daedalus* 140(4), pp49–58

Cox, M. and Slee, T. 2016 *How Airbnb's data hid the facts in New York City.* http://whimsley.s3.amazonaws.com/wordpress/wp-content/uploads/2016/02/how-airbnbs-data-hid-the-facts-in-new-york-city.pdf

Frenken, K. and Schor, J. 2017 Putting the sharing economy into perspective, *Environmental Innovation and Societal Transitions* 23, pp3–10

Giddens, A. 1990 *The Consequences of Modernity*, Polity Press, Cambridge.

Gilmore, J.H. and Pine, B.J. 2007 Authenticity: What Consumers Really Want, Harvard Business Press

Gorenflo, N. 2015 *How Platform Coops Can Beat Death Stars Like Uber to Create a Real Sharing Economy*, November 4, 2015: https://www.shareable.net/how-platform-coops-can-beat-death-stars-like-uber-to-create-a-real-sharing-economy/

Goulden, M. 2017 Uber can't be ethical – its business model won't allow it. The Conversation. October 4, 2017. https://theconversation.com/uber-cant-be -ethical-its-business-model-wont-allow-it-85015

Hawlitschek, F., Teubner, T. and Weinhardt, C. 2016 Trust in the Sharing Economy. Die Unternehmung – Swiss Journal of Business Research and Practice, Vol 70, pp26–44

Kenton, W. 2021 Greenwashing. *Investopedia*: https://www.investopedia.com /terms/g/greenwashing.asp

Lampinen, A. and Brown, B. 2017 Market Design for HCI: Successes and Failures of Peer-to-Peer Exchange Platforms. *CHI'17*, New York, NY: ACM

Lawson, S. 2010 Warner's Mistakes, *Steve's Blog*, 10th Feb 2010: www.stevelaw son.net/2010/02/warners-mistakes

Lewis, J.D. and Weigert, A. 1985 Trust as a social reality. *Social Forces*, 63(4), pp967–985

Light, A. 2019 Designing the Economics of the Sharing Economy: Towards Sustainable Management. *Handbook of the Sharing Economy*, (eds) Russell Belk, Giana Eckhardt and Fleura Bardhi, Edward Elgar.

Light, A. and Akama, Y. 2019 The Nature of 'Obligation' in Doing Design with Communities: Participation, Politics and Care (eds) Tom Fisher and Loraine Gamman,. *Tricky Design: ethics through things*. London: Bloomsbury

Light, A., Egglestone, P, Wakeford, T. and Rogers, J. 2011 Participant-Making: bridging the gulf between community knowledge and academic research, *J. Community Informatics*, 2011, 7:3.

Light, A. and Miskelly, C. 2014 *Design for Sharing, Sustainable Society Network+:* https://designforsharingdotcom.files.wordpress.com/2014/09/design-for -sharing-webversion.pdf

Light, A. and Miskelly, C. 2015 Sharing Economy vs Sharing Cultures? Designing for social, economic and environmental good, *IxD&A*, 24, pp49–62

Light, A. and Miskelly, C. (2019) Platforms, Scales and Networks: Meshing a Local Sustainable Sharing Economy. *JCSCW*, Summer 2019

Light, A., Wakeman, I., Robinson, J., Basu, A. and Chalmers, D. 2010 Chutney and Relish: Designing to Augment the Experience of Shopping at a Farmers' Market, Proc. OzCHI'10, pp208–215, New York, NY: ACM

Luhmann, N. 1979 *Trust and Power*. Chichester: John Wiley.

McAllister, D.J. 1995 Affect- and Cognition-Based Trust Formations for Interpersonal Cooperation in Organizations, *The Academy of Management Journal* 38(1): pp24–59

Möhlmann, M. 2021 Unjustified trust beliefs: Trust conflation on sharing economy platforms, *Research Policy*, 50(3), 104173, https://doi.org/10.1016/j .respol.2020.104173.

Owyang, J., Tran, C. and Silva, C. 2013 A Market Definition Report The Collaborative Economy: Altimeter Research Theme: Digital Economies, June 4, 2013

Räisänen, J., Ojala, A. and Tuovinen, T. 2021 Building trust in the sharing economy: Current approaches and future considerations, *Journal of Cleaner Production*, 279, 123724. https://doi.org/10.1016/j.jclepro.2020.123724.

Russell, B. 2014 Sharing Versus Pseudo-Sharing in Web 2.0, *The Anthropologist*, 18:1, 7–23, DOI: https://doi.org/10.1080/09720073.2014.11891518

Sennett, R. 2013 Together: The Rituals, Pleasures and Politics of Cooperation, Penguin Books

Sherry Jnr, J.F. 1990 A sociocultural analysis of a midwestern American flea market. *J. Consumer Research*, 17, 1.

Slee, T. 2015 *What's Yours Is Mine: Against the Sharing Economy*. Or Books

Sharing and Collaboration in European Ecovillages: Breadth, Enablers and Limitations

Dicte Frost
University of Southern Denmark, Denmark

Abstract

The chapter examines sharing and collaborative practices within the context of European ecovillages. The research is based on interviews and participant observation in five European ecovillages, located in Spain, Slovenia, Ukraine, Germany and Denmark. In total, 74 interviews were carried out, encompassing the levels of 1) community members, 2) enterprises or organisations located in the ecovillages and 3) the ecovillage. The chapter describes the sharing realities in the ecovillages, the sharing methodologies and the enablers of and limitations to sharing practices in the communities. Results show that, in contrast to other social structures that push 'members' towards competition, ecovillages offer incentives for collaboration. In these contexts, collaboration and sharing are the main trajectory to ensure sustenance, making ecovillages unique incubators for sharing and collaborative practices. As such, the communities merge

---

How to cite this book chapter:
Frost, D. 2022. Sharing and Collaboration in European Ecovillages: Breadth, Enablers and Limitations. In: Travlou, P. and Ciolfi, L. (eds.) *Ethnographies of Collaborative Economies across Europe: Understanding Sharing and Caring.* Pp. 31–50. London: Ubiquity Press. DOI: https://doi.org/10.5334/bct.c. License: CC BY-NC-ND

collaborative and market-based economies, and so function as intermediate, or transitioning, spaces. Two frameworks are birthed: 1) A framework that outlines the sharing methodologies applied in the ecovillages and 2) a framework that positions the social and institutional enablers of sharing practices in the ecovillages. The research stresses the importance of aligning the mentalities of individuals with the sharing and collaborative values in the communities, and of carefully designing community structures to incentivise desired sharing and collaborative activities, while being flexible to change with the 'sharing maturation' of the community or group.

Introduction

Sharing and collaboration are surfacing as guiding principles moving towards the future of European livelihoods. However, complex, multilevel and long-term cases of sharing and collaboration are rare within Western industrial spheres, where single area cases involving carpooling, food-sharing or house exchanges have taken centre stage. In this context, ecovillages provide a unique example of place- and community-based sharing and collaboration practices. This chapter explores and delimits novel developments with regard to collaborative and sharing economies adopted in European ecovillages.

An ecovillage is defined as 'an intentional, traditional or urban community that is consciously designed through locally owned participatory processes in all four dimensions of sustainability (social, culture, ecology and economy) to regenerate social and natural environments' (GEN Europe 2021). Alice Brombin offers a description of ecovillages that captures some essential traits of the phenomenon:

> ecovillages practice a holistic view of living, characterized by a new political-aesthetics in which pleasure, conviviality and restoring relationships of trust and sharing become essential in the pursuit of personal satisfaction ... following a process of individual and environmental renaturalization. (Brombin 2015: 471, 468).

In focalizing the collaborative economy, values characteristic of economic practices in ecovillages include *fairness, equity, transparency, low carbon emissions, inclusiveness* and *participation* (Frenken & Schor 2017). Furthermore, members of ecovillages consciously and unconsciously engage in discourses of 'collaboration and community in order to reject stories of the economy as engendering isolation and separation' (Richardson 2015: 122), thereby actively challenging neoliberal capitalist assumptions and biases. With a unique merging of a spatially embedded, intentional community with sustainability-oriented values, ecovillages and ecovillage members are engaging with collaborative economy practices on a daily basis. Such extensive and continued engagement with sharing practices is unique in the Western industrialized social landscape,[1] amplifying the role of ecovillages as living laboratories for technological and sociocultural transitions towards a more collaborative culture.

The research presented in this chapter was collected during a field study of five European ecovillages[2] located in Spain, Slovenia, Ukraine, Germany and Denmark. These cases were selected because they represent the diversity of ecovillages in terms of size, age, economic organization and range of economic activities.

Data collection took place over seven months between 2018 and 2019 and combined semi-structured interviews with participant observation. A main demographic trend was that interviewees were highly educated, mainly with completed bachelor or master's degrees in diverse fields. In total, the researcher carried out 74 interviews,[3] covering three levels of the ecovillage phenomenon: (1) *the individual level,* (2) *the enterprise/organization level* and (3) *the community level.*

This chapter describes the sharing economy of European ecovillages in four main stages. It first positions the communities studied within their socio-historical contexts and clarifies the main characteristics of each. Secondly, it outlines the collaborative and sharing practices documented in the ecovillages researched. It then elaborates on how these practices are enabled by the structures and cultures of these communities, including a discussion of their limitations. Finally, it considers the relevance of its findings in the context of a wider transition towards a collaborative economy.

Contexts and Characteristics of Case Ecovillages

Prior to the elaboration of trends and differences in the sharing practices of the ecovillages studied, it is important to ascertain in part the socio-historical contexts and defining characteristics of these communities. Each community

---

[1] Indigenous communities have merged these characteristics outside of and prior to Western industrial, cultural and political spheres. Arguably, the definition of an 'intentional community' does not apply to indigenous communities. The need for intentional communities generally arises where traditional communities have faded or been diminished.

[2] The terms 'ecovillage' and 'community' are applied indifferently in the remainder of this chapter.

[3] The 74 interviews include 53 interviews with different community members, 16 interviews with enterprises or organisations located in the ecovillages, and five interviews with economic representatives of the ecovillages. All ecovillages and interview participants are anonymous.

is operating within considerably different national and subcultural contexts, although they are bound together by a European genesis. The cultural clues explained below have been distilled from the fieldwork and follow-up interviews.[4] Accordingly, they are ethnographic accounts of the experiences and perspectives of the ecovillage members rather than a literature review of the national histories of ecovillages, intentional communities and the communitarian movement. This choice has been necessary as literature on ecovillage history is largely non-existent.

Denmark

The Danish ecovillage, established in 2002, was home to 72 adults and 30 children at the time of the field work. The community is characterized by individual plots of land[5] occupied by families with fairly large self-build houses, all constructed of natural and sustainable materials. These planning and architectural characteristics are echoed in most Danish ecovillages. The planning aspect is mirrored in an individual- and family-based economy, where households each pay a yearly fee to the community and otherwise keep their economies separate. Freedom and voluntariness are central values in the community. Since the 1960s and 1970s, Denmark has seen a socio-political expansion of communitarian and ecological sentiments manifested through a widespread co-housing[6] culture (Jakobsen & Larsen 2019). This trajectory has generally created fertile grounds for the growth of ecovillages and Denmark is at present the country with the highest number of ecovillages per capita. The narratives of ecovillage members emphasize a desire to make ecovillage life 'mainstream' and to show that 'the normal Dane' can live in an ecovillage too. Societal antisocial

---

[4] Follow-up interviews were conducted with members from the case communities and members of other ecovillages located in the same national contexts. These interviews were centred on illuminating historical traces in the ecovillage movement in each of the countries. In total, seven follow-up semi-structured interviews were carried out.

[5] The property is owned by a community fund, while the built structures on it are owned by the individual households. The households pay a one-time rent (entrance fee) for the usage of the property.

[6] Co-housing can be defined as individual homes linked by shared facilities and certain shared activities (Beck, 2019). The main difference between co-housing and ecovillages is that ecovillages consist of an intentional community, whereas co-housing is often a collective of a randomised group of people (based on the market). Furthermore, co-housing initiatives do not necessarily include an ecological or sustainability dimension, whereas ecovillages do. Various forms of co-housing can be found in Europe (Tummers, 2015).

behaviour, such as paying less tax, not sending children to the neighboring village school or promoting the image of creating a separate society, is deprecated. As such, community members are attempting to make the ecovillage lifestyle culturally accessible by integrating widely accepted elements of social life into the ecovillage model, reflected in the work of Anette Høite Hansen (2019).

Germany

The German ecovillage was founded in 2009 and during the period of research had 36 inhabitants, 21 adults and 15 children. Located in the western part of Germany, this ecovillage practices a shared income economy[7] and functions rather like a commune, with three or four large buildings that existed on the property upon purchase, plus a few additional tiny houses built after the community moved in. The project was initiated as an agricultural community and later evolved into an ecovillage largely focused on agriculture and education. The ecovillage is part of a network of 'sister' ecovillages located within the same region and which share a similar political affiliation and economic structure.

Contemporary Germany offers a diverse ecovillage and co-housing scene. Four main branches of ecovillages were identified by the interview informants and each of them was traced back to distinct subcultures and periods of time. Inspired mainly by political Marxism, politically left-wing communities appeared in Germany following the Second World War. Political and systemic change generally forms the community basis. Some of these communities define themselves as ecovillages, while others do not. The interview informants explained that the 1970s, 1980s and 1990s saw the rise of ecologically informed community initiatives driven by sustainability. These communities have a strong focus on organic and regenerative food systems, ecological building and lowering their CO_2 footprint over time.

Several communities driven by the impulse to instigate cultural change through personal and interpersonal processes appeared more or less at the same time, partially inspired by movements of sexual liberation. Finally, spiritual ecovillages arose within the German community landscape. These ecovillages include communities based on Eastern or Neo-Eastern traditions, as well as Neo-Christian communities and modern monasteries. Over time, knowledge exchange between communities has stimulated a merging of the various

---

[7] The community practises a shared income economy, but not a shared savings economy. In practice, this means that newcomers to the ecovillage transfer their income to the common account from the day that they are accepted into the community, but they do not transfer their savings into the community account. As such, community members can hold private savings that they have secured prior to integration in the community.

branches in newer ecovillages and an integration of practices across existing ecovillages of different branches. This account is largely supported by Marcus Andreas' historical tracing of German ecovillages in his book *Vom neuen guten Leben* (2015). The case ecovillage is an example of a politically left-wing, ecologically based community.

Spain

The youngest of the communities considered here, the Spanish ecovillage was founded in 2014 and at the time of research had around 50 inhabitants, including 25 adults, 15 children and a group of long-term volunteers. The community was established in existing buildings in need of renovation, in which community members live in apartment-like housing. The interview informants regard the ecovillage movement in Spain as defined by two main trajectories.[8] Similar to one of the German branches, one trajectory is characterized by spiritual communities, or communities that have been started from the desire of working with personal growth within a community setting. Examples of such ecovillages can be found in most European countries. The second and most prominent trajectory arose in the aftermath of the Franco regime. According to the narrative of the interview informants, the deep political divisions that provoked the Spanish Civil War lingered on after the dictatorship, when political disentanglement allowed left-wing representatives of the middle and lower classes to look for alternative ways of self-organizing. The movement is inspired by anti-Franco, anarchist and anti-militarist sentiments and is experienced as a radical political activity. Accordingly, it separates itself from society in general, accentuating its distinctiveness.

Given the concurrent conditions of high land prices[9] and a rise in the number of abandoned villages in rural Spain due to urban migration, this trajectory has manifested itself through the (often illegal) occupation of abandoned villages and a type of self-governance largely characterized by common economies, anti-private property ideals and deeply rooted political engagement. This nonconformity is driven by a will to be autonomous and by the associated values of living off-grid and being self-sufficient. Among these communities, some identify as ecovillages, while others do not. The case ecovillage is a rare example of a 'median' community that does not follow one of the trajectories but focuses on social processes mainly though experimental systems of governance (sociocracy), common educational projects and balancing individual

---

[8] A third trajectory might be defined as communities formed by Northern Europeans who have purchased land and migrated to Spain, creating enclaves of migrant communities.

[9] As compared to the average wage in Spain.

space and communal spaces. This translates into a rent-based economy: members hold private accounts and pay a monthly rent to the community.

Ukraine

The Ukrainian ecovillage was initiated in 2012 and at the time of field work had 22 members, including children. The community was established through the private purchasing (by members of the community) of properties and existing houses in three traditional rural villages in close proximity to one another. As such, all ecovillage members live in separate, family-centred housing. The sense of community is thus transferred to common activities and shared agricultural land, showcasing how an ecovillage approach to the collaborative economy can be applied to traditional villages.

The ecovillage movement in Ukraine started in the 1990s in the wake of both economic and systemic instability and a newly gained sense of freedom and opportunity precipitated by Ukrainian independence. Within the urban middle class an environmental awareness has been progressively growing, along with an appreciation of clean air and water and fresh food. This demographic accounts for most of the community members. Despite this trend, ecovillage members generally feel distanced from and rejected by Ukrainian society. The narratives of the interview informants tell the story of a contemporary Ukraine that is experiencing a massive urban drift with a lingering memory of USSR policies, so that any voluntary shift to community life and 'moving back to the country-side' is deprecated. The Ukrainian ecovillage movement is characterized by a clearly defined ideopolitical split between pro-Russian ecovillages, commonly called 'Anastasia communities',[10] and pro-European communities inspired by European ecovillages and often aspiring to integrate similar politics.[11] Structurally, the Anastasia communities are separated into family 'homesteads', each on approximately one hectare of land. Individuals in the community consider each other as neighbours who individually strive for self-sufficiency, rather than 'community members'. This structure eases the complexities of sharing, whereas pro-European communities vary extensively in terms of ownership and economic structures, as well as the integration of sharing practices. The Ukrainian ecovillage in this study is defined as pro-European.

---

[10] Anastasia ecovillages are ideological communities informed by the 'Ringing Cedars of Russia' book series. The first book in the series is called *Anastasia* (Megré, 1995).

[11] Examples of such politics include the status and positioning of women, acceptance of unconventional sexualities and family structures, governance methodologies, and the practice of affectionate non-romantic physical touching between community members.

Slovenia

Founded in 2013, the Slovenian ecovillage was the home of 15 adults and children at the time of research. The interview informants understand that communitarianism is a concept distrusted by the Slovenian public as a result of socialist political rule in former Yugoslavia. The cultural, ethnic and religious diversity of the population, and the history of recurring conflicts between these groups, have resulted in a general suspicion towards inter-group community building and sharing practices in general. This intersection of cultural influences has allowed enclaved ideologically based and religious communities to surface in larger sizes. Communities without a strong ideological affiliation are typically smaller family-sized units of five or six members. The Slovenian ecovillage studied here is an atypical case of a less ideologically driven community that has grown to a total of 15 members. The community shares a common house rebuilt from ruins and a few smaller housing structures such as yurts. Individuals live in private or shared rooms while the kitchen and other living spaces are communal. Permaculture and voluntary simplicity are central values, as well as creating partnerships locally, nationally and internationally to advocate for ecovillage and community lifestyles.

Ecovillage Sharing Practices

This section describes the sharing and collaborative practices performed in the case study ecovillages. Collaborative and sharing practices were evident in all three levels of analysis: the individual, the enterprise/organizational and the community. Sharing and collaboration are mainly centered upon providing livelihoods in terms of facilities, goods and services. In pooling several forms of capital,[12] the ecovillages have acquired ownership, or common rental, over spatial resources, making a range of facilities available to their members. As such, the ecovillages engage in a variety of 'commoning' practices, described as 'the social process of creation and reproduction of the commons' (LeVasseur 2013: 255, cited in Esteves 2017) and are developing 'alternative economic and social arrangements, such as inclusive decision-making, cooperative enterprise, collective consumption, and "economic communalism"' (Mychajluk, 2017: 181).

The commune-like communities are highly integrated and have a large number of communal assets (shared facilities, goods and services), while the communities with individual housing lean more towards private ownership. These levels of 'commoning' are in alignment with previous research in the field (e.g., Mychajluk 2017; Lockyer, 2017; Ergas 2015; Moravčíková & Fürjészová 2018). In the commune-like communities, individuals and businesses alike share

---

[12] Including financial, social, and human capital.

resources and facilities. Several community members use the metaphor of 'one big family' to explain this sharing reality. Examples of shared resources include living and common spaces (leisure rooms and multi-purpose spaces such as dining rooms, bars, meeting rooms, playrooms for children, saunas and swimming pools), hardware (kitchen equipment, washing machines, garden tools and tools such as those in sewing and carpentry workshops), mobility (cars and car sharing) and shared infrastructure (electricity, heating, water, biogas, internet and roads). One Slovenian ecovillage member describes it accordingly:

> Almost everything which is not in this room, is common and we all use it together … because we do everything like in one big family, you know? Because heating, washing things, cooking, these are all things that we do together.

Although the communities with individual housing are separated into individualized housing units, they have assimilated certain sharing solutions. For example, in the Danish community, a 'freezer community' exists where community members can store food, along with a consumer group that allows for collective bulk purchase of food by members. Additionally, the community owns a communal garden, a fruit orchard, chickens, and other facilities like a sauna, playgrounds, campfire, shelter, a lake and table tennis, as well as a 'free shop' and recycling centre where members can share clothes and items with each other. Community members of all five ecovillages engage in a high degree of sharing and gifting of personal belongings and a variety of homemade products through various sharing pathways (further discussed below). A Danish community member describes their gifting culture:

> The email system has been used a lot to say 'now we have five boxes, does anybody want them? Pick them up for free', or 'we need to get rid of this couch or this table, is anybody interested?'

Collaboration and sharing also takes place through activities or 'services'. A good example of this is communal cooking and meals. This is an important social meeting point that has been institutionalized in several of the ecovillages. The Spanish community shares a common lunch every day, albeit on a voluntary basis, whereas the Slovenians share lunch and an evening meal daily. The German community shares all meals, while in the Danish and Ukrainian communities, on the other hand, communal meals happen on an ad-hoc basis and are arranged by members who volunteer (non-institutionalized). A Spanish ecovillage member expresses her appreciation of this exchange of services:

> I love that I have to cook today for example, and the rest of the month I go to eat. Without cooking, without buying groceries, without thinking about

it. I just go and eat. 29 days and only one day of cooking. For me that is very good. And that doesn't happen in other situations or in the city.

Other services are self-organized within the community by a group of community members as a response to a shared need or desire (e.g., childcare, consumer and production groups, football or board game clubs, movie nights, singing circles and yoga classes). Services are also provided by individual members to the community. These services similarly include cultural activities such as yoga and contact improvisation classes, theatre training, drawing lessons and crafts workshops, as well as various alternative treatment and therapy methodologies. It is also a common practice for members to participate in the courses and events hosted in their communities. In the business and organizational realm, community members will typically cook for visitors who attend courses and events hosted by the ecovillage, be responsible for event logistics and facilitation, and host participants in their private homes. These customs indicate that the 'business' realm and the community realm are highly intertwined and are rarely strictly separated. Businesses are mainly understood in terms of the community members who own them and are treated accordingly. As such, sharing and collaboration take place between individuals and businesses. This includes the use of technical assistance and specialized knowledge within the community, such as legal support, translation, IT services or administration by businesses. In some cases, human resources have also been translated into financial resources such as investments or informal loans. The communities also foster productions and activities otherwise unavailable in rural areas. As the community members constitute 'immediate customers', it is easier for household productions, cottage industries or small businesses to venture out. In return for their customer loyalty, community members are granted access to in-house products and services, to acquire which they would otherwise have to travel.

The most prominent shared service is 'human resources', the immediate or organized availability of assistance in the shape of hands or heads for advice, ideas and solutions. 'Help and assistance' is a fluid currency that is constantly in use. During communal meals requests for help are often called out, such as 'two or three hands are needed for this or that task', and in most cases help is to be found. Another embodiment of non-institutionalized shared human resources is exemplified by a Ukrainian ecovillage member:

I know I can count on the help of my neighbours [community members]. Our house is cold now, it is an old house, and I know that if I came here [from our urban home] I could ask to stay for a night at some of the neighbours' places. It would be pleasant for me and for them also.

Services also extend to the numerous informal learning opportunities that frequently emerge in the ecovillage environment through interpersonal relations. A Slovenian ecovillage member explains this continuous dynamic:

> There are so many different little bits of knowledge! You know, you can ask one person about sociocracy or dragon dreaming, another person told me about facilitation, and another person told me about building and wood carving, and parenting, a lot, a lot. I've never been a babysitter before, so this is for me really big. And [someone is] teaching music sometimes because she's playing the violin, just all of these tools ... all this for me is a service, you know? I'm learning all this stuff.

One essential 'human resource' is community work. Lisa Mychajluk defines it as 'the unpaid, intra-organizational work that is commonly undertaken by members in a cooperative' (Mychajluk 2017: 184). On average, community members in the five ecovillages dedicate 42.6 hours[13] of work to the community every month. Community work is integrated into a narrative of 'mutual benefit', whereby members 'transfer' work that would normally provide a personal livelihood to the livelihood of the community. These are mainly household activities that have been expanded into the wider community. Community work is experienced as a part of 'normal life': chores that must be dealt with independently of living in an ecovillage or not, but that are often more effectively handled in a community setting. Cleaning, cooking and maintenance are common cases of community work typically organized through rotation or shared responsibility schemes. For example, in the Slovenian ecovillage, each week a new 'couple' is responsible for daily cleaning and every Tuesday all members are invited to take part in an extensive cleaning of the premises.

As such, the community members have access to a wide range of facilities, activities, goods and services that would not be available to the vast majority of, or to any, members outside of the community setting – due to financial constraints or lack of availability. Many of these facilities would also be available to individuals in urban spatialities, albeit based on monetary exchange. One Spanish ecovillage member explains this financial dimension:

> The difference for me is money. I can do all the things I do here in the city, but here with less money. In the city there are consumer groups, and ecological groups, and a network to take care of the children, but to sustain that economically you need to put in a big amount of money.

---

[13] This average is based on the monthly estimate of the 53 community members interviewed.

In pooling their financial and human resources, the ecovillages provide a continuum of shared facilities and services that are cost-free (apart from rent, initial entrance payments or other financial agreements) and continually available for members. As Karen T. Litfin eloquently writes in her book *Ecovillages: Lessons for Sustainable Community*:

> In the affluent countries, many ecovillagers are living comfortably on incomes that place them well below the poverty line. Their secret? A combination of self-sufficiency, sharing and elegant simplicity. (Litfin 2014: 81).

Sharing Methodologies

Apart from sharing through common ownership and lending/borrowing, the types of sharing documented here are indicative of various other sharing methodologies. Ecovillages apply these methodologies within the community, as well as in their external relations. The lines between methodologies (sharing, gifting, bartering and monetary exchanges) are blurred and often situationally dependent. To understand the reality of community life, these levels of sharing methodologies should be imagined as interactive and fluid concepts, illustrated in Figure 2.1.

The service of offering drawing lessons, for example, is typically given as a gift to one person, bartered for some good with another and exchanged for money with a third person. The pathway chosen is usually determined by the depth of personal relationships and the means and capabilities of the recipient, along with the community norm. Bartering is a common practice in ecovillage settings; members exchange products for products, services for services or products for services and vice versa. In terms of products, this method is especially used in Ukraine, where members grow produce on individual plots, and then barter to diversify their food supply and attain greater self-sufficiency. The German ecovillage, on the other hand, operates on the basis of shared income, in which context bartering becomes insignificant. Gifting is a level of the sharing culture in which community members give their private belongings or services to other community members. This procedure is especially normative in the income-sharing community, as individuals are increasingly aware of the needs, wants and consumption of others and try to reduce the total consumption. It is also employed in the Ukrainian ecovillage, where self-sufficiency is highly valued. Gifting can also take the shape of 'free flow' economies, where members give what they are able to without expecting direct reciprocity, or as part of a generalized reciprocity. This economic attitude is explained by Tobias from the Danish ecovillage:

> When I was about to put on the roof here, I had no idea how to put on this kind of roof, then I asked my neighbour and he said 'Oh I'm not that good, but I know this other person in the community, he is good at it'. I had never even met this person, and then the person comes and he is

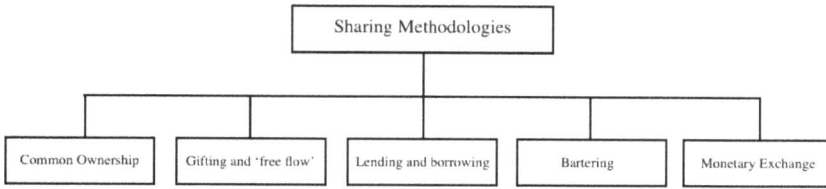

Figure 2.1: Sharing methodologies applied in ecovillages.

super busy with his own house, and then he spent half a day helping me with the roof. And I'm like 'shouldn't I pay you anything for this?' and he is like 'no no, you will just help some other time'.

The 'free flow' mentality is apparent in all the communities; however, it is especially present in the income-sharing setting and in settings involving greater financial individuality (Ukraine and Denmark). On a slightly different level, the communities create stable and beneficial relations to the external world. The ecovillages situate themselves within a wide pattern of linkages, so as to extend their sharing practices beyond community borders and to obtain greater self-sustainability through common sustenance practices, the sharing of advice and experience, funding opportunities and the amassing of collective social capital. These relations, or linkages, include ecovillage to ecovillage relations; national, European and global networks and associations; collaborations with organizations, businesses and governments; and relations with local villages. The depth of linkage embeddedness varies between ecovillages, but they are all actively engaging in external relations to expand their sharing practice reach and to provide non-monetary paths for sustenance. The trend of establishing linkages and networks is reflected in the findings of Robert Hall (2015), Susanna Waerther (2014), Shahrzad Barani et al. (2018) and Robert Boyer (2014).

Enablers of Sharing

The breadth of collaborative and sharing practices in ecovillages has important social and technological implications. Ecovillages have developed social norms based on, and continually reinforced by, the shared values of the individuals in the community. The themes of 'limiting resource use' and 'sustainable alternatives'[14] guide these values, and are also supported by previous ecovillage research (e.g., Brombin 2015; Esteves 2017; Ergas & Clement 2015; Waerther 2014). Tension between these values and social norms and the surrounding reality has motivated innovation and experimentation and has led to novel sharing solutions. These solutions, social norms and the enabling social context

---

[14] Including social, cultural, environmental and economic sustainability.

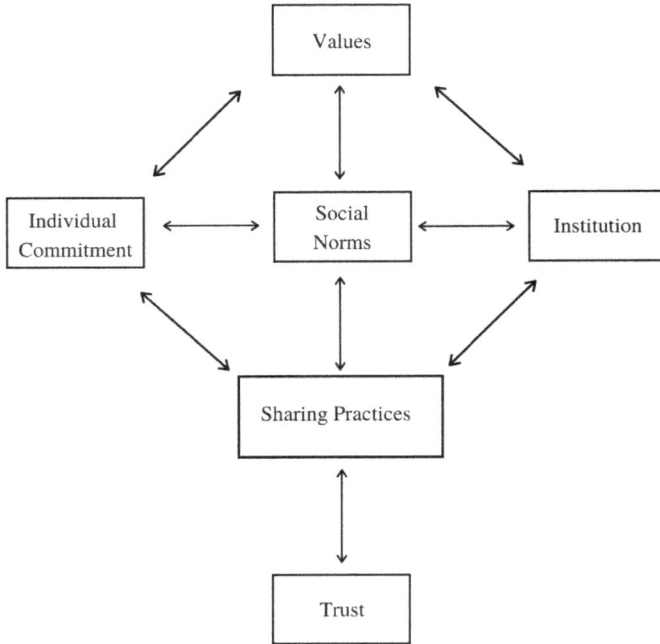

Figure 2.2: Cultural and institutional enablers of sharing and collaboration in ecovillages.

reinforce each other and, together, stabilize the sharing reality of the ecovillage. Figure 2.2 illustrates the enabling social 'cultures' (*individual commitment and trust*) and the enabling structures (*institution*).

Enabling cultures

The use and development of sharing and collaborative practices are enabled by a high level of commitment on the part of community members to the project/ ecovillage and the common intentions. Many state that they do not experience the ecovillage as separate from themselves, but as part of their immediate reality. They perceive it as their own project and take ownership of its continuation and success, with the result that they are willing to devote large quantities of time and energy to its realization. Most members report that they are willing to do more community work than they do at present. A large number of the members are thus willing to 'sacrifice' immediate self-interest for the collective good, if they see a pressing community need, reflecting their commitment. Via carefully structured phases of social inclusion and membership processes, ecovillages can ensure that members are committed, are aligned with the common vision and fit in socially. Membership processes are relatively long and require multiple steps that will normally take more than a year. Common features are initial visits, written or verbal applications, probationary periods and a community decision.

The community setting itself generates other ways for the members to relate to each other. Relations among community members are constantly revitalized as continual interaction and collaboration are necessitated by common activities and simply through living in close physical proximity. Ecovillage members commit themselves to staying within a web of relationships. This commitment entails participating in social processes of all kinds, from sharing personal emotions and states of mind to engaging in, sometimes uncomfortable, conversations and resolving conflicts.

Where ecovillages depart most markedly from more conventional social trajectories is in the commitment by the members to resolve tensions and continually re-evaluate their ways of relating to each other. Ecovillages are thus places where personal spheres increasingly become the property of, or held by, the collective. Such continual and deep sharing requires trust and generates trust in return. It surfaces through normalized, daily practices such as leaving doors unlocked. This, however, is not the case in the Ukrainian ecovillage because the community is only partially spatial, and community members are living among residents who are not part of the community. In all five ecovillages, children roam around freely within the community perimeter, and parents trust that all community members are observant of their wellbeing. These practices, considered normal in the eyes of community members, indicate a high level of trust within the community. Individuals in the community setting generally enjoy a deeper level of intimacy, based solely on the fact that simply by being members of the community they immediately own a commonality, a shared commitment and common frames of reference.

The high level of trust spills over into the businesses and organizations located in the communities. The businesses and organizations in the ecovillages actively attempt to change the competitive status quo of business environments. Accordingly, sharing, trust and openness are valued principles. Many enterprises and organizations are even willing to share their ideas and information freely, making no distinction between businesses outside of or inside the community. Trust and collaborative practices are seen to reinforce each other in the ecovillages, so that trust among community members is essential for the deepening of sharing practices.

Enabling structures

The technical structures mainly consist of the formal and informal institutions that the communities have devised through legal setups, community constitutions and community rules. Central to all of this, the ecovillages constitute various degrees of common ownership. The wider the extent of a co-owned livelihood (financial means/housing/productions/facilities …), the greater is the incentive for the community members to collaborate and engage in sharing practices. Common ownership entails common responsibility and legitimizes the right of community members to request or demand cooperation from the others. Waerther (2014) also emphasizes the fact that through common ownership, members share the economic risk. Furthermore, the institutionalization of sharing activities is a practical and symbolic tool, enabling ecovillages to ensure the continuation of key values, standards and activities. Examples of these enabling structures are community work and working groups, which are structured spaces for ongoing collaborations.

The Spanish and Slovenian ecovillages have written agreements establishing the minimum hours of community work expected from members, whereas other communities have institutionalized working groups. In these models, community members volunteer for different activity groups, such as cooking, cleaning, mobility or communications. These groups have responsibility and decision-making authority within their field of work, and distribute these responsibilities to individual community members. Meetings for emotional sharing have also become structured practices for the ecovillages and are used to facilitate social cohesion through conflict resolution, deepening relations and inducing trust. Emotional support is institutionalized in three of the ecovillages, through weekly or monthly meetings that facilitate emotional sharing and processing.

Limitations to Sharing Practices

An underlying challenge to sharing practices is the need for individuals to change mindsets that generally reflect the surrounding culture. The ecovillages have clearly established their intention to engage in sharing practices and to shift from a competitive to a cooperative culture. However, for this intention to be realized, each community member needs to shift their own mindset in a similar direction. Many community members relate that such mental and emotional change is the greatest barrier to the further development and entrenchment of sharing practices in their communities. This challenge is hinted at in the work of Waerther (2014) and Mychajluk (2017), though without further elaboration. Mental barriers to the deepening of collaboration and sharing activities surface within the context of community work. All the ecovillages report conflicts related to reaching a common definition of community work, as well as controlling and tracking the amount of community work contributed by each member. Tension arises from comparisons between individual contributions to community work and perceived inequality in this area. These social and personal barriers limit further collaboration between members because they generate a growing distrust.

Furthermore, sharing practices in the communities do not stretch beyond immediate realities, evidenced by the fact that none of the communities have institutionalized any comprehensive social security systems.[15] This is challenged by Geseko von Lüpke's (2012) testimony to the fact that social securities exist in other ecovillages. Certain social security[16] elements are, however, incorporated in the ecovillage structures. By sharing income, inhabitants of the German ecovillage are able to support each other economically if members are temporarily out of employment. Pensions and eldercare have been the centre of discussion in several of the ecovillages. These have been especially pressing topics in the income-sharing community, as although members are officially not allowed to save money outside of the community account, they are at the same time not obliged to share savings. The Danish ecovillage is discussing whether to impose an internal insurance scheme, under which community members would insure each other, instead of taking out household insurances with external companies. In general, social security functions of the communities are currently limited to case-by-case scenarios, which emphasizes the limits of ecovillage sharing practices.

Various other factors limit the deepening of sharing practices in the ecovillages. None of the sample communities have developed a way to sustain themselves economically without being dependent on the external financial incomes of their members. This means that most of the community members must travel outside the ecovillage to work. The daily commute and economic pressures leave the members less opportunity to create daily sharing practices. For example, the Spanish ecovillage shares a daily lunch, which, however, is only a 'common' activity for the individuals who work within the community perimeter and thus excludes community members who work elsewhere. This is partially because the communities have not created a common source of income able to sustain the entire community (or have not achieved self-sustainability), but it also results from a particular accounting system that separates personal and collective incomes. Accounts related to sustaining the ecovillages and accounts covering designated income-generating activities are typically separated and do not spill over into each other. This dilemma can also be traced back to the lack of property ownership or the holding of loans in multiple communities.

---

[15] It should be noted that the ecovillages are embedded within the social security systems in force in their national contexts, and that what is offered by these systems varies.

[16] Examples of 'social securities' are health care, child care and schooling, unemployment support, sick leave support, pensions, elderly care and insurances.

Conclusion

Ecovillages facilitate sharing practices through a range of elements that can be transferred to other fragments of the sharing and collaborative economy movement. However, the unique combination of a place-based intentional community and sustainability-oriented values allows for the emergence of beneficial social norms and institutions, and the creation of a fertile experimental space. The diverse and intricate economic structures and institutions simultaneously enable and restrict the sharing and collaboration practices in the community. Sharing and collaborative structures should thus be carefully designed to incentivize desired sharing and collaborative activities, while being flexible enough to change with the 'sharing maturation' of the community or group.

Apart from working with enabling institutionalizations, this research stresses that the main limitation, and/or opportunity, with regard to developing sharing and collaborative practices is the *mindset* of the individuals or community members. To shift mindsets, the importance of exposure to cooperative and sharing cultures, mindsets and practices is indicated in the research. Furthermore, by being engaged in a community of shared values, members reinforce the legitimacy of these practices and assist each other in shifting mindsets from competitive to cooperative. As such, the research emphasizes the importance of an intentional community; although the research findings might be relevant in any setting, the fact that ecovillages are spatially bounded enables greater interaction, trust and cooperation. Sharing common values, building mutual trust and asserting a certain level of exclusivity through group membership ensures commitment to the shift in mindset, behaviour and structures and allows community members to develop solutions together.

Certain solutions, especially concerning social security, delimit current sharing practices in the ecovillages studied. Identifying ways to address this is an area for potentially fertile engagement with research in other fields of collaborative economy.

References

Andreas, M. 2015 *Vom neuen guten Leben: Ethnographie eines Ökodorfes.* Bielefeld: Transcript.

Barani, S., Alibeygi, A.H. and Papzan, A. 2018 'A framework to identify and develop potential ecovillages: Meta-analysis from the studies of worlds ecovillages.' *Sustainable Cities and Society*, 43(November): 275–289. https://doi.org/10.1016/j.scs.2018.08.036

Beck, A.F. 2019 'What Is Co-Housing? Developing a Conceptual Framework from the Studies of Danish Intergenerational Co-Housing. Housing.' *Theory and Society*, 37, no. 1(June): 40–64. https://doi.org/10.1080/14036096.2019.1633398

Boyer, R.H. 2015 'Grassroots Innovation for Urban Sustainability: Comparing the Diffusion Pathways of Three Ecovillage Projects.' *Environment and Planning A: Economy and Space*, 47, no. 2(January): 320–337. https://doi.org /10.1068/a140250p

Brombin, A. 2015 'Faces of sustainability in Italian ecovillages: Food as 'contact zone'.' *International Journal of Consumer Studies* 39, no. 5(June), 468–477. https://doi.org/10.1111/ijcs.12225

Ergas, C. and Clement, M.T. 2016 'Ecovillages, Restitution, and the Political-Economic Opportunity Structure: An Urban Case Study in Mitigating the Metabolic Rift.' *Critical Sociology*, 42, no. 7–8(January): 1195–1211. https:// doi.org/10.1177/0896920515569085

Esteves, A.M. 2017 ''Commoning' at the borderland: Ecovillage development, socio-economic segregation and institutional mediation in southwestern Alentejo, Portugal.' *Journal of Political Ecology*, 24, no. 1: 968–991. https:// doi.org/10.2458/v24i1.20978

Frenken, K. and Schor, J. 2017 'Putting the sharing economy into perspective.' *Environmental Innovation and Societal Transitions*, 23(June): 3–10. https:// doi.org/10.1016/j.eist.2017.01.003

GEN Europe. n.d. 'Ecovillages: What is an Ecovillage?' Accessed April 3, 2021. https://gen-europe.org/ecovillages/what-is-an-ecovillage/

Hall, R. 2015 'The ecovillage experience as an evidence base for national well-being strategies.' *Intellectual Economics*, 9, no. 1(April): 30–42. https://doi .org/10.1016/j.intele.2015.07.001

Hansen, A.H. 2019 ''It has to be reasonable': pragmatic ways of living sustainably in Danish eco-communities.' In *The Role of Non-State Actors in the Green Transition*, 86–104. London: Routledge.

Jakobsen, P. and Gutzon Larsen, H. 2019 'An alternative for whom? The evolution and socio-economy of Danish cohousing.' *Urban Research & Practice*, 12, no. 4: 414–430. https://doi.org/10.1080/17535069.2018.1465582

Litfin, K.T. 2014 *Ecovillages: Lessons for Sustainable Community*. Cambridge: Polity Press.

Lockyer, J. 2017 'Community, commons, and degrowth at Dancing Rabbit Ecovillage.' *Journal of Political Ecology*, 24 no. 1: 519–542. https://doi.org /10.2458/v24i1.20890

Losardo, M. 2016 ''New Ways of Living, as Old as the World' Best Practices and Sustainability in the Example of the Italian Ecovillage Network'. *Studia Ethnologica Croatica*, 28, no.1(January): 47–70. https://doi.org/10.17234 /sec.28.3

von Lüpke, G. 2012 'Ecovillages Islands of the Future?' *RCC Perspectives: Realizing Utopia: Ecovillage Endeavors and Academic*, 8: 73–78. https://doi.org /10.5282/rcc/6182

Megré, V. 1996 *Anastasia*. South Lake Tahoe: Ringing Cedars Press.

Moravčíková, D., and Fürjészová, T. 2018 'Ecovillage as an Alternative Way of Rural Life: Evidence From Hungary and Slovakia.' *European Countryside*, 10, no. 4: 693–710. https://doi.org/10.2478/euco-2018-0038

Mychajluk, L. 2017 'Learning to live and work together in an ecovillage community of practice.' *European Journal for Research on the Education and Learning of Adults*, 8, no. 2: 181–196. https://doi.org/10.3384/rela.2000-7426 .rela9092

Richardson, L. 2015 'Performing the sharing economy.' *Geoforum*, 67(December): 121–129. https://doi.org/10.1016/j.geoforum.2015.11.004

Tummers, L. 2015 'The re-emergence of self-managed co-housing in Europe: A critical review of co-housing research.' *Urban Studies*, 53, no. 10(May): 2023–2040. https://doi.org/10.1177/0042098015586696

Waerther, S. 2014 'Sustainability in ecovillages – a reconceptualization.' *International Journal Of Management and Applied Research*, 1, no. 1(August): 1–16. https://doi.org/10.18646/2056.11.14-001

CHAPTER 3

Easy Sharing: A Sharing-Economy Pilot Service in Areas of Multiple Deprivation in West Edinburgh

Catherine Lyons
Independent Consultant, UK
Morgan Currie
University of Edinburgh, UK

Abstract

This chapter describes Easy Sharing, a pilot service from the Edinburgh Tool Library (ETL). ETL lends from a library of 1000 tools and has made more than 13,000 loans in four years. Over a 20-week period, Easy Sharing provided pick-up and drop-off of reserved ETL items at four community organizations in areas of multiple deprivation in West Edinburgh, combining a digital platform with social engagement and transport logistics. The goal of Easy Sharing was to introduce an alternative economic infrastructure, a Library of Things, that can engender sharing over time. Through ethnography, surveys, and focus groups, we investigate the drivers and barriers to participation in the sharing economy, interrogating the receptiveness and capacity of people facing barriers to using a library of things over retail consumption and other forms of

How to cite this book chapter:
Lyons, C. and Currie, M. 2022. Easy Sharing: A Sharing-Economy Pilot Service in Areas of Multiple Deprivation in West Edinburgh. In: Travlou, P. and Ciolfi, L. (eds.) *Ethnographies of Collaborative Economies across Europe: Understanding Sharing and Caring*. Pp. 51–71. London: Ubiquity Press. DOI: https://doi.org/10.5334/bct.d. License: CC BY-NC-ND

reuse. We report stories of reception by members of these communities. We conclude with the argument that a platform-mediated sharing economy would be not so much an innovation as in fact a restoration of historic social bonding, mitigating the pressures of current deprivation by introducing infrastructure to strengthen community.

Introducing Easy Sharing

This chapter reports on a pilot Library of Things (LoT) service, Easy Sharing, from the Edinburgh Tool Library (ETL). Easy Sharing extended the geographic reach of ETL beyond its two current lending locations in Edinburgh during a 20-week period, from 24 May till 4 October 2019. Using participant observation and surveys, the authors spoke to community members who were being introduced to the platform to gauge receptiveness in the four areas of multiple deprivation where Easy Sharing was implemented. At follow-up focus groups at two of the lending locations, the authors asked participants more general questions about sharing and reuse and what shape they would like a LoT in their community to take. This research adds to a small body of literature that has sought to understand societal willingness to engage with sharing initiatives, the role of community and place in fostering sharing, and what barriers might prevent these shifts (Cherry and Pidgeon 2018; Amelie 2017; Alibinsson and Perera 2012).

Making sharing a social norm poses challenges, compounded by the difficulty that among the people spoken to for this chapter, most had never heard of LoTs. In the face of these hurdles, we ask:

- How receptive are community members to the sharing economy and Easy Sharing. and what barriers might prevent membership?
- What role might community bonds play in developing sharing initiatives?

We hypothesize that a complex interplay between new infrastructures and existing community relationships will influence cultural reception of LoTs. By drawing on the strength of existing local ties, Easy Sharing might incrementally create cultural receptiveness to sharing. Below we position Easy Sharing within literature on the 'sharing economy' before providing greater detail on Easy Sharing and the Edinburgh context. We then detail our methods, findings, and conclusions.

Libraries of Things in the Sharing Economy

Around the world, sharing economies present alternative consumption models that suppress the market for new consumer goods and reduce the cost of post-consumer processing. Examples of the sharing economy include sharing events, such as bartering and auction sites and swap meets (Albinsson and Perera 2012), and peer-to-peer (p2p) sharing communities. The appetite for these alternative forms of exchange appears to be growing; surveys conducted by Nielsen (2014) in 60 countries revealed that two-thirds of participants claimed they would share products through a p2p system.

LoTs are proving to be one of the more tractable models for establishing a sharing economy. LoTs lend items such as tools or toys, often in exchange for a membership fee; they are often run by volunteers, typically build inventory from donated items, and have curtailed hours. Ameli (2017) notes that LoTs offer stable locations and hours and an online platform to manage loans, all of which reduce the burden of exchange logistics present in p2p sharing, while centralising liability and maintenance. The hub-and-spoke architecture of the LoT is much more scalable than a p2p service, which would require repeatedly collecting single items from multiple locations. Further, many LoTs host workshops and social playtime with toys, fostering a sense of community that commercial retail does not offer (Albinsson and Perera 2012). LoTs therefore have the potential to destigmatize second-hand goods and promote common borrowing behaviour as a form of social inclusion.

We view LoTs and other sharing cultures as distinct from commercial platforms that have taken hold in the mainstream through companies such as Airbnb, Uber, and Taskrabbit. International commercial platforms manage the idle capacity of a resource or person — whether unused apartments, cars, or someone with both skill and time on their hands — and they help clients exploit these resources across distance (Light and Miskelly 2015). Light and Miskelly (2019) distinguish these online for-profit platforms, which commodify otherwise private resources, from 'caring-based sharing' initiatives that are embedded in a locality. Caring-based sharing is non-rent seeking, not-for-profit, and focused on giving and reciprocating items in a manner that builds relations over time. Rather than growing to international scale, to levels where exchange is highly or entirely impersonal, these initiatives are ideally local. If these projects grow, they are best done through what Light and Miskelly (2019: 598) call 'meshing', through an 'ecology of mutually-supportive systems' that grow across a locality. A healthy sharing ecosystem will yield many local collectives along with several technical and social scaffolds between them.

In this chapter, we distinguish not only between sharing and renting, but also between sharing — as in both shared *use* and shared *ownership* — and p2p lending, which entails shared use but private ownership. When items are donated to a community-run LoT, ownership transfers to the community; the donor has rights to the item that are equal to but not greater than the rights of others in the community.

In the next section we describe in greater detail the mechanics of Easy Sharing and its implementation in four locales. We then use this case study to show how Easy Sharing aligns with a caring-based sharing vision that will succeed, we believe, by drawing on existing community bonds to normalize the virtues of buying less, whether for economic or environmental reasons or both.

The Easy Sharing Pilot

> If we are to re-frame consumption, borrowing has to be easy and social. Easy means logistics are simple and reliable. Social means that your local libraries of things are a household name in your community; borrowing means less effort for you and your friends. (Lyons, 2019)

ETL's Easy Sharing pilot ran from May to October 2019. ETL lends from a library of 1000 tools covering woodwork, gardening and bicycle repair, and has made more than 12,000 loans in four years. The workshops at ETL's locations encourage skill-sharing and provide classes, open sessions and social-inclusion projects. Regular members pay an annual subscription fee for unlimited loans (like an all-you-can-eat buffet).[1] The service this buys is scalable for the member in that additional tool use does not incur additional cost. Subscriptions fund storage space for tools and the licence for the library-management software, myTurn. The tools come from donations, and library processes are run by volunteers. ETL's model stands in contrast to LoTs that charge pay-per-use fees to their members.[2] Access to ETL's platform is revenue-generating, but its material resources in themselves are non-revenue-generating.

Easy Sharing received funding from Nesta's Sharelab in Scotland on behalf of the Scottish Government. The project arose partly in reaction to a report commissioned by the Ministry for Economy, Jobs and Fair Work, which warns Scotland's government against reactively regulating 'new collaborative platforms that land in this country' (Goulden 2018). The report urges Scotland to pioneer home-grown collaborative platforms that deliver social value and inclusive economic growth; Sharelab Scotland funded five such projects, of which Easy Sharing is one (NESTA, 2018).

Easy Sharing offered a technical platform and a physical borrowing service along with opportunities for community engagement. The pilot supported pickup and drop-off of reserved items once a week at four West Edinburgh community organisations: Wester Hailes Arts for Leisure and Education (WHALE Arts), Broomhouse Hub, North Edinburgh Arts (NEA) and granton:hub. All are outside the social orbit of the Edinburgh Tool Library and too far away for transport to be quick and easy. All are among the 20 per cent most deprived areas of Scotland, according to the Scottish Index of Multiple Deprivation (SIMD); Wester Hailes and Muirhouse are in the top 5 per cent (SIMD 2016[3]) (Figures 3.1 and 3.2).

---

[1] £30 in the first year; £20 subsequently. A pay-it-forward fee of £40 subsidizes a £10 concessionary fee for students and people who are receiving benefits, unemployed or over 60. Tool donors get free membership.

[2] ETL has other revenue streams, including third-sector partnerships, specialist worshop courses and consultancy, which are separate from LoT operation. Pay-per-use sharing libraries include Share Oxford (shareoxford.org) and the Library of Things in London (www.libraryofthings.co.uk).

[3] The Scottish Index of Deprivation was since revised in 2020.

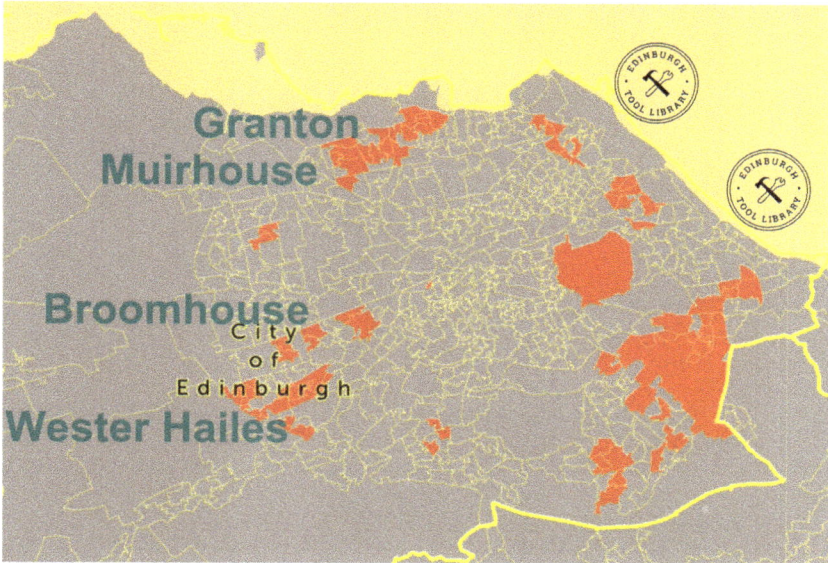

Figure 3.1: City of Edinburgh: areas falling within the top 20 per cent of multiple deprivation are shown in red (SIMD, 2016). Easy Sharing communities are indicated; ETL locations (Leith and Portobello) are marked by a logo.

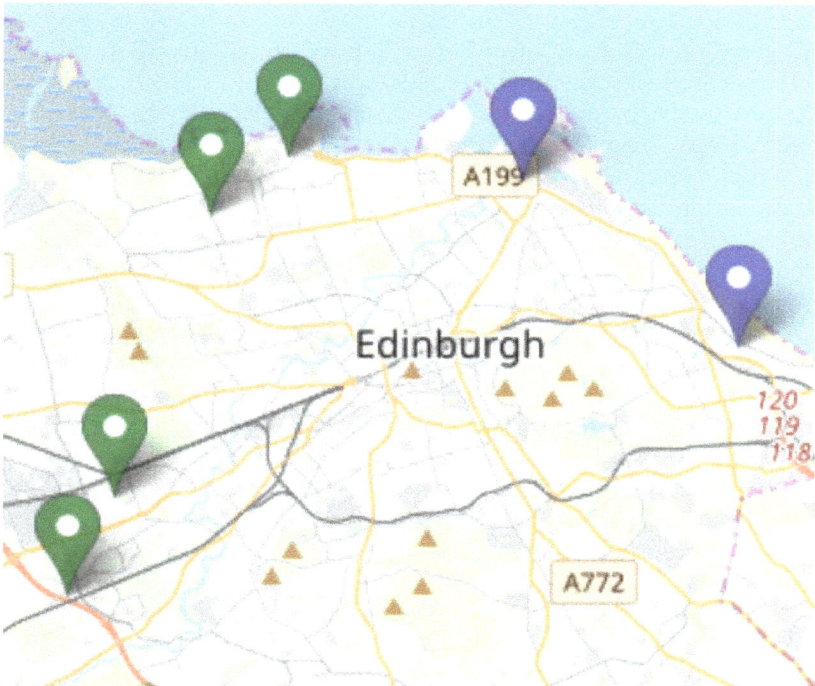

Figure 3.2: The map at easysharing.org. ETL locations are blue; Easy Sharing locations are green.

Figure 3.3: Easy Sharing postcard.

Under Sharelab funding, Easy Sharing created a free membership category and therefore presented no financial barrier to potential members. Because ETL's business model already offered members unlimited loans rather than pay-per-use, Easy Sharing membership likewise did not deter repeated use of the service.

To use Easy Sharing, participants would visit easysharing.org and select an Easy-Sharing pick-up location on a map, which linked them to ETL's myTurn catalogue with that location set. myTurn is the leading LoT software, used in over 400 LoTs on five continents. The project funded myTurn to support multi-location delivery logistics, which makes ETL the first LoT to build this option into its online platform.

Easy Sharing employed a part-time coordinator who delivered and collected loans at each of the community organisation's Easy Sharing stations every Friday over the course of the 20 weeks; he was met at each location by a local coordinator, an Easy Sharing Liaison Officer, appointed by the centre for the partnership. To pick up and return tools, Easy Sharing members visited during the Easy Sharing hour assigned to each centre. In effect, the project tested a hub-and-spoke model via community organisations.

The project promoted the service by distributing 1500 postcards throughout the centres (Figure 3.3). As hubs of community activity, the centres allowed Easy Sharing staff to reach many locals who offered to promote the service through schools and churches and by word of mouth. At WHALE Arts and Broomhouse Hub, Liaison Officers distributed the cards locally through a housing association; at the local library, where 20 postcards were taken away in a week; and door to door.

Methodology

Researchers adopted a mixed-method approach that combined participant observation and surveys at six events at the four community hubs between May and July 2019, and follow-up focus groups at two of the hubs, Broomhouse Centre in October and NEA in December 2019.[4] We detail the findings from the community events first, before describing the focus groups. In our findings we also draw from loan statistics collected by myTurn (Appendix II).

Community events and surveys

ETL hosted four Community Making days, one at each hub, to introduce Easy Sharing in each location, between 31 May and 17 July 2019; researchers also conducted surveys at two community days at NEA and WHALE

The five-minute surveys allowed researchers to engage in conversation and gather stories about people's willingness to borrow. The surveys (see Figure 3.4) asked people questions about digital exclusion by enquiring if they use online services and social media, about whether they use the public library and shop second-hand, about whether they have heard of LoTs before and what items they might use a LoT to borrow, and any barriers they could foresee to Easy Sharing adoption, such as stigma about second-hand borrowing, lack of confidence with tools, or lack of internet access. Survey findings are in Appendix I. The two researchers who conducted fieldwork are employees of the project, one as project researcher and one as project manager.

Focus groups

Researchers also held focus groups with local residents at two of the community centres that hosted Easy Sharing, to gather more ideas about the reception and use of a local LoT. One took place at Broomhouse Hub on 8 August 2019, as part of a community garden party and during the Easy Sharing pilot; the other was at NEA on 16 December 2019, following the conclusion of the pilot in October. Both focus groups had five participants – two women and three men.

The focus groups began with the researchers explaining the Easy Sharing project and the purpose of the research. Researchers then asked participants to tell 'sharing stories' — to talk about their feelings and experiences with sharing and reuse, from buying and receiving second-hand items to donating or giving away their own second-hand goods. In the second part of the focus group, researchers introduced the concept of LoTs and managed sharing. Participants discussed

---

[4] Plans for a March focus group at granton: hub were cancelled due to the Covid-19 lockdown.

EASY SHARING

easysharing.org

Thank you for answering this survey for an Edinburgh Tool Library pilot service

1. Which of these do you use online?
- ○ Social Media
- ○ Email
- ○ Online shopping
- ○ Banking/Bills/Government services
- ○ Games and Entertainment
- ○ Other, write here: _____

2. Do you use the public library?
○ Often   ○ Rarely   ○ Not registered

If you do, what for?
- ○ Books
- ○ DVDs/Music/Audiobooks
- ○ Computer/Internet
- ○ Events/Classes/Workshops
- ○ Other, write here: _____

3. *Everything in the tool library is secondhand and maintained.* It helps to know if you buy from Gumtree, charity shops, etc.?
○ Often   ○ Rarely   ○ Never

4. Before this project, had you heard of a *library of things* other than books?
○ No   ○ Yes

5. What kind of equipment would you be interested in borrowing, as needed?
- ○ Tools/Gardening   ○ Bikes
- ○ Sewing/Knitting   ○ Wedding/Formal clothes
- ○ Baby things   ○ Cookware/Partyware
- ○ Toys   ○ Camping/Picnic
- ○ Other, write here: _____
- ○ Not interested in borrowing

6. Is there anything that would prevent you from using this pilot service?
○ No   ○ Yes

If yes:
- ○ Access to the internet is difficult
- ○ Not interested in tools
- ○ Not interested in borrowing
- ○ Other, write here: _____

Figure 3.4: Easy Sharing survey.

Figure 3.5: Examples of the sharing shapes.

types of items they could imagine borrowing, including items they wouldn't ordinarily buy, and what a sustained library of things in their community might look like. Participants talked about the nuts and bolts of a hypothetical LoT, from opening hours to location, and also considered barriers to its adoption.

Physical prompts in the form of cardboard cut-outs using printed icons from the Noun Project,[5] dubbed 'sharing shapes', were used to support dialogue. Sharing shapes (see Figure 3.5) exemplified the kinds of things that might be

_____

5 http://thenounproject.com

shared and helped the researchers to model processes by which sharing could be managed and imagined.

Outcomes: Early Reports on Easy Sharing

In the West of Edinburgh, Terence drives to WHALE Arts to leave DIY and woodworking tools with Fabien. Fabien will drop off a couple of them with a neighbour. He makes a phone call and another man comes to collect some of the tools. Terence will come back next week to pick them up. Meanwhile, he is also arranging to deliver an angle grinder to Broomhouse Hub for a lady who is trying to remove the stubborn remains of a broken fence. In Muirhouse, there's a man who is interested in borrowing a lawnmower after his was stolen. In Granton, there's a woman who says, 'I wouldn't have bought a lawnmower if I had known I could borrow one.' (Lyons, Easy Sharing blog 2019)

In this section we describe the four community making days, summarise the results of our surveys and focus groups with community members, and offer some preliminary data on platform use.

Making days

The WHALE making day took place on 24 May; we timed it to coincide with a free community lunch that an estimated 25 people attended. Outside the lunch hall, ETL staff were building a little free library that members of a WHALE place-making group would later decorate. A small number of people walked over to talk to us, but not as many as we would have liked, though we did speak to all the lunch attendants and invited them to sign up. A woman from the Mums into Business programme told us she plans to make and sell herbal teas, and she was interested in borrowing a strimmer to renovate her garden and grow herbs. At the second WHALE event, a participant told us she would like to use Easy Sharing because 'My husband spends a fortune on tools ... it would keep him out of B&Q.'

Easy Sharing at WHALE also inspired existing community making activities, particularly a men's making group started by a local resident and WHALE's community link worker. WHALE gave the men a storage room holding items that were to be relocated, and the group has persisted, curtailed only by Covid lockdown. Anticipating access to 'a pool of resources' has motivated the group to clear the room, borrow tools and launch projects. One in the group commented that Easy Sharing has made a 'huge impact' on this initiative. Another outcome of Easy Sharing at WHALE was that the local resident employed to work on Easy Sharing has remained an employee since, working front of house.

At the Broomhouse making event, ETL staff constructed an outdoor bench for the Broomhouse Hub's new building. The event attracted around 15 people, including a local councillor and a community policeman. Several people spoke to us with ideas about how they might support the service. A mum who had just collected her children from primary school and was on the parent council told us that the school would be interested in promoting Easy Sharing. Two retired ladies, both church elders, thought the minister would be willing to promote Easy Sharing to the parish. One of them signed up and reserved an angle grinder to remove a broken chainlink fence since she had no suitable tools.

Granton:hub's making event attracted the fewest participants, with around five. The event centred on building a bench for the large community garden, and, perhaps unsurprisingly, all participants were interested in gardening equipment. One told us 'If I had known about Easy Sharing I would not have bought a lawnmower – you need to have lived in my neighbourhood for 10 years before I'd have been comfortable asking my neighbour.'

At NEA's making event, 12 participants built a coat stand. We spoke to parents, mostly mothers, who frequently visited public libraries with their children to look at books and play with toys, and they readily saw the possibilities of LoTs for baby accessories, toys and bikes. Children accompanying a parent-respondent joined in to express their views; one nine-year old suggested that roller skates could be added to the library, and another, a four-year old, asked to go to a toy library that day. We met a man whose lawnmower had been stolen and who wanted to use Easy Sharing since he could not afford a replacement.

Surveys

According to the surveys, very few of our participants had heard of LoTs; among the few who indicated prior knowledge were those who had already heard of ETL or toy libraries, and a small number knew of the musical instrument library in Muirhouse public library in partnership with NEA. This finding indicates that Easy Sharing has been a means to introduce the sharing economy concept to participants. With only a few exceptions, participants were interested in borrowing rather than buying at least some items, especially gardening tools and camping gear, which ranked highest among items people wanted to borrow.

Originally, we had hypothesized that difficulty using online platforms and stigma about using second-hand goods might hinder participation. According to the surveys, however, neither of these assumptions proved to be true. Participants did not feel opposed to second-hand use, nor did they report trouble with online shopping or using social media. The survey results did find that a few people saw other barriers to participation or found no motivation to participate. At Broomhouse a participant was concerned about the short collection time, which reflects other studies that show LoTs' limited hours preventing accessibility for some (Ameli 2017). At WHALE and NEA, some felt either that their family members could lend them tools or that many items, such as baby things, could be easily sourced from neighbours and friends.

Focus groups

With the focus groups, three main themes emerged around sharing and LoTs: (1) *material* value and maintenance, (2) *social networks* and social values in sharing and reuse, and (3) concerns around *processes*, such as management, transport and storage.

The *material* items that candidates suggested for managed sharing included tools for woodwork, decorating, and gardening. Both groups agreed that ladders, while seldom needed, were particularly expensive and very difficult to store at home, making them a good item to borrow, though they would need particular transport and safety information if lent. Participants suggested leisure items would work well at a local LoT, including camping, fishing, and golfing equipment, and they suggested items that would support trying out hobbies such as painting equipment and musical instruments, before committing to spending money on them. Participants also proposed toys and children's equipment, including buggies, waterproof clothing, and hiking equipment for young people, and school uniforms. The Broomhouse group suggested barbecues as an occasional-use item, especially to replace non-recyclable disposable barbecues.

Participants at both places talked about the material value of electrical items, especially power tools, and the reliability of second-hand electricals, and they thought that a guarantee of reliability – such as working batteries – was more important than newness, since new budget tools might not be reliable. Said one participant, 'I don't think of it as second hand if it's from the tool library. You need an instrument to do a job, and as long as it works properly there's no need to complicate matters further.' There was some scepticism, however, that reliable tools would be donated to a LoT. Both groups pointed out the need for clear user instructions and Portable Appliance Testing for electrical safety. The Broomhouse group talked about the prohibitive cost of getting things fixed, which raised the prospect of a repair service to complement the library.

Both groups also talked about social networks and the social value of reusing goods, which led to discussions around the differences between sharing something, selling it, and giving it away. Participants felt that direct sharing between people plays an important role in their communities, which indicates degrees of trust. For instance, charity-shop donation, participants thought, could be less rewarding for a donor than giving to someone they know — a point that mirrors scholarship on the emotional rewards of giving to friends and acquaintances (Aknin et al. 2013). Children's clothes and toys especially are subject to close-knit social networks of handing down. Some participants pointed out they would always try borrowing from a neighbour before a LoT. On the other hand, participants also talked about how recipients might actually prefer the anonymity of receiving items through a mediating agent, such as a charity shop or LoT, rather than receiving what is perceived as charity by someone they do not know well; one gave food banks as an analogy.

There was also discussion around how a local LoT would benefit and grow from people finding value in the prognostic use of the donated item — that is, the knowledge that its functional value will be retained by a new owner. When contemplating a LoT that would be embedded in the community, value in this prognostic use of a donated item could offset the monetary loss of selling that item, if it was sufficiently small, so that donating would be motivated by enlightened self-interest. An exchange at Broomhouse illustrates this point:

> P4: Aye, you might be thinking, I want rid of this. You might think, see if I can get something for it; stick it on eBay or that. But if it's —so nobody else in the area gets to benefit from that you know — but if there's a library and people are able to borrow it and give it back and things, like, if you know that stuff's getting tested and things regularly as well, you know that it's gonna be decent equipment, it's gonna be —
>
> P5: Yeah, so that's what I'm saying, you know, the equipment's gonna be tested and things so that's —
>
> P1: Yeah that's a major thing aye
>
> P5: That's your membership yeah, like I say if you've given something to the centre then you've got a bigger toolbox —
>
> P1: And you feel like it's yours as well, which gives you more sense of keeping that safe as well, and making sure that other tools come back and stuff like that and so on and so forth — it kinda gives you more of an attachment to it.

The above exchange also indicates how donating could be an act of trust. Other statements reinforced this point that social cohesion is necessary to trusted sharing and is a function of settled communities and neighbourly bonding; on the other hand, where neighbours are new to each other, there is less trusted sharing. One participant at NEA reflected on how things used to be in the 1960s and 70s, when organic social networks obviated the need for formal organisation:

> Sharing's not a new thing in this community. That goes back … the front garden was always flowers for your mum. Back garden was vegetables. Everybody grew vegetables. You had a fork and spade, but Johnny down

the road had a wheelbarrow. There was an exchange system, shall we say, and the planting season, you always had too much, too many seeds, so you shared the plants with your neighbour. Or you borrowed a wheelbarrow, a horse's stable down the road. That system was going. Neighbours swapped furniture. Didn't have money to buy new furniture, so swapped furniture. People did these things at that time. I'm talking late 60s early 70s because there was community; it wasn't organised.

By contrast, younger participants who were less settled felt less able to ask neighbours to lend them items. Participants pointed out, with reference to a new housing development near the community centre, that new housing also lacks these organic sharing networks. Participants also observed that the distinction between settled community networks in the past and greater residential mobility now correlated with ownership versus tenancy, and the difference in responsibility and autonomy in home maintenance. Said one, 'it used to be, like, if you owned your house and stuff and you do your DIY and whatever, but now there's so many people who can't afford to buy a place, so just renting.'

Strengthening cohesion in order to support trusted sharing was a theme of both focus groups. To Broomhouse participants, the mediated sharing that a well-organised LoT would provide was analogous to the dignity afforded by charity shops. And at NEA, the outreach needed to make a LoT succeed provided the opportunity to build cohesion in areas that have lost it over time.

Finally, both focus groups envisaged themselves as stakeholders in the *processes* of running a community asset, not as service users. A participant at Broomhouse Hub speculated:

Just say it was a coping saw that you needed to dae a job, so you got the coping saw, and then you gave that to the library, that kind of makes the rest of the tools in the library yours as well. So you're givin your saw away, but at the same time you're gaining a whole toolbox.

At NEA, a participant proposed that there was obvious readiness for a local LoT and how to build momentum and outreach:

[It would] need a panel of people, group of people who are the drivers, who will think of the organisational aspects, saying what has worked before, why isn't this thing already happening? There's the desire for it to happen … There's a sense in this community, so why has this not happened?

Both groups speculated that the LoT would be run by a combination of paid staff and volunteers, and that the LoT would need to consider storage and delivery needs. For instance, some of the items that people would want to borrow, such as ladders and lawnmowers, would be bulky to move or store, and that was precisely why they made good candidates for sharing. Transport of bulky items, especially for use by people with mobility issues, led to a detailed discussion of a possible delivery service from Broomhouse Hub and the immediate vicinity and its natural boundary, a discussion that would determine which areas should be part of the catchment for a local LoT.

Platform analytics

In all, the project helped grow ETL membership, with the first loan occurring two weeks after the first making event. Eventually, over the course of the project, 80 people registered with Easy Sharing and 186 loans were made by 39 people, which means almost half of the new members joined because they wanted access to Easy Sharing without having an immediate need. The data indicates strong take-up in WHALE, reflecting the activity of the men's maker group. NEA had a smaller number of loans, an unintended consequence of partnering directly with the Shed, a wood workshop there that is detached from the main building. We had hypothesized that Shed users would be interested in Easy Sharing, but this was not borne out.

Conclusion

In the first phase of the project, researchers interrogated local residents' exposure to LoTs and their receptiveness to them. In the second phase, focus groups made an extended investigation into experiences, feelings, and attitudes about sharing, and elicited ideas from local people about creating a possible sharing-economy community initiative that could have sustained presence in the community.

Easy Sharing was a delivery service from elsewhere in the city, brought into areas of multiple deprivation; it was not an organic grassroots initiative. As a delivery service, Easy Sharing did not engender the social amenities of ETL's permanent locations, with open-access workshops, classes, and volunteering opportunities. Rather, Easy Sharing was a service sent into communities, a hub-and-spoke logistics model that was adequate for operating a pilot. In contrast, a sustainable embedded local amenity would of necessity be co-created and owned by local people. The focus groups evidence a way forward for participatory design, should funding become available, towards building community-owned and -run LoTs.

Further, as mentioned, Easy Sharing was funded under NESTA's Sharelab, 'to grow evidence and understanding of how collaborative digital platforms can deliver social impact', rather than commercial gain. That framing of the pilot service emphasised user experience, service design, and process. This technical focus, however, was too narrow, and did not interrogate what social impact might mean in a community of multiple deprivation.

The focus groups afforded us a much deeper examination of the social significance of sharing, without getting bogged down with the workings of technological platforms. There, participants painted a vivid picture of what a thriving local sharing economy looks like: locals knowing which neighbours to approach for a loan of a tool; people swapping, bartering, and receiving children's clothes and toys and handing things on in turn. People with practical skills helping others to learn, knowledge of who had mobility problems and would need support if they were to be included, informally arranged local events, and intimate knowledge of local geography for a feasible delivery service. In short, both focus groups described a dynamic network of relationships of trust grounded in a stable community.

Participants assumed that the people running a LoT, whether paid or as volunteers, would be familiar and well connected locals. Donating items to the LoT would not feel the same as giving them away anonymously to a charity shop, but rather like putting them in an extra-large toolbox that belongs as much to the donor as to anybody else. This sense of being part of a network of trusted relationships carried over from depictions of local community to visions of what a community-owned LoT would feel like.

The SIMD data is an instructive indicator for a locally created sharing economy; it points to both the need and the potential of a community-owned LoT. SIMD divides Scotland into 6976 data zones, each with an average population of 760, which are ranked across seven domains: income, employment, education, health, access to services, crime and housing. Each community centre where Easy Sharing operated serves more than one datazone. Figures 3.6 and 3.7 indicate the ranking of the datazones of the community centres' locations. NEA, in Muirhouse, is in the top 10% of multiple deprivation; Broomhouse is in the top 20%.

The focus groups shed light on vibrant community cohesion, despite high levels of deprivation, and the contrasts between the past and the present: residential stability and high levels of trust are being replaced with greater residential transience, poverty, and subsequent dependence on landlords for household maintenance, along with less time to build trusted bonds for sharing with neighbours. In this context, a LoT could amplify existing social capital, in addition to reducing the urban carbon footprint.

We can contrast the findings of the focus groups with those of the surveys carried out in phase 1. The surveys interrogated awareness and receptiveness of local people for LoTs, with emphasis on their openness to second-hand use, borrowing from a LoT, and using an online platform. The phase 2 focus groups prompted people to imagine habitual sharing through potential LoTs and provided a more systemic scoping of sharing-economy capacity and the social significance of community-mediated reuse.

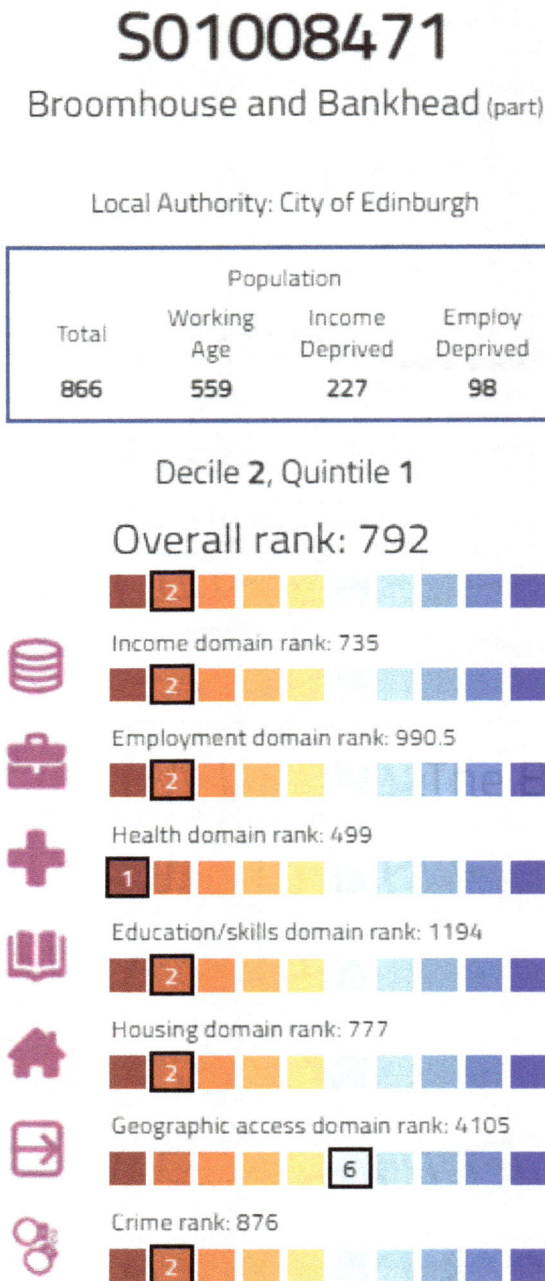

S01008471

Broomhouse and Bankhead (part)

Local Authority: City of Edinburgh

Population			
Total	Working Age	Income Deprived	Employ Deprived
866	559	227	98

Decile 2, Quintile 1

Overall rank: 792

Income domain rank: 735

Employment domain rank: 990.5

Health domain rank: 499

Education/skills domain rank: 1194

Housing domain rank: 777

Geographic access domain rank: 4105

Crime rank: 876

Figure 3.6: Broomhouse SIMD ranking.

S01008930

Muirhouse (part)

Local Authority: City of Edinburgh

	Population		
Total	Working Age	Income Deprived	Employ Deprived
876	527	321	117

Decile **1**, Quintile **1**

Overall rank: 228

Income domain rank: 149

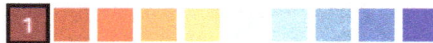

Employment domain rank: 444

Health domain rank: 487

Education/skills domain rank: 182

Housing domain rank: 588

Geographic access domain rank: 6613

Crime rank: 101

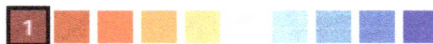

Figure 3.7: Muirhouse.

The contrast points to the following insights. A sharing economy is already embedded in the communities of multiple deprivation we researched, even though online sharing platforms are a little-known innovation. The social significance of sharing an item, whether as a loan or a gift, is informed by the degree of trust between the parties. Donors value the prognostic use of an item, sometimes more highly than its resale value, when prognostic use will remain within the donor's social network. It follows that a community-owned LoT can be conceived of as an extended social network, and, as such, it offers greater potential for valuing prognostic use than a charity shop does.

The phase 2 research allows us to reframe the proposition of a platform-mediated sharing economy not as *innovation* but in fact as *restoration*. It offers the possibility of mitigating the pressures of deprivation by introducing infrastructure to strengthen social bonding. A strategic goal of Easy Sharing was to test scalability and replicability of LoTs organically without mimicking highly centralised commercial platforms, which value economy of scale above other benefits. The concept of restorative infrastructure for the sharing economy points the way to further research and community development.

Acknowledgements

The authors wish to thank the Easy Sharing Coordinator and the Easy Sharing Liaison officers at WHALE Arts and Broomhouse Hub. The authors thank NESTA for project funding.

References

Albinsson, P.A., and Perera, B.Y. 2012 Alternative marketplaces in the 21st century: Building community through sharing events, *Journal of Consumer Behaviour, 11*, 303–315.

Aknin, L.B., Dunn, E.W., Sandstrom, G.M. and Norton, M.I. 2013 Does Social Connection Turn Good Deeds into Good Feelings? On the Value of Putting the 'Social' in Prosocial Spending. International Journal of Happiness and Development 1, no. 2: 155–171.

Ameli, N. 2017 Libraries of Things as a new form of sharing: Pushing the Sharing Economy, *The Design Journal, 20*:sup1, DOI: https://doi.org/10.1080/1460 6925.2017.1352833.

Cherry, C.E. and Pidgeon, N.F. 2018 Is sharing the solution? Exploring public acceptability of the sharing economy, *Journal of Cleaner Production, 195*.

Goulden, H. 2018 Scottish Expert Advisory Panel on the Collaborative Economy Report, The Scottish Government, ISBN 9781788515610

INGDiba. 2015 Economic Research: "My car is my castle" Retrieved November 16, 2019, from https://www.ing-diba.de/pdf/ueber-uns/presse/publikationen/ing-diba-studie-sharing-economy-31-07-2015.pdf

Light, A. and Miskelly, C. 2015 Sharing economy vs sharing cultures? Designing for social, economic and environmental good. *Interaction Design and Architecture(s), 24*(Spring), 49–62. ISSN 1826-9745

Light, A. and Miskelly, C. 2019 Platforms, scales and networks: meshing a local sustainable sharing economy. *Computer Supported Cooperative Work.* ISSN 0925-9724

Lyons, C. 2019 Easy Sharing: Making sharing simpler than shopping. Nesta Blog, retrieved 30 July, https://www.nesta.org.uk/blog/easy-sharing-making-sharing-simpler-shopping/

NESTA. 2018 Sharelab Scotland, retrieved 19 July 2019, https://www.nesta.org.uk/project/sharelab-scotland/

Nielsen. 2014 Global Share Community Report. Retrieved November 16, 2019, from   http://www.nielsen.com/us/en/insights/reports/2014/is-sharing-the-new-buying1.html

Seyfang, G. 2008 The New Economics of Sustainable Consumption: Seeds of Change. Springer.

SIMD. 2016 Scottish Index of Multiple Deprivation. Scottish Government. Retrieved 30 July, https://simd.scot/

Appendix I: Survey Data

N:60 unless indicated otherwise

Proportion of respondents using the internet

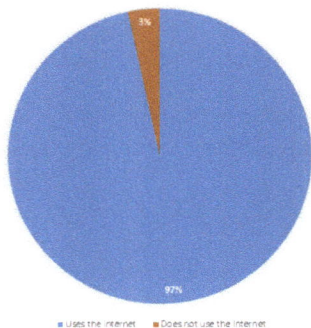

3%

97%

■ Uses the internet   ■ Does not use the internet

Proportion of respondents' purchasing secondhand goods

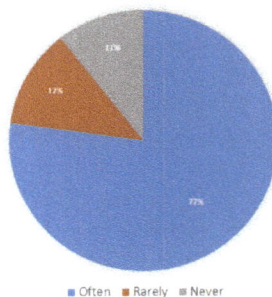

11%

17%

72%

■ Often   ■ Rarely   ■ Never

Proportion of respondents with previous knowledge of 'libraries of things'

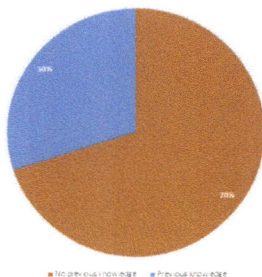

30%

70%

■ No previous knowledge   ■ Previous knowledge

Proportion of respondents interested in borrowing things

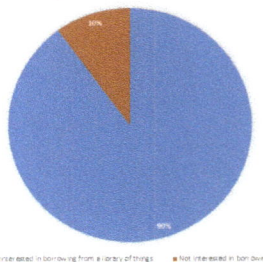

10%

90%

■ Interested in borrowing from a library of things   ■ Not interested in borrowing

Frequency of respondents' interest in different equipment (n: 54)

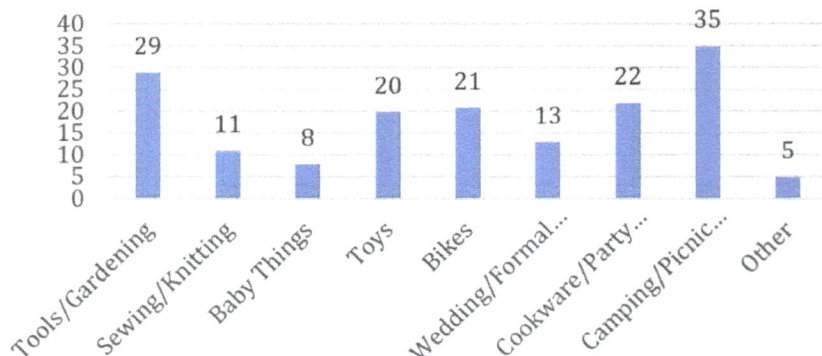

40							35	
35	29							
30								
25						22		
20			20	21				
15		11			13			
10		8						5
5								
0								

Tools/Gardening Sewing/Knitting Baby Things Toys Bikes Wedding/Formal... Cookware/Party... Camping/Picnic... Other

Appendix II: Easy Sharing Borrowing Statistics
7 June–30 July 2019

Items checked out per location

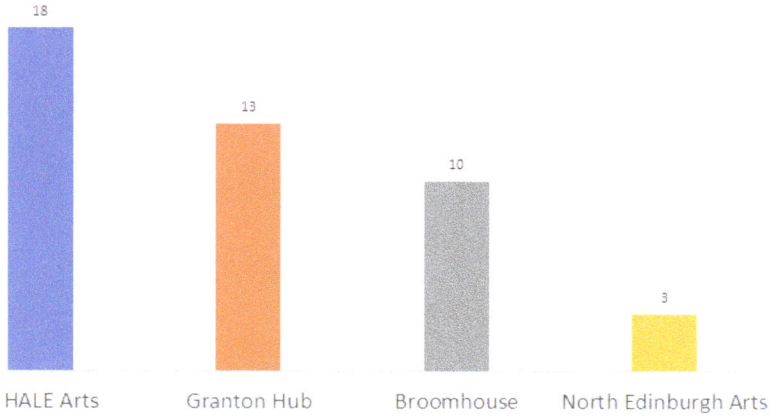

Borrowing interactions per user

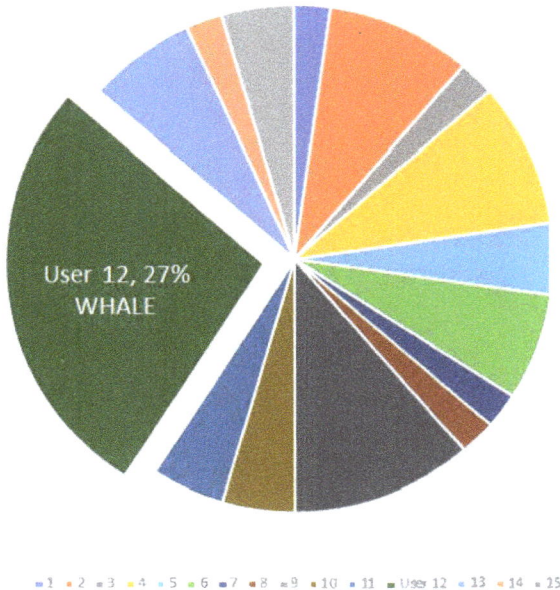

CHAPTER 4

Making Space for the Sharing Economy: Fablab Torino and the *Performativity* of Democratized Production

Samantha Cenere

University of Turin, IT

Abstract

The spreading of collaborative practices in the production and consumption of goods and services constitutes an unavoidable challenge to researchers aiming at understanding the sociospatial dynamics of economic life. Fablabs in particular are identified as expressions of a new form of material production pivoting on collaboration and democratised innovation. Embracing a recent claim in economic geography for an appreciation of the relevant role of spatial dynamics in organizations (Müller 2015), I argue for an investigation of collaborative workplaces through an ethnographic research of the situated practices involved in the process of organising a Fablab. Drawing on Actor-Network Theory and the 'performativity programme' launched by Michel Callon (1998), the chapter argues that collaborative economies could be analysed as the emergent outcome of the interaction between economic theories and heterogeneous sociotechnical arrangements through which they are brought into being, showing

How to cite this book chapter:
Cenere, S. 2022. Making Space for the Sharing Economy: Fablab Torino and the
    Performativity of Democratized Production. In: Travlou, P. and Ciolfi, L. (eds.)
    *Ethnographies of Collaborative Economies across Europe: Understanding Sharing and
    Caring.* Pp. 73–92. London: Ubiquity Press. DOI: https://doi.org/10.5334/bct.e.
    License: CC BY-NC-ND

how economics performs the economy. In order to unpack the contingent, situated, and fragile nature of this process with regards to Fablabs and Makers, the chapter discusses the data from an ethnographic investigation of a Fablab in Turin, Italy, working on two levels. Firstly, it identifies the economic theories involved in the process of performing Fablabs as collaborative and open spaces within contemporary urban economies. Secondly, it shows how sociospatial processes of organizing participate in the enactment of an economy where production and innovation have been 'democratised' and where collaboration and sharing are at the core of value production. However, the chapter highlights also how the process of actualization is never stable, resulting sometimes in failures and 'misfires' (Callon 2010).

Introduction

So-called sharing and collaborative economies represent one of the most relevant transformations in the economy of the last decades. Usually, digital technologies are considered the main trigger of this innovation, enabling the collaboration of heterogeneous economic actors. Although the labels 'sharing economy' and 'economies of collaboration' have become widely employed, these new forms of coordinating economic activities are characterised by a high degree of internal variety and heterogeneity. What is shared could be either material goods, such as houses and cars, or something immaterial, such as digital objects or services. At the same time, the spatialities related to practices of sharing are multiple, ranging from pure digital space – as in websites such as Wikipedia – to the bounded physical space of an organization – as in coworking spaces – and to the hybrid spatiality of platforms used to share physical goods or experiences – such as Airbnb and social eating platforms. Moreover, understandings of the sharing economy as a form of economic exchange alternative to the capitalist market have been widely disputed (Shor et al. 2015). Thus, claims have been made to conceive the sharing economy as something that is *performed* in multiple, contingent, and situated ways (Richardson 2015), rather than as an economic object that is distinctly identifiable. These multiple performances depend not only on what is shared, but also on the material and immaterial devices for sharing, the values inscribed in those practices, the economic discourses and imaginaries behind them, and the space through which sharing happens.

   Among these multiple examples of sharing and collaborative economies, spaces for making and coworking spaces are frequently read as part of the same phenomenon, corresponding to the spreading of urban alternative spaces of work where flexible, entrepreneurial, and collaborative forms of value production can be fostered by the multiple potentials of digital technologies (Mariotti et al. 2021). In particular, the practices performed by the members of the so-called Maker Movement and the spaces they use are considered a new urban form of small manufacturing pivoting on collaboration and sharing (Davies 2017; Gauntlett 2011). The label 'Maker' is usually applied to people engaging in various ways in a high-tech version of DIY (do-it-yourself), employing digital machines such as 3D printers, CNC milling machines, Arduino microcontrollers and laser-cutters to autonomously produce customised artefacts. The work and activities performed by Makers are usually associated with small workshops called Makerspaces and Fablabs, which provide access to digital fabrication machines and other tools.

Despite the rise of these spaces specifically devoted to Makers, the spatial dimension of the phenomenon is still a poorly explored topic, and the mainstream literature stresses instead that the heavy reliance on communities of peers connected through online open platforms makes the geography of Makers an irrelevant issue. On the contrary, scholars in both economic geography and urban studies have recently drawn attention to the spatial dimension of the phenomenon, claiming that the rise of Makers represents an innovation in the production system that entails important socio-spatial transformations too. However, these works generally assume that the most relevant spatial dimension of the phenomenon is constituted by the city, considering Makers as part of a univocal shift in contemporary urban economies in the era of digital capitalism (Armondi & Bruzzese 2017; Armondi & Di Vita 2017; Capdevila 2018). In so doing, they also take for granted the relevance of the phenomenon in terms of its capacity to constitute a shift in contemporary urban economies, usually drawing on a mainstream discourse that portrays Makers as examples of democratization of production and a new way of organizing the innovation process (cf. Doussard et al. 2017; Powell 2012; Vicari et al. 2015). Considering the rise of Makers and Fablabs as a relevant economic transformation, this literature pigeonholes Fablabs through the mobilization of concepts such as open innovation, sharing economy, and collaborative production.

However, works inspired by a post-structuralist approach to the study of economic geography have stressed that the economy is something that *is done* through practices and performances that depend on specific socio-material orderings (Jones & Murphy 2010; Müller 2015). Indeed, as the sharing economy should be used 'as a prompt rather than the target of geographical research' (Richardson 2015: 128), the extent to which a Fablab could be considered a workplace and a space of production that participates in new urban economies should be proved rather than postulated. In other words, drawing on analytical approaches that 'investigate the formation of economic realities through contingent, heterogeneous, and local processes' (Barry & Slater 2002: 180) would allow us to overcome the use of concepts such as open innovation, sharing economy, and collaborative production as explanatory categories from which to start in investigating the role of a Fablab. Rather, the present chapter claims that these concepts come from economic theories that frame the activities of Makers and contribute to the coming into being of a Fablab.

To illustrate this process, the chapter draws on the performativity programme in economic sociology and on Actor-Network Theory (ANT) in arguing that a Fablab is performed as a space of collaborative production and open innovation through a precarious process of socio-material ordering. This performance is produced precisely by the economic theories on Fablabs and Makers as harbingers of a democratization of production that are usually used to *describe* them.

The chapter starts with an introduction on the rise of Makers and Fablabs and situates them within the spreading of economic theories on a paradigm shift in the economy, pivoting on sharing practices and an open ethos towards production and innovation. The following section is dedicated to the description of the case study and the methodology employed. Showing the dialectical movement between the evidence from the field coming from the ethnographic research and the theoretical framework employed, the chapter then introduces the performativity programme in economic sociology and post-structuralist geography of organization as original theoretical frameworks to reconceptualize the relationship between economic theories on Fablabs and Makers and the concrete reality of specific Fablabs. The final sections discuss the empirical material. After showing how economic theories on collaborative economies, open innovation, and autonomous production have contributed to the creation of Fablab Torino in Turin, Italy, the discussion of the empirical findings highlights how the socio-technical arrangement constituted by the Fablab has partially failed to enact these theories. Thus, the chapter claims that, rather than being mere descriptions of what Fablabs and Makers are, economic theories envisaging the rise of collaborative economies and democratization of production participate in bringing this transformation into being. Moreover, the discussion of the empirical findings highlights that a Fablab could fail in performing this shift when the human and non-human entities that are part of the organization do not act in the way described by the theories themselves.

Collaborative Production in the Digital Age:
The Rise of Makers and Fablabs

During the past decade, innovation in digital technologies and the rise of entrepreneurial forms of work, together with the increasing dematerialization of value production, have fostered highly autonomous forms of production. At the same time, the shift towards the individualization of work and production typical of this phase of capitalism has paradoxically 'produced an idealisation of community in different ways' (Rossi 2017: 179), thus combining with a simultaneous rising importance of various forms of collaboration and sharing (Gandini 2015; Schor et al. 2015).This transformation is frequently labelled "sharing economy" or "economy of collaboration", thus stressing the advent of material and immaterial platforms that enable new forms of production, consumption, and distribution among networks of peers (Ramella & Manzo 2021).

Within urban contexts, transformations in the practices of work and production have brought with them the proliferation of coworking spaces and sites of open production and open innovation, such as Makerspaces and Fablabs.

The first Fablab opened in 2001 out of a course on digital fabrication organised at the Massachusetts Institute of Technology (MIT), in which Prof. Neil Gershenfeld set up a small workshop made of personal digital fabrication technologies through which everyone can produce physical objects autonomously. Since then, the label 'Fablab' has been used to identify open workshops where people can have access to machines such as 3D printers and laser cutters, learn how to use them thanks to ad-hoc courses and to the experience of other Makers, and produce digitally fabricated artefacts either independently or working on a collaborative project with others. The MIT, the US company *Make Media* and some business consultants contributed to the rise of a discourse that praises the innovative potential held for the future of work and production by Fablabs and the people attending them, called Makers (Anderson 2012; Dougherty 2012; Hatch 2013). According to this discourse, the availability of shared digital fabrication machines and the diverse practices of knowledge sharing performed at Makerspaces and Fablabs make these sites the drivers of a democratization of production (Anderson 2012) and the catalysts of an open innovation ecosystem (Chesbrough et al. 2006). Thus, Makers are considered 'hi-tech do-it-yourselfers who are democratizing access to the modern means to make things' (Gershenfeld 2012: 48). For this reason, Makers are depicted as bearers of a 'third industrial revolution' (Rifkin 2011) that holds at its core the encounter between digital technologies and the organizational innovation represented by forms of commons-based peer production (Benkler 2006). According to the ideologists of the Maker Movement:

> everything that the web has enabled – new forms of collaboration, easy sharing of designs, readily available desktop tools – can now be used to support digital production and entrepreneurial activities connected to such production. (Davies 201: 6)

Indeed, the sharing dimension is considered particularly relevant for Makers. On the one hand, the very organising principle of a Fablab lies in the opportunity to use shared machines and to share knowledge with other Makers locally. On the other hand, Makers could rely on various online tools that constitute a crucial part of the infrastructure that sustains the global community of Makers, such as open sources to share the code or the instructions of a project.

The discourse that incorporates Makers and Fablabs into a broader structural change in the production of artefacts and in the way economic value is produced pivots on two pillars coming from recent theories in economics. The first is the mantra according to which collaborating with others who have different skills and sharing knowledge and material assets represent the main economic transformations of the present time. Sharing and collaboration as sources of value production are said to go beyond the walls of these organizations too, giving birth to a form of collaborative production among distant peers, as in the case of commons-based peer production (Benkler 2006; Tapscott & Williams 2006). According to these theories, the contemporary organization of value production has changed, giving birth to a form of 'open innovation' in which:

> useful knowledge is widely distributed and … even the most capable R&D organizations must identify, connect to, and leverage external knowledge sources as a core process in innovation.' (Chesbrough et al. 2006)

In line with these theories, the economic discourse that portrays coworking spaces as accelerators of serendipity has been extended from immaterial labour (Moriset 2014) to material production with Fablabs.

The second economic discourse that resonates with the birth of Fablabs and Makers focuses on the role of individuals within a broader reconfiguration of the productive paradigm, theorising the fall of the boundaries between experts and amateurs, consumers and producers. Albeit strongly interlinked with the former, these theories focus on the changing role of the individual and the rise of a new *Homo economicus*. The division between who produces and who consumes and the clear distinction between what is produced within a capitalist economy framework and what is done out of passion during free time are increasingly undermined by those digital technologies that facilitate participation in the production of immaterial contents and material devices. The 'prosumption' (as a mix of production and consumption) discussed by critical sociologists (Ritzer & Jurgenson 2010) was preconceived in the 1980s by the futurologist Alvin Toffler, who claimed that the old distinction between work and leisure would fall apart thanks to technologies enabling people to produce almost everything autonomously (Toffler 1980). In line with Toffler, the recent theorisation of the Pro-Am, that is, the professional-amateur (Leadbeater & Miller 2004) and cognate economic theories on the changing relationship between consumers and companies concerning the process of value production (Prahalad & Ramaswamy 2004; Von Hippel 2005) have contributed to defining how the role of consumers has been progressively transformed by their involvement in the production process.

Most of the analyses conducted on Makers and Fablabs from the perspective of social sciences employed the analytical lenses provided by these economic theories to read the phenomenon as part of this broader transformation in the economy. Notably, these works took for granted that labels such as 'open innovation', 'commons-based peer production' or 'prosumption' could be used to *describe* Makers' production and the role of Fablabs. Some authors mobilize the framework of commons-based peer production and open innovation to look at the experience of the first Makerspaces (Arvidsson et al. 2015; Smith et al. 2013), eventually stressing their role to act as alternatives to the capitalist economy (Chiappini & Törnberg 2018). Others emphasize the capacity of these spaces to create new urban and regional entrepreneurial ecosystems

(Doussard et al. 2017; Fiorentino 2018) and to contribute to the rise of new urban economies in the era of digital capitalism (Armondi & Di Vita 2017). These double, contradictory frameworks resonate with the apparent paradox that characterizes the so-called sharing economy, defined either as an alternative to capitalism or as part of a digitalized form of it (Richardson 2015).

In general, a key assumption underlying much research is that these spaces actually succeed in fostering a reconfiguration of production and innovation processes that would transform the market economy as we know it. These studies on Makers and Fablabs take for granted that the discourse on Makers and the actual creation of open workshops such as Makerspaces and Fablabs should be assumed as starting points, providing the analytical lenses useful to read the experience of all Fablabs and Makers.

However, this approach does not leave room for interpreting those cases in which the relevance of Makers and Fablabs to the urban economy is unclear. Indeed, sharing economy in general and Maker production specifically are better understood not as labels that describe coherent sets of economic practices but as heterogeneous performances that configure production and its spatialities in multiple and contingent ways (Richardson 2015). In line with this perspective, recent studies on Makers have stressed the importance of focusing on the practices and place-based specificities of each Fablab in order to deconstruct the homogenizing narrative that sees them as all belonging to the same democratizing turn in production and innovation (see, for example, Johns & Hall 2020).

The present chapter situates within this body of works, sharing with them not only the claim that more empirical, place-based analysis of what occurs in different Makerspaces and Fablabs is needed but also a connected conviction that alternative methodological approaches would help to reach the goal. Notably, rather than relying exclusively on interviews with founders and managers of these workshops, ethnographic research on Makers' practices and the organisational life of a Fablab allows providing more nuanced accounts of the actual innovative scope of Makers and Fablabs as transformative economic subjects and organizations.

Case Study and Methodology

The chapter is based on ethnographic research conducted at Fablab Torino in Turin, Italy. The fieldwork was conducted over a period of 18 months, between November 2016 and June 2018, and employed a mixed-method approach. Both participant and non-participant observations were conducted three times per week, usually during the evening and the night, the Fablab being open to the standard members from 4 pm onwards. Observations were supported by secondary data such as online projects' documentation and websites, and 36 semi-structured interviews with Fablab Torino members, managers, and founders. Besides conducting participant observation during the hours devoted to independent production, I attended both community nights (i.e., self-managed meetings of Makers sharing an interest in either the same technology such as Arduino or the same application of digital fabrication techniques) and workshops.

Opened in 2011 as a temporary Fablab within a one-year exhibition on the future of work, Fablab Torino's location changed one year later, becoming permanently hosted by a coworking space. The same building also hosts a start-up that used to have strong ties with Arduino, the company producing the single-board microcontroller renowned among Makers and born near Turin.

Members are mainly men, of an average age of 40. The youngest members (in their 30s) are designers who either use the space for their professional activity or work for the connected start-up. Three female members regularly attended the space. The association counts approximately 200 members, whereas the messaging chat of Fablab Torino gathers approximately 100 people. However, during my fieldwork, I used to meet no more than 30 people.

Indeed, the most pressing challenge was the fact that during the afternoons barely two or three people were using the space, which used to become more crowded after 6 pm, especially during the communities' nights. For this reason, I shared the puzzling feeling described by Kohtala and Bosqué when facing a lack of attendance at the lab, since:

> what was at first problematic from the perspective of ethnographic research (but something that emerged as a key finding) is that there was surprisingly little activity ongoing in the Lab during our visits that we could observe. (Kohtala & Bosque 2014: 2)

Moreover, even during the night gatherings, it was rare for me to observe someone making a prototype or working on a project. Thus, an important part of my fieldwork was based on 'netnographic explorations' (Smith 2020; see also Kozinets 1998) through members' chats occurring in groups on instant messaging platforms, used both to share useful information and advice and to simply chat about daily lives. The observation of what happened on the chats, together with the interviews, allowed me to go beyond the apparent lack of activity at the Fablab, following the practices beyond the physical space of the organisation, which consequently appeared instead 'as a nodal point of momentary contact' (Johns & Hall 2020: 25).

Thus, in a sort of dialectical movement between theory and empirical work, the scarce evidence of Fablab Torino as an innovative workplace and the more general lack of productive activities demanded a critical approach towards the actual correspondence between the descriptions of Makers as a relevant economic phenomenon and the case investigated. The inconsistency between, on the one hand, the descriptions of the phenomenon provided by both the mainstream literature and the first studies in social sciences on the topic and, on the other, the specific case I was investigating triggered a reformulation of the research question. Therefore, rather than asking which kinds of transformations Fablab Torino and its Makers represented for Turin's urban economy, the research focus shifted to the relationship between the description of Makers and Fablabs as innovative subjects and spaces of contemporary (urban) economies and the contingent, situated evidence of a specific Fablab. In other words, the research question became: How do the spaces and practices of Making become (or, eventually, fail to become) a relevant economic transformation, corresponding to the autonomous, highly digitalized production of physical artefacts enabled by sharing practices and the collaboration of communities of peers? And how does a Fablab become a space for open innovation, collaborative economy, and democratized (eventually, entrepreneurially oriented) production?

Theoretical Framework: How Economics Performs the Economy

Considering both the rise of Fablabs as collaborative spaces for digital fabrication and the individual practices constituting customized and autonomous production, the phenomenon has been read as part of a broader transformation in the economy, merging the increasing openness and accessibility of knowledge and tools of production with the rise of the entrepreneurial self as the contemporary form of *Homo economicus*. Moreover, as discussed in section 2, the academic literature that investigates the spatialities of the new form and organisation of production fostered by Makers and Fablabs assumes that they represent important economic transformations in urban economies in the era of digital capitalism, thus identifying 'the city' as the exclusive spatial dimension to refer to in conducting a geographical analysis of the phenomenon.

However, as the previous section illustrated, the first evidence from the field showed that the discourse that portrays Fablabs as sites of open innovation and sharing economies could not be seen as a mere description of the place-based practices performed by the Makers attending a specific Fablab, since the reality investigated does not always fit these definitions.

An alternative theoretical approach, developed in the field of economic sociology and then adopted by economic geography, allows to understand the role played by economic discourses and theorisations differently. This approach to the relationship between economic theories and economic phenomena derives from the performative programme in economic sociology, inspired by the work of Michel Callon (1998). Theories on economic performativity contend that 'economics, in the broad sense of the term, performs, shapes and formats the economy, rather than observing how it functions' (Callon 1998: 2). In other words, the way the economy functions is *performed* by economic theories, rather than being described by them.

This body of work is inspired by the tradition of Actor-Network Theory (ANT), specifically by its emphasis on socio-technical networks as the locus of agency and the refusal to consider the relation between theoretical constructs and the reality they refer to as one of representation (Callon 1986, 1987; Latour

2005). The semiotic understanding of agency developed by ANT views an actor in relational terms, as an *actor-network* whose coming into being depend on the material ordering established among the heterogeneous entities that constitute the network itself. The agency of an actor-network is therefore distributed among different human and non-human actants.

In line with that, performative understandings of economic theories read the relationship between economic descriptions and the economy as practice in terms of performance and enactment, claiming that economic discourses materialize into complex socio-technical systems (*agencements*) that enact those theories, that is, that make those theories true. Practices and socio-material arrangements consisting of buildings, devices, texts, rules, human agents, etc. make the economy (Mitchell, 2008); that is, they make specific economic entities emerge through a *performativity* process (Callon 2007) that aligns humans and non-humans (Callon 1986, 1987) in actualizing the world described by theories. In ANT's vocabulary, this corresponds to a process of *translation* (Callon 1986), through which heterogeneous entities are enrolled into an actor-network that assigns roles to them, producing specific socio-material orderings. The successful enrolment of all the entities allows the stabilization of an actor-network (or *agencement*).

When it comes to the translation of economic theories into concrete economic subjects and organizations, the socio-technical arrangements through which they are enacted are made also of specific non-human entities such as rooms, spatial configurations, and tools (Beunza & Stark 2004; Garcia-Parpet 1986/2007). Indeed, a branch of organizational studies and cognate research in the geography of organizations argue that organizations represent typical economic *agencements*, and organizing processes are crucial components of the *performativity* process, highlighting how organizations come into being also as the result of a complex array of socio-material and spatial practices. An organization is therefore 'a sociomaterial accomplishment, in which things – whether mundane such as partition walls or complex such as software – often provide the cohesive glue to make organizational arrangements durable at least for some time' (Müller 2015: 305).

Framing Fablab Torino as a Space for Open Innovation and Collaborative Production

As anticipated, the history of Fablab Torino started in a temporary exhibition on the future of work. The decision to build a Fablab as an example of the evolution of work and production was strongly influenced by the mainstream, US-based discourse on Makers and Fablabs that represents them as harbingers of an economic revolution.

> When [the tech-magazine] Wired Italia was launched and Riccardo Luna became the director, he came to Milan and asked people to be

introduced to someone who was doing something ... So, he said to Chris Anderson, *Wired America's* editor-in-chief: but we're doomed in Italy, there's no innovation! And he replied: are you kidding? Don't you know Massimo Banzi and Arduino? ... So, Riccardo was asked to organise the exhibition for the 150th anniversary of Italy in Turin and he asked me to collaborate for the part on the future of work ... I said: let's build a Fablab there! But it cannot be something where people go and there's a turned-off 3D printer and that's all. We should have something alive!' (Interview with Massimo Banzi, CEO of Arduino, December 2017)

In this narrative of Fablab Torino's origins made by one of the main figures of its foundation, the active role played by specific economic theories in the decision to build a Fablab is apparent. This discourse was firstly moved from the US to Turin via some *intermediaries* (Latour 2005) constituted by the exhibition and two key persons who were variously connected to the sites where theories about the potentialities of Makers for the economy were developed. One of these people, Massimo Banzi, was already familiar with the Maker Movement thanks to his experience in the US, where he used to attend the first fairs of Makers, described by him as a moment that was 'needed mainly by us, to count us as Makers'. In particular, when a permanent Fablab was built after the exhibition, the idea inspiring Banzi was to foster a community of Makers as a sort of external R&D for Arduino,[1] as he explains in the interview: 'I wanted to build a community. Cause I wanted to have a space where ... actually, in the past, we [Arduino] did manage to glean from the Fablab culture to look for people who could do things.' Thus, Fablab Torino was conceived and designed as an organisation responding to the principles of open innovation, according to which amateurs that have access to material and immaterial tools of production and knowledge could be incorporated into the innovation process.

The other founder, Riccardo Luna, had a crucial role too, being at that time the director of the Italian branch of the tech-bible *Wired*. Indeed, the magazine represents an important example of the large plethora of subjects that nowadays 'make the economy' by producing economic discourses and theories. As stressed by Barry and Slater (2002: 189–190), economic theories and discourses are no longer produced exclusively by academic economists; they are also the outcome of the work of regulatory institutions, public debates and non-scientific magazines such as *Wired*, in which non-economists too contribute to defining the changing shape of the economy. Thus, the role of the director of a specialized magazine such as *Wired* is indeed crucial for the diffusion and reproduction of theories on Makers that frame them as innovators, empowered

---

[1] Retrieved from: https://www.youtube.com/watch?v=4F0BrhVLDQQ. Last access: 25 April 2021.

by a facilitated access to tools that enable the production of immaterial and material artefacts.

> There's something different, something that has changed. Today ... we can do a lot of things by ourselves. We can make a website by ourselves; we can make an app by ourselves, we can make a cup, we can start a business ... Today that the means to produce objects or bits have become so less expensive and easy to use, the barrier of entry to put us to the test and do something by ourselves has become a lot lower ... The ones who are now changing the world are [people like] a hacker from a basement in Brooklyn. (Riccardo Luna at the event Giovedì Scienza – La Terza Rivoluzione Industriale, Turin, 23 January 2014)[2]

Notably, *Wired* magazine and, more generally, the kind of 'economists at large' (Callon, 2009) connected to it, provide the economics background that also inspired future interventions performed at Fablab Torino on what a Fablab is, in which ideas about open innovation and customization were backed up by concepts such as the third industrial revolution and democratic access to the means of production.

> We used to buy games, now we build them, we make them in 3D ... here's my son, he took this toy car and added a star on it. From that moment, the car became his car, it became customised ... This has been defined as the third industrial revolution. As you can see easily from this cover of The Economist, it is a revolution where you have direct access to the means of production ... In this book by Rifkin, he deals with the topic more holistically: it's also a revolution of democracy, of trade ... This is the title of a book that Chris Anderson wrote in 2012, The Long Tail, a book that I warmly suggest you read. (Fieldnote, member of the Fablab board delivering a speech for a school visiting the space, February 2017)

Summing up, through the 2011 exhibition and the circulation of non-human intermediaries represented by dedicated books and magazines, the Fablab model was introduced in Turin (and in Italy) as an example of the trajectory that the economy and the nature of work and production were about to take. A new socio-technical arrangement was built through, on the one hand, the assemblage in the same place of innovative digital machines that constituted a sample of Fablab and, on the other, the framing of these pieces of machinery as part of a transformation in production and work, thanks to the circulation of economic theories on the role of sharing and collaboration in innovation

---

[2] Retrieved from: http://www.giovediscienza.it/old/modules/conferenze/article .php?storyid=11. Last access: 14 August 2018.

processes, the increasing relevance of digital fabrication, and the democratization of production.

Enacting: Alignments (and Misalignments) in Organizing a Space for Open and Collaborative Production

Theories on open innovation, sharing economy, the changing role of the consumer and self-entrepreneurialism clearly framed the organizational structure
and mission of Fablab Torino. According to the intent of one of the founders
who was already part of the US-based Maker Movement, Fablab Torino should
have been a space where people with different backgrounds, interests, skills and
levels of familiarity with digital fabrication and Arduino could meet and experiment together.[3] Therefore, in line with the abovementioned economic tenets,
the main features of the space should have been great accessibility to the space
itself, free encounter between users and producers of Arduino, and provision of
open access to various digital fabrication machines not only to work but also to
experiment in a playful way. These three features were inscribed in the material
constitution of the space itself, thanks to some non-human entities that took
part in the creation of an *agencement* of open innovation and commons-based
peer production.

Specific spatial practices of organizing were put in place, aimed at the facilitation of networking in order to foster open innovation (cf. Lorne 2019), thus
performing the serendipitous encounter not only between people working in
different sectors but also between professionals and amateurs. Starting from
the inner architecture, the premises of the Fablab are connected with both the
ones of the coworking space and the room on the second floor occupied by a
start-up that used to be the research branch of Arduino. This spatial organization aimed at creating a material connection between the two main business
actors participating in the creation of the Fablab. Indeed, this double connection would have spatially enacted both the concept of open innovation and
the basic tenets of the collaborative economy, thanks to the facilitated flux of
knowledge and information but also material instruments among the various
communities inhabiting the building.

According to the performativity theory, one of the most important aspects
of making the economy is constituted by the creation of new organizations
whose physical space's characteristics have inscribed within them the kind of
actions and interactions described by economic theories (Garcia-Parpet 2007).

---

[3] http://ed2013.makerfairerome.eu/2013/06/25/che-cosa-vi-siete-persi-a
-innovazione-dal-basso-e-arduino-camp/.   https://www.businessadvisor.it
/notizie/wbf-news/massimo-banzi-arduino-e-le-officine-nuove-idee-e
-prodotti. Last access: 15 March 2019.

Fablab's walls, desks, and doors participated in organizing a space that performed the unprecedented falling of the boundaries that used to separate consumers and producers. This distinction had to be substituted with the reference to an ill-defined idea of 'community', which the spatial configuration of the organisation aimed at performing. In the original idea of the Fablab creators, spaces for learning, spaces for production and spaces for business had thus to be entangled for the opening up of production to be obtained. Indeed, a Fablab is not only conceived as a space for production but also as a space where knowledge is freely shared in a horizontal way in order to foster innovation. Thus, a room was specifically devoted to workshops.

However, over the years, the architectural design of the space has jeopardized the enactment of an open form of innovation through unpredictable spatial and temporal practices. Besides the clear obstacle represented by the fact that most of the Fablab members use the space after the coworking's closing hour, the material artefacts and the technologies in charge of creating an organizational arrangement enabling the free encounter between people using the coworking space and the Makers actually fail. The coworking space is separated from the Fablab premises by a big empty room, employed as an occasional garage for loading and unloading. No sign indicates the directions for the coworking, and the fact that the Fablab has an independent entrance sometimes leads newcomers to be to unawarene of the very presence of the coworking space. Even more strikingly, sometimes the fact of being under the same roof makes the materiality of the two spaces – i.e., furniture, utilities, cleanliness, and level of care – a source of comparison, which undermines the identification of Fablab Torino as an organisation suitable for working on a project.

> Gregorio asks me to go for a coffee at the coworking space … 'They [the coworking's management] did a great job with the space! And this relaxing area … I like it a lot!'; me: 'Um … but you have one too, at the Fablab'; Gregorio laughs: '… I don't like that … It's too … meagre'. Fablab's relaxing area is actually constituted by two leather armchairs and a sofa, the three of them all evidently second-hand and marked by wear and tear. (Fieldnote, October 2017)

> I visited a Fablab in Porto. It's kind of an ex-firm … the furniture is not very different from ours, very meagre … even if it's much cleaner and more orderly, with many more tools … But they're still wooden axes with nails, with the drill inserted on it, that is, that's the drill-holder. It's very functional, let's say. Low budget. But … but it looks like a space that works, where there is someone with an idea … with entrepreneurial interests. (Interview with Vincenzo, Maker, November 2017)

DIY furniture was conceived as a crucial and symbolic component of the organization. A cloud-shaped open-source toilet paper holder, 3D printed tap handles, tables, and laser-cut speakers belong to a specific design style that performs the paradigm of openness and collaboration. Together with some artefacts on display that were fabricated at Fablab Torino in recent years, DIY furniture contributes to actualizing the democratization of production. Notably, the entanglement between artefacts and practices of display aims at eliciting inspiration through imitation, thus producing an arrangement of open production in which artefacts directly affect Makers and translate into visible, material form Gershenfeld's motto on digital fabrication capacity to allow people 'to make almost anything' (Gershenfeld 2005).

Nevertheless, when the basic provisions of the space become intertwined with a diminished functionality, the net result is the organisation failing in being perceived and attended 'like a space that works', as complained by Vincenzo. Indeed, digital fabrication itself is undermined by the misalignment of some non-human entities, as the frequent breakdowns of both machines and the heating system and a general negligence towards shared tools exemplify.

> When they laugh, a puff of smoke comes out of their mouths. We all wear scarves and wool hats. 'Come on, let's finish! I want to go back to my desk [N/A at the coworking space], it's freezing!' (Fieldnote, January 2017)

> If you go there, you won't find pliers. A hammer? Forget about it! Screwdrivers properly working? Extremely rare!' (Interview with Tiberio, Maker, May 2017)

While sometimes the performance of a democratized production may go adrift due to some 'glitches' in the internal socio-spatial processes of organizing, it could also result in a 'misfire' (Callon 2010), that is, a partial *performativity*, when a proper arrangement to guarantee accessibility fails to emerge. Indeed, while Fablabs and Makerspaces have been considered in the literature parts also of the so-called 'access-based economy', the way this access gets to be assured is usually overlooked.

> On the wall next to the door there's an intercom with the names of the various organisations hosted in the building. The sign 'Fablab Torino' is barely readable. No other signs outside help the newcomer ... Laura, a newcomer, suggests to better signal it. Adriano, laughing 'Yes, it's kind of an intelligence test!! Like: if you manage to get here ...' (Fieldnote, November 2016)

An automated door-opening system was developed in the early years of the organization and then continued to be implemented, inscribing into the material artefact a particular social order, and delegating to the technology the accomplishment of a task (i.e., assuring the accessibility of the space in order to allow people to self-organize and self-manage their productive activities). This system should represent an important factor in performing self-organized production, enacting the Fablab as an organization that takes part in a new economic model in which everyone can have easy access to the means of production. However, the delegation to a non-human agent does not always work as expected. Indeed, the automated entrance system of Fablab Torino was frequently out of order.

The misalignment of the automated door paired with the shortcomings in the role of the most important human actant of the Fablab's actor-network, namely the host, and many complaints were raised about the lack of a proper welcome at Fablab Torino, something that is supposed to be at the core of collaborative workspaces.

> Other friends have a little bit suffered from this fact ... that nobody is welcoming you, that nobody is curating the human side. (Interview with Michele, Fablab Torino Maker, March 2017)

Indeed, the role of managers and hosts in collaborative spaces is crucial in organizing a space that performs a form of value production based on openness and collaboration (Brown 2017; Merkel 2015). Therefore, when accessibility is poorly enacted, the net result is that some people are excluded from production, thus making the actualization of the so-called democratization of production partially fail.

Conclusion

Fablabs and Makers are portrayed as part of a broader shift in urban economies characterised by the increased autonomy of the individual in producing value thanks to digital technologies and the rise of collaborative and sharing practices. Although these readings may well describe the role of Fablabs in some typical creative cities, the process needed for a Fablab to be part of this transformation as a space of open innovation and collaborative production usually goes unnoticed. In particular, the chapter has stressed how theories on the increased participation of amateurs into innovation processes and collaborative forms of work cannot be adopted as mere descriptions of what a Fablab represents.

Rather than either considering economic theories simply a wrong description of the phenomenon or interpreting as isolated cases the experience of Fablabs whose inner functioning does not correspond to those theories, the chapter has proposed an alternative analytical path. Drawing on the performativity programme in economic sociology and on the poststructuralist stream of geography of organizations, the chapter has shown how economic theories on open innovation and collaborative production were constitutive components of the rise of Fablab Torino as a new economic organization. The role of two persons belonging to the global network of 'economists at large' that frame Fablabs and Makers as part of an economic revolution was crucial in the opening of Fablab Torino as an organization that embodied the future of work and production.

However, the discussion of the empirical findings has also stressed that the actual enactment of what those economic theories describe depends on the role played by all the human and non-human entities that should take part in the coming into being of Fablab Torino as an organization typical of the sharing economy era. Indeed, although specific socio-technical systems were created to perform collaboration, open innovation, and commons-based peer production, some entities failed to align to the network, thus making the performativity process go adrift. As discussed, not only the socio-spatial practices of the Fablab members compromised the enactment of Making as a form of entrepreneurially oriented open innovation. Also, the frequent breakdown of the machines and the very materiality of the space prevented Fablab Torino from performing a reconfiguration of urban spaces of work and production. Thus, the chapter has shown that it is precisely through the acknowledgement of the performative and contingent nature of economies and the possibility of failure in the performativity process that a more nuanced understanding of Fablabs and Makers could be provided.

Concluding, the adoption of a theoretical framework informed by Actor-Network Theory and by the performativity programme in economic sociology and post-structuralist geography has allowed to provide a nuanced understanding of the role of Fablabs and Makers within new urban economies; one that, although not adopting a normative approach that locates the experience of a Fablab within either true or false forms of the sharing economy (cf. Ramella & Manzo 2021), stresses how economic discourse and theories on collaboration and openness variously take part in bringing into being a Fablab in always contingent and uncertain ways.

References

Anderson, C. 2012 *Makers: The New Industrial Revolution.* Random House.

Armondi, S. and Bruzzese, A. 2017 Contemporary production and urban change: The case of Milan. *Journal of Urban Technology, 24*(3), 27–45.

Armondi, S. and Di Vita, S. 2017 Contemporary Production, Innovative Workplaces, and Urban Space: Projects and Policies. *Journal of Urban Technology, 24*(3), 1–3.

Arvidsson, A., Caliandro, A., Cossu, A., Deka, M., Gandini, A., Luise, V. and Anselmi, G. 2016 Commons-based peer production in the information economy. Available at: https://www.researchgate.net/profile/Alessandro _Caliandro/publication/310624903_Commons_Based_Peer_Production _in_the_Information_Economy/links/5834403108ae004f74c85030.pdf

Barry, A. and Slater, D. 2002a Introduction: the technological economy. *Economy and society, 31*(2), 175–193.

Benkler, Y. 2006 *The wealth of networks: How social production transforms markets and freedom.* Yale University Press.

Beunza, D. and Stark, D. 2004 Tools of the trade: the socio-technology of arbitrage in a Wall Street trading room. *Industrial and corporate change, 13*(2), 369–400.

Bosqué, C. and Kohtala, C. 2014 The story of MIT-Fablab Norway: community embedding of peer production. *Journal of Peer Production, 5,* 1–8.

Brown, J. 2017 Curating the 'Third Place'? Coworking and the mediation of creativity. *Geoforum, 82,* 112–126.

Callon, M. 1986 *Some elements of a sociology of translation: domestication of the scallops and the fishermen of St Brieuc Bay.* In Law, J. (Ed.) (1986) *Power, action and belief: a new sociology of knowledge?* London, Routledge, 196–223.

Callon, M. 1987 Society in the making: the study of technology as a tool for sociological analysis. *The social construction of technological systems: New directions in the sociology and history of technology,* 83–103.

Callon, M. (Ed.). 1998 *The laws of the markets.* Blackwell Publishers/Sociological Review.

Callon, M. 2007 *What does it mean to say that economics is performative?.* In MacKenzie, D., Muniesa, F., & Siu, L. (2007). *Do economists make markets? On the performativity of economics.* Princeton University Press. 311–357.

Callon, M. 2010 Performativity, misfires and politics. *Journal of Cultural Economy, 3*(2), 163–169.

Capdevila, I. 2018 Knowing communities and the innovative capacity of cities. *City, Culture and Society, 13,* 8–12.

Chesbrough, H., Vanhaverbeke, W. and West, J. (Eds.). 2006 *Open innovation: Researching a new paradigm.* Oxford University Press on Demand.

Chiappini, L. and Törnberg, P. 2018. 'Deus ex machina'. In *The Production of Alternative Urban Spaces: An International Dialogue,* edited by Fisker, J. K., Chiappini, L., Pugalis, L., and Bruzzese, A. London: Routledge.

Davies, S.R. 2017 *Hackerspaces: making the maker movement.* Cambridge: Polity Press.

Doussard, M., Schrock, G., Wolf-Powers, L., Eisenburger, M. and Marotta, S. 2017 Manufacturing without the firm: Challenges for the maker movement in three US cities. *Environment and Planning A: Economy and Space, 50*(3), 651–670.

Fiorentino, S. 2018 Re-making urban economic geography. Start-ups, entrepreneurial support and the Makers Movement: A critical assessment of policy mobility in Rome. *Geoforum, 93,* 116–119.

Gandini, A. 2015 The Rise of Coworking Spaces: A Literature Review. *Ephemera, 15*(1), 193–209.

Garcia-Parpet, M.-F. 2007. *The Social Construction of a Perfect Market: The Strawberry Auction at Fontaines-en Sologne*. In MacKenzie, D., Muniesa, F., & Siu, L. (2007). *Do Economists Make Markets? On the Performativity of Economics*. Princeton University Press, 20–53.

Gauntlett, D. 2011 *Making is connecting. The social meaning of creativity from DIY and knitting to YouTube and Web 2.0*. Cambridge: Polity Press

Johns, J. and Hall, S.M. 2020 'I have so little time […] I got shit I need to do': Critical perspectives on making and sharing in Manchester's FabLab. *Environment and Planning A: Economy and Space, 52*(7), 1292–1312.

Jones, A. and Murphy, J.T. 2010 Practice and economic geography. *Geography Compass, 4*(4), 303–319.

Kozinets, R.V. 1998 On Netnography: Initial Reflections on Consumer Research Investigations of Cyberculture. *Advances in Consumer Research, 25*, 366–71.

Latour, B. 2005 *Reassembling the social: An introduction to actor-network-theory*. Oxford university press.

Leadbeater, C. and Miller, P. 2004 The Pro-Am Revolution: How enthusiasts are changing our society and economy. London: Demos.

Lorne, C. 2019 The limits to openness: Coworking, design and social innovation in the neoliberal city. *Environment and Planning A*. https://doi.org /10.1177/0308518X19876941

Mariotti, I., Di Vita, S. and Akhavan, M. (Eds.). 2021 *New Workplaces— Location Patterns, Urban Effects and Development Trajectories. A Worldwide Investigation*. Switzerland, Springer.

Mitchell, T. 2008 Rethinking economy. *Geoforum, 39*(3), 1116–1121.

Moriset, B. 2014 Building new places of the creative economy. The rise of coworking spaces. In *Proceedings of the 2nd Geography of Innovation, International Conference 2014, Utrecht University, Utrecht (The Netherlands)*.

Müller, M. 2015 *Organization, Geography of*. In Wright, J. (2015). *International Encyclopedia of the Social & Behavioral Sciences, 2nd Edition*. Elsevier. 301–306.

Powell, A. 2012 Democratizing production through open source knowledge: from open software to open hardware. *Media, Culture & Society, 34*(6), 691–708.

Prahalad, C.K. and Ramaswamy, V. 2004 Co-creation experiences: The next practice in value creation. *Journal of interactive marketing, 18*(3), 5–14.

Ramella, F. and Manzo, C. 2021 *The Economy of Collaboration. The New DigitalPlatforms of Production and Consumption*. Oxon-New York, Routledge.

Richardson, L. 2015 Performing the sharing economy. *Geoforum, 67*, 121–129.

Rifkin, J. 2011 *The third industrial revolution: how lateral power is transforming energy, the economy, and the world*. Macmillan.

Rifkin, J. 2014 *The zero marginal cost society: The internet of things, the collaborative commons, and the eclipse of capitalism*. St. Martin's Press.

Schor, J.B., Walker, E.T., Lee, C.W., Parigi, P. and Cook, K. 2015 On the sharing economy. *Contexts, 14*, 12–19.

Smith, A., Hielscher, S., Dickel, S., Soderberg, J. and van Oost, E. 2013 Grassroots digital fabrication and makerspaces: Reconfiguring, relocating and recalibrating innovation?. *University of Sussex, SPRU Working Paper SWPS, 2.*

Smith, T.S. 2020 'Stand back and watch us': Post-capitalist practices in the maker movement. *Environment and Planning A: Economy and Space, 52*(3), 593–610.

Tapscott, D. and Williams, A.D. 2006 *Wikinomics: How mass collaboration changes everything.* Penguin.

Toffler, A. 1980 *The third wave* (Vol. 484). New York: Bantam Books.

Vicari, S., Colleoni, E. and D'Ovidio, M. 2015 *Makers. The making of the human city.*, Feltrinelli, Milano.

Von Hippel, E. 2005 *Democratizing innovation.* MIT press.

PART 2

Ethnographies of Grassroots Local Initiatives

CHAPTER 5

The Online–Offline Hybrid Model of a Collaborative Solidarity Action: Migrant Solidarity Grassroots Groups in Hungary

Anikó Bernát
TÁRKI Social Research Institute, Hungary

Abstract

The migrant and refugee crisis that culminated in 2015–2016 brought about a number of new phenomena and lessons for Europe. Hungary also experienced an intense, albeit relatively short period of the crisis in 2015 as a transit country, but the impact of this period goes beyond its duration. One remarkable new phenomenon of the migration crisis was the emergence of a volunteer grassroots solidarity movement that operated large-scale aid activities by using a hybrid online–offline model. The volunteers formed and maintained their grassroots groups online, via Facebook, to organize their daily activities, logistics and fundraising in order to provide an effective on-site, offline aid activity for migrants and refugees. The spontaneous solidarity movement emerged from nowhere provides an example of how activity through social media platforms interacts with offline humanitarian aid activity in the framework of a 'go online to act offline' model and how the relationship is transformed by the proliferation of the online activity.

How to cite this book chapter:
Bernát, A. 2022. The Online–Offline Hybrid Model of a Collaborative Solidarity Action: Migrant Solidarity Grassroots Groups in Hungary. In: Travlou, P. and Ciolfi, L. (eds.) *Ethnographies of Collaborative Economies across Europe: Understanding Sharing and Caring.* Pp. 95–107. London: Ubiquity Press. DOI: https://doi.org/10.5334/bct.f. License: CC BY-NC-ND

Introduction and Background

Migrant solidarity grassroots groups as collaborative action groups emerged from nowhere in some major Hungarian cities during the summer of 2015 as a response to the migration and refugee crises, in a hostile political and public context. Hungary has been affected by the crisis as a transit country, but the thousands of refugees and migrants who crossed and temporarily stayed in Hungary at that time were left without sufficient provisions and aid by the state and official aid providers. State and municipality organizations as well as major NGOs and charities that were originally working in this field were not responding sufficiently to the unmet needs of migrants and refugees, which became highly visible when hundreds of them started to 'live' in central public open-air spaces in downtown Budapest, mostly around major railway stations. Local civilians with no organizational ties and often without any professional background started to provide aid to migrants and refugees, mainly to express solidarity and provide immediate relief. Soon these independent actors contacted each other on Facebook, and various types of Facebook groups started to connect individuals who wanted to help in some way.

Social media platforms (predominantly Facebook) were used by both the volunteer activists and the asylum seekers at an intensity and with an effectiveness never witnessed before in humanitarian activities in Hungary, and this was one of the most relevant lessons that Hungarian civil society learnt from this crisis. For the volunteers, Facebook was the core platform for establishing their groups, and it had a central role in sharing information, developing contacts and membership, organizing activities and collecting and distributing donations during the entire crisis. Furthermore, these were highly effective communication channels outside the grassroots groups to inform and also shape public opinion about the migration crisis and the activity of the solidarity grassroots. For refugees and asylum seekers, Facebook, Twitter and a number of new and already established user-driven mobile phone applications were extremely helpful: call and chat software programs (ICRC 2017) and other information applications directly targeted migrants, while online maps, GPS and other practical applications created radically different opportunities compared to those available during previous waves of migration.

In sum, without Facebook, the other social media platforms and mobile applications, the development, patterns and scale of the migration flow probably would have been significantly different. In contrast, established NGOs and large charities – which might have taken a more relevant role due to their profile and previous activity but were hardly involved in the mitigation of the crisis – used social media less intensively and in a more conservative manner, in line with their lower activity level in the refugee crisis compared to the volunteer groups.

Questions and Methods

This chapter explores the 'go online to act offline' model, by investigating how the efficiency of using social media platforms can fuel and interact with the offline activity of solidarity-driven humanitarian aid movements in a crisis. Moreover, this case can contribute to the discussion on how online and offline activities can reinforce each other in such a context, as, in addition to the online tool facilitating the offline activity, an interaction between the online and offline activities might occur.

The backbone of this study is empirical research[1] that was carried out between September 2015 and January 2018 in three Hungarian cities (Budapest, Szeged, Debrecen), by applying mainly qualitative social research methods, with an emphasis on ethnographic methods. Fifty-six semi-structured individual interviews were carried out with stakeholders and actors in the refugee solidarity movement: 19 with leaders or prominent members of grassroots groups and other NGOs and charities; and 37 with grassroots volunteers. Furthermore, three focus groups were organized with volunteer activists in the three major cities where these grassroots operated. The primary evidence collected through these methods was complemented by on-site and online participant observation during the aid activities, and also by the information gathered in public (offline) events where the volunteers and the grassroots groups presented their activities to a wider non-professional audience.

The Evolution of the Solidarity Movement in the Context of the Migration Crisis and Hungarian Politics

The migration crisis that peaked in 2015 and the following years was unprecedented in Europe since World War II. The number of asylum seekers in the EU increased steadily from the early 2010s, and an initially moderate upward trend accelerated and more than quadrupled by 2015 and 2016 (from 282,000 asylum applications in 2011 to 1,283,000 in 2015 and 1,221,000 in 2016). The year 2015 was also a milestone in the refugee and migrant crisis in Hungary with an even steeper upward trend, as the number of registered asylum seekers increased a hundredfold within four years (from 1,690 in 2011 to 177,000 in 2015) (Eurostat 2021): the highest number of asylum seekers and migrants recorded in an EU member state, and in Hungary since World War II. The number of asylum seekers, however, then shrank radically (by 29,000 first time

---

[1] The chapter is based on the broader research project entitled 'The social aspects of the 2015 migration crisis in Hungary' (Simonoivits and Bernát, 2016). I would like to thank Fruzsina Márta Tóth and Anna Kertész for their contribution in the research and in previous studies.

applicants in the next year, and to 115 people by 2020); the drastic decrease was the result of rigorous legal and political measures as well as the physical border fence implemented by the Hungarian state from the autumn of 2015 in order to literally close off Hungary and prevent further waves of migrants.

As a transit country, Hungary was affected by the migration flow in a different way than target countries: migrants usually spent only the necessary minimum time in Hungary until they were able to continue their trip towards their target countries, which also required assistance and aid. Furthermore, migrants generally wanted to avoid having to apply for asylum in Hungary, as this was not their country of destination and, under the Dublin Convention, the asylum procedure would in principle have tied them to Hungary and not to their country of destination. Most migrants and asylum seekers were interested in getting through Hungary as quickly and with as little official administration as possible. The Hungarian state initially pursued the same goal, backed with a strong anti-migration campaign: the state also aimed to admit or administer the fewest possible asylum seekers, and thus it did not prevent migrants from crossing the country or essentially provide any assistance.

However, the need for aid and assistance became apparent by early summer 2015, as more and more migrants and asylum seekers stayed for several days instead of transiting the country immediately, and lacked accommodation and other basic amenities or needed health provision. Local individuals noticed and reacted to these situations in growing numbers and it soon turned to a collaborative effort organized via online channels (mainly Facebook groups) and realized on-site, offline. Finally, the humanitarian aid provided to migrants and asylum seekers who transited through Hungary largely relied on the activities of civil volunteers and grassroots organizations. This movement emerged rapidly and unexpectedly across the country at the beginning of the 2015 summer migration crisis, especially in cities where these people spent several days before they could continue their journey to their destinations.

Similar grassroots solidarity movements, also applying an online–offline combination of aid activity, emerged in many countries along the migration route from Greece to Serbia, as official aid providers were not prepared to adequately provide aid for the migrants and refugees arriving in such numbers. Therefore the migrants and the local volunteers soon established direct contact, and locals started to provide assistance in multiple countries and cities in a very similar way to what happened in Hungary.

The evolution of the solidarity and aid movement, including both the new grassroots and traditional aid organizations, is embedded in a particular sociopolitical context in Hungary. The stark contrast between the pro-migration EU approach and the anti-migration Hungarian state approach was apparent, which combined with inaction from both sides initially. The Hungarian state then took pivotal steps to realize its politics through strict legal and physical barriers to hamper migration, while the EU remained ineffective in managing the refugee crisis with legal and political instruments.

The Hungarian domestic anti-immigration governmental campaign started via all political and public media channels before the first visible signs of the migration crisis in Hungary, and accelerated in the following years, although the number of asylum seekers shrank radically and thus immigration was not a reality for Hungary due to the strict legal and physical barriers (including a defence fence built at the southern borders) implemented by the Hungarian government from the fall of 2015. The introduction of these legal and physical barriers instantly cut the migration flow at the borders of Hungary, which ended the mission and thus the work of the refugee solidarity movement but did not put an end to governmental anti-immigration propaganda, which continued even years later, although without any measurable immigration flow (see Juhász, Hunyadi & Zgut 2015; Kallius, Monterescu & Rajaram 2016 for more details on the political context and impact).

Although the general political landscape in Hungary was dominated by the anti-migrant campaign of the government before the migration crisis could have been noticed on the streets of Hungary, in the wake of the crisis of the summer of 2015 the migrant crisis and refugee aid movement have been embedded in a highly polarized political context, which also provided some opportunity for the expression and activity of pro-migration solidarity advocates. This exceptional solidarity movement of new civilian volunteers and their organizations emerged from an inherently anti-refugee country with low level of interpersonal and institutional trust. The Hungarian population has a tendency to demonstrate xenophobic attitudes (Sik 2016), and exclusionary behaviour towards marginalized groups (e.g., various nationalities, ethnicities, religions or lifestyles) in general. It is combined with a low level of trust in general (Tóth 2009; Boda & Medve-Bálint 2012; TÁRKI 2013) as well as a low level of civilian activity (KSH 2012). However, 3 per cent of the Hungarian adult population reported that they participated in refugee relief work or made donations in some form during the summer and early autumn of 2015, and 7 per cent claimed to have a friend or an acquaintance that participated, according to self-reported responses of a representative survey. At the time around 5 per cent of the population could be considered 'xenophiles' in a survey denoting those who would accept any asylum seekers to enter the country, and this group could overlap significantly with those that volunteered (Bernát et al. 2015).

A further aspect to understand about the Hungarian reception of the migration flow is the limited experience of both immigration and emigration: the last large-scale immigration flows happened several decades earlier and mainly involved Hungarians fleeing from neighbouring countries where they lived as a minority (in the late 1980s and early 1990s from Transylvania, Western Romania; in the early 1990s asylum seekers, many of whom were ethnic Hungarians, from the war zones of Yugoslavia). Accordingly, Hungary is a homogeneous society with a very low number of non-nationals (200,000 people in 2020), which is one of the lowest levels in the EU (2 per cent of the population) (Eurostat 2020). Hungary is also a latecomer to emigration, boosted mainly due to the protracted financial crisis around 2010, and despite the recent increase Hungary has always been a less significant source of Eastern European immigrants into Western European countries. The rise in the number of migrants in the 2015 crisis thus was unprecedented in Hungary as well as in Europe in terms of the order of magnitude, composition and processes. Although governments had information about migrants heading towards Europe, they may have underestimated the possible effects of such a large-scale and heterogeneous migration flow with some links to human trafficking.

Underestimating the migration flow, combined with the purposeful reluctance and lack of official aid, finally led to a spontaneous and highly effective refugee solidarity aid movement in Hungary. The aid activity followed a hybrid online–offline model that had never been used at this scale in any Hungarian humanitarian crisis.

The Social Media Imprint of the Grassroots Organizations

The unexpected grassroots solidarity movement emerged in the early summer of 2015: several migrant solidarity grassroots, operated exclusively by volunteers, appeared out of nowhere, without any history, with the direct goal of providing relief to migrants who transited through Hungary. In a surprisingly short span of time these new grassroots groups managed to formulate a wide agenda, significantly raise public awareness and obtain influence by voluntarily filling a service gap that became increasingly apparent, and fulfilling a mission that should have been served by paid, professional state agencies and charities. Neither state institutions nor professional, established civilian and charity organizations provided sufficient humanitarian aid to the migrants transiting the country, partly due to adapting to the anti-immigration state approach and partly for infrastructural reasons. Moreover, some general public services, such as some of the public transportation companies and the public sanitation services, were unprepared and seemingly less motivated to cope with this challenge, which made relief work even more difficult.

The discrepancy between the often reluctant official and professional aid organizations and the non-professional but committed volunteers gained much public and political attention in the context of an already highly politicized atmosphere as the grassroots' pro-migration approach sharply contrasted with the anti-immigration message of the government. The activities of volunteering civilians were covered significantly in social media and in both pro- and anti-migration political sides' media outlets, but with a strong headwind against the aid-provider civilians due to the general dominance of the governmental media in Hungary (Bernáth & Messing 2015; Barta & Tóth 2016).

The relief work by newly emerged grassroots groups was solely organized via Facebook: besides some independent (and often closed) Facebook groups there was a hierarchical alliance of location-based groups (also often closed groups). Until the reduction in the presence of migrants in Hungary, the larger

groups, the individual Segítsünk Együtt a Menekülteknek – Let's Help the Refugees Together (SEM) and the core group of the alliance Migration Aid (MA),
based their operations in Budapest and had an online membership of 10,000
each in closed Facebook groups that were established to help active members to
organize effective operational work. The open Facebook page of MA supported
the closed group. This initiative was the easiest to join and was designed to
provide an open space for discussing pro-migrant opinions; it reached 35,000
'likes' within a few months. The closed operative groups tied to specific aid
locations usually had a few thousand members: the closed groups of Migration
Aid dedicated to the three largest Budapest railway stations were MA Keleti/
Eastern (2,500 members), MA Nyugati/Western (2,900 members) and MA
Déli/Southern (1,200 members). One of the main MA bases outside Budapest
was in Debrecen (600 members), the second largest Hungarian city, where a
reception camp also operated at that time. The largest grassroots group outside
the capital, MigSzol Szeged (as Szeged is the first city where migrants enter
Hungary on the Balkan route), was founded at the end of June 2015 as the first
such grassroots group on Facebook during the Hungarian phase of the refugee
crisis, and had around 2,500 members. Membership of the individual groups
rose remarkably fast until October 2015 (when the borders of Hungary closed
and the migration flow decreased significantly), although there were over-
laps between the groups. The Hungarian migrant solidarity grassroots groups
shrank fast after the migration crisis bypassed Hungary as they decreased
or completed the migrant-focused activity or shifted their attention towards
local vulnerable groups. Most groups, except for Migration Aid, finished or
minimized any other kinds of activity, for several reasons. Initially, most of
the refugee solidarity groups tried to shift their activity towards local vulnerable target groups, but these attempts faded and disappeared in the long run. The
only Hungarian migrant solidarity Facebook group, MA still exist, six-seven
years after the migration flow gripped Hungary, but its activity was limited to
requests for some support for the remaining few refugees or awareness-raising
related to the milestones of the migration crisis in other countries until the
Ukrainian migrant crisis of 2022, when MA continued its refugee relief activities, but in an even larger volume. It set up a temporary refugee shelter for
260 people, an afternoon school, a long-term accommodation search and men-
toring team for the fullest possible aid provision, exclusively with volunteers
and civilian donations, and without any state support.[2]

---

[2] This chapter is focusing on the refugee solidarity aid activities during the
2015 crisis and not dealing with the Ukrainian refugee crisis started in
February 2022, in which Migration Aid and other civil and grassroots organizations and volunteers provided a wide range of aid provisions to refugees. As the crisis is still ongoing at the time of finalizing the manuscript,
this case will be analysed in other research papers.

The Hybrid Online-Offline Model of Aid Activity
and Its Drivers

One of the most important features of the refugee crisis was the use of new internet-based technologies. In addition to Facebook, call and chat software programs and other information exchange applications (such as an information app directly targeting migrants on their way into Europe) directly targeted migrants, while electronic maps created radically different opportunities compared to those available during previous waves of migration. All this was complemented by the intense presence of commercial and public media (television, radio, online and print media) which simultaneously shaped public opinion and events. But above all, the exploitation of Facebook as a multi-faceted tool used by the new grassroots to 'go online to act offline' was among the most important outcomes, as it made the offline activity so effective that it was able to compensate for the lack of experience, resources and infrastructure of the reluctant professional aid providers.

The migration crisis articulated in 2015 in Europe was not the first crisis that used social media effectively, as several social movements are conceptualized as having been given life through social media (e.g., the Arab Spring), or have referred to the crucial importance of social media (Castells 2012; Fuchs 2014), but this was the first time that social media played a central role in a social movement in Hungary. The former cases prove that social networking sites can function as counter-power to the official channels of (political) communication, and can turn up the volume of oppositional views so that it better reflects the real political flow (Castells 2012). This can apply even to an EU member state where the power and media dominance of the democratically elected government could create highly biased coverage. However, as the grassroots' media use was dominated by Facebook, this limited their possibility to dominate the field of communication in general. Media content analysis shows that, even though the new grassroots initiatives used social media frequently and quite successfully to spread their messages and mobilize resources, most of their content was framed by official governmental communication (conveyed via both offline and online media), which led to a reactive strategy of communications that failed to create an independent narrative and framing (Barta & Tóth 2016; Bernáth & Messing 2015). The limited reach to a wider audience beyond its membership or Facebook users, even given the dominant role of Facebook in everyday communication, suggests that it was not a game changer in political communication in general: rather a 'connective action' (Dessewffy & Nagy 2016), which refers to a new type of collective action based on social networking sites.

Moreover, some critics of the positive approach attributed to the role of social media in political action suggest that such activity is often superficial or less effective and thus may be labelled as 'slacktivism', 'clicktivism' or 'feel-good online activism', which they claim has little or no effect on real-life events (Morozov 2010; Fuchs 2014).

Social media, which is represented almost exclusively by Facebook in Hungary, primarily served as a multifunctional tool with applications to recruitment, management, fundraising and awareness raising. There have been no similar groups in Hungary since, or before, the Facebook refugee solidarity groups. These online activities initially responded directly to the needs of offline, on-site aid provision in terms of involving more activists, organizing the aid activity and donation supply more effectively and inducing a more positive public reception of the migration crisis in a hostile political climate. Later, the online activity became so intensive and effective that it had to be more responsive to needs generated by the online activity itself. In terms of recruitment and involvement, the management of the online membership by moderation increased significantly and thus was not limited to the original goal, the recruitment of more volunteer workers as on-site aid activists who worked face-to-face with the migrants. In terms of management, the accelerated online activity of the Facebook groups triggered further online organizational activity. Furthermore, in terms of awareness raising, the influence and volume of the online groups' activity induced more and more Facebook posts and comments as a self-generating loop that also required more moderation and staff hours by the volunteers operating the groups. These processes thus gradually transformed the relation between the online and offline activity of the solidarity groups: the original clear role of the online activity to support the offline action in a 'go online to act offline' manner shifted to a more blurred and mixed pattern, with increasing and self-supporting online activity beyond the support of the offline aid provision. This highlights that not only can online activity drive the offline action, but it can be realized in the opposite way, as initially the causal interaction was driven by the offline activity and the online tool supported it according to the need of the offline activity.

The various facets of the Facebook groups as a multifunctional tool provide further examples of how the hybrid online–offline activity was realized. In terms of recruitment and involvement, most activists joined the aid providers via the Facebook groups and not offline. However, the mobilizing effects of social media should not be exaggerated, as evidence from qualitative research suggests that only one Hungarian group, albeit the largest and most influential one, established itself exclusively through social media, while in other groups some of the core members and founders had been in contact before. However, Facebook provided a low entry threshold to join the mission: by just one click anyone could feel that they supported or were part of an errand, although most people who joined these groups remained less active online and not active at all offline, confirming the validity of the 'clicktivism' argument. A low entry threshold is also applicable to offline activity: those who wanted to go beyond armchair activism could easily join on-site relief activity by donating a bag of food or a pair of good shoes or working a few hours as donation distributor or administrative staff, or practising their profession or skills if relevant (as medical staff, translator or social worker).

The organizational function of the Facebook groups covered a wide range of activities and the portfolio as well as the workload also proliferated in line with the increase in online activity, both in terms of the types and the volume of the tasks. The organizational portfolio covered a wide range of administration, such as keeping track of the online and offline volunteer activists and their work schedules as well as donation lists, donation demand and supply by locations, or providing up-to-date and practical legal or travelling information.

The awareness-raising facet of the Facebook groups covered an increasing range of communication tasks in line with the proliferation of the groups' activity. It served as an internal information source related to the relevant events and news of the migration crisis in Hungary and beyond, targeting the membership, and also functioned increasingly as a representation platform informing outsiders about the groups as well as promoting the pro-migration and solidarity perspective in contrast to the anti-migration state politics.

Finally, the link between online and offline activity at an individual level can be induced by an unconscious process aiming to make our online activity consistent by reinforcing it with offline activity. As evidenced by the interviews with volunteers, the activists often referred to their previous social media activity related to the migration crisis prior to joining any solidarity group on Facebook as a driver to the offline involvement, although most online group members never became active in the actual relief work. The term 'slacktivism' (Morozov 2010) encompasses these earlier forms of engagement exclusively through social media and refers to an online activism with little to no effect on actual events, but which later can lead to commitment to humanitarian work in the offline sphere. This also suggests a hierarchy of online activities in social media activism, ranging from low-cost, lighter activities such as post likes via activities that require more engagement, like commenting or sharing posts, up to the highest cost activities, e.g., joining a group or attending a Facebook event, with a constantly decreasing number of activists towards the higher levels of the activity pyramid. An analysis based on the actual Facebook activity data of the pro-refugee activists disproved the theoretical model of the hierarchy of online activities that is based on the theory of slacktivism in the case of Hungarian pro-refugee Facebook groups. The dominant activity was attending a Facebook event, followed by liking posts (these should be in reverse order according to the theory), while Facebook group membership indeed covers fewer activists but it is not a marginal group; rather, it is significant in terms of number of activists (half of the only-liking group). This also suggests that online and offline activism (e.g., liking, commenting, sharing a post or joining a group and participation in an event) are not separate, but rather complementary elements in a humanitarian action that reinforces the framing of hybrid activism in the Hungarian migrant solidarity movement (Dessewffy, Nagy & Váry 2017).

Another critique of slacktivism theory and a possible reason why the mere online activity of sharing or commenting on others' posts, media contents or own thoughts can later lead people to join actual aid work is the inner striving for consistency in terms of commitment: society rewards consistency and condemns inconsistent behaviour (Cialdini 2007). This suggests that the engagement in an idea or mission through social media might be the first step of civic involvement, if the actors of that cause provide the possibility of joining their work, and thus social media activity to support a mission cannot be simplified as mere armchair activism.

Conclusion

The inevitable role of social media, especially Facebook, in the Hungarian refugee solidarity movement was to link to support of on-site relief activity by exploiting social media skills in a crisis, involving independent individuals often from widely spread locations but with similar principles. Facebook offered a high level of efficacy in terms of recruiting offline (and online) activists and volunteers, to make on-site aid provision more effective in terms of staff, task and donation management and also to provide an efficient tool for internal and external communication.

The relief activity thus relied on a hybrid model that aimed to utilize the advantages of both the online and offline facets in this crisis, but the sudden and unexpected growth of the movement led to unforeseen difficulties. The proliferation of the groups in terms of membership, online activity (posts, comments, etc.), reach, and public and political attention shifted the online–offline division of work towards a less clear model, where the relation between the two spheres became blurred: the online activity no longer only supported offline work but also maintained a self-boosted overflow that consumed resources from the group and distracted attention from the original aim of on-site humanitarian aid provision to a more political focus. The online boom that shifted resources and capacities from the offline work outside the scope the movement but it was also impossible to neglect it, in case the Facebook pages and groups would slip out of control. This sheds light on additional vulnerability of a system that was inherently vulnerable, being a spontaneous grassroots movement, which multiplied the organizational challenges of the stakeholders. These processes could be sufficiently followed by the combination of online and offline ethnography, dominated by participant observation, that would ensure the most beneficial tools to understand the complexity of the hybrid operation of pro-refugee activism.

References

Barta, J. and Tóth, F.M. 2016 Online media coverage of humanitarian organizations and grassroots groups during the migration crisis in Hungary. In B. Simonovits and A. Bernát (Eds), *The social aspects of the 2015 migration*

crisis in Hungary. Budapest: TÁRKI Social Research Institute, http://www
.tarki.hu/hu/news/2016/kitekint/20160330_refugees.pdf

Bernát, A. 2016 Hosts in hostility: the new forms of solidarity and the role of
volunteer and civilian organizations in the migration crisis in Hungary. In
B. Simonovits and A Bernát (Eds), *The social aspects of the 2015 migration
crisis in Hungary*. Budapest: TÁRKI Social Research Institute, http://www
.tarki.hu/hu/news/2016/kitekint/20160330_refugees.pdf

Bernát, A., Kertész, A. and Tóth, F.M. 2016 Solidarity reloaded: volunteer and
civilian organizations during the migration crisis in Hungary. *Review of
Sociology of the Hungarian Sociological Association*, 26(4):29–52.

Bernát, A., Sik, E., Simonovits, B. and Szeitl, B. 2015 *Attitudes towards refugees, asylum seekers and migrants*. Budapest: TARKI Social Research Institute. http://www.tarki.hu/hu/news/2015/kitekint/20151203_refugee.pdf

Bernáth, G. and Messing, V. 2015 Bedarálva. A menekültekkel kapcsolatos
kormányzati kampány és a tőle független megszólalás terepei [The bulldozer:
the government's anti-immigration campaign and platforms for independent voices]. *Médiakutató [Media Research]*, 16(4): 7–17. http://www.media
kutato.hu/cikk/2015_04_tel/01_menekultek_moralis_panik.pdf

Boda, Z. and Medve-Bálint, G. (2012). Intézményi bizalom a régi és az új
demokráciákban (Institutional trust in old and new democracies). *Politi-
katudományi Szemle (Hungarian Political Science Review)*, 21(2):27–54.
http://www.poltudszemle.hu/szamok/2012_2szam/boda.pdf

Castells, M. 2012 *Networks of outrage and hope: social movements in the internet age*. Cambridge: Polity Press,

Cialdini, R.B. 2007 *Influence: the psychology of persuasion*. New York: Harper
Collins.

Dessewffy, T. and Nagy, Z. 2016 Born in Facebook – the refugee crisis and grassroots connective action in Hungary. *International Journal of Communication*, 10:2872–2894. http://ijoc.org/index.php/ijoc/article/view/4884/1684

Dessewffy, T., Nagy, Z. and Váry, D. 2017 Where are those better angels of
our society? Subaltern counterpublics in Hungary during the refugee crisis.
Bulletin of Science, Technology & Society, 37(2):112–123. DOI: https://doi
.org/10.1177/0270467618783944

Eurostat. 2020 *Migration and migrant population statistics*. Brussels: European
Commission. https://ec.europa.eu/eurostat/statistics-explained/index.php
?title=Migration_and_migrant_population_statistics#Migrant_population:
_23_million_non-EU_citizens_living_in_the_EU_on_1_January_2020

Eurostat. 2021 *Asylum statistics*. Brussels: European Commission. https://ec
.europa.eu/eurostat/statistics-explained/index.php/Asylum_statistics

Fuchs, C. 2014 *Social media: a critical introduction*. London: Sage.

ICRC. 2017 The Engine Room and Block Party, humanitarian futures for messaging apps. January. https://reliefweb.int/sites/reliefweb.int/files/resources
/4299_002_Humanitarian-Futures-for-Messaging-Apps_WEB_.pdf

Juhász, A., Hunyadi, B. and Zgut, E. 2015 *Focus on Hungary: refugees, asylum and migration.* Prague: Heinrich Böll Stiftung. https://www.boell.de/sites /default/files/2015-focus-on_hungary_refugees_asylum_migration.pdf

Kallius, A., Monterescu, D. and Rajaram, P.K. 2016 Immobilizing mobility: border ethnography, illiberal democracy, and the politics of the 'refugee crisis' in Hungary. *American Ethnologist,* 43(1):25–37. https://www.academia .edu/20386757/Immobilizing_Mobility_Border_Ethnography_Illiberal _Democracy_and_the_Politics_of_the_Refugee_Crisis_in_Hungary _American_Ethnologist_43_1_1-12_

KSH. 2012 *Önkéntes munka Magyarországon – A Munkaerő-felmérés 2011. III. negyedévi kiegészítő felvétele (Volunteer work in Hungary – Labour Force Survey Q3 2011, supplementary survey).* Budapest: Központi Statisztikai Hivatal (Central Statistical Office). https://www.ksh.hu/docs/hun/xftp/idoszaki /pdf/onkentesmunka.pdf

Morozov, E. 2010 *The net delusion: how not to liberate the world.* London: Allen Lane.

Sik, E. 2016 The socio-economic basis of xenophobia in contemporary Hungary. In B. Simonovits and A Bernát (Eds), *The social aspects of the 2015 migration crisis in Hungary.* Budapest: TÁRKI Social Research Institute, http://www.tarki.hu/hu/news/2016/kitekint/20160330_refugees.pdf

Simonovits, B. and Bernát, A. (Eds). 2016 *The social aspects of the 2015 migration crisis in Hungary.* Budapest: TÁRKI Social Research Institute. http://www.tarki.hu/hu/news/2016/kitekint/20160330_refugees.pdf

TÁRKI. 2013 Értékek 2013. Bizalom, normakövetés, az állam szerepéről és a demokráciáról alkotott vélemények alakulása Magyarországon. *A gazdasági növekedés társadalmi / kulturális feltételei c. kutatás 2013. évi hullámának elemzése.* (Values 2013. Trust, observance of norms, opinions on the role of the state and democracy in Hungary. *Social/cultural conditions of economic growth. Analysis of the 2013 wave of research).* Budapest: TÁRKI. http:// www.tarki.hu/hu/research/gazdkult/2013/2013_zarotanulmany_gazd _kultura.pdf

Tóth, I.G. 2009 Bizalomhiány, normazavarok, igazságtalanságérzet és paternalizmus a magyar társadalom értékszerkezetében. *A gazdasági felemelkedés társadalmi felemelkedés társadalmi-kulturális feltételei című kutatás zárójelentése.* (Lack of trust, norm disorders, injustice and paternalism in the value structure of Hungarian society. *Final report of the research entitled Socio-Cultural Conditions of Economic Ascension and Social Ascension).* Budapest: TÁRKI Social Research Institute.

CHAPTER 6

Building a Collaborative Community Economy: The Case of La Comunificadora

Vera Vidal
Open University of Catalonia, SP

Abstract

This chapter reflects on the role of accelerator programmes and entrepreneurship training in fostering the emergence of collaborative economy projects. More specifically it interrogates the mechanisms enabling a process usually criticised for (re)producing capitalism to produce other understandings and practices of the economy. It uses the example of Barcelona's La Comunificadora accelerator program. Instead of reinforcing capitalist understandings of the economy and a model of entrepreneurship tied to it, it can be the site of producing a diverse economy (Gibson-Graham 2006), thanks to a politics of language, of the subject and of collective action. Through the values conveyed by the teaching team, participants can resignify and reappropiate a series of notions, such as community. This reframing process is also that of themselves as an ongoing process. Nonetheless, resistances and non-recognitions of the framework presented to the participants, coupled to the precarious conditions of existence of the programme, limit the possibility of transformation of the

How to cite this book chapter:
Vidal, V. 2022. Building a Collaborative Community Economy: The Case of La Comunificadora. In: Travlou, P. and Ciolfi, L. (eds.) *Ethnographies of Collaborative Economies across Europe: Understanding Sharing and Caring.* Pp. 109–124. London: Ubiquity Press. DOI: https://doi.org/10.5334/bct.g. License: CC BY-NC-ND

individuals and of the projects. There is no singular outcome but rather a variety of paths taken.

Introduction

How do collaborative economy projects take shape and what type of collaborative economy do they end up embodying? As pointed out by Acquier et al. (2017), the collaborative economy – or sharing economy – is a contested umbrella construct at the intersection of three cores: the access economy, the platform economy and the community-based economy. All three have different, or even contradictory, promises and potentials. This leads to possible tensions, namely between ideals of empowerment, emancipation, decentralization, solidarity and social change and practices of value extraction and capture via capitalist markets.

Research on the collaborative economy has been carried out mostly on platforms and projects themselves, their potentials and impacts. In the course of the past few years, titles of academic papers on the collaborative economy, also known as the 'sharing economy', went from the approach 'sharing economy: a potential pathway to sustainability' (Heinrichs 2013) to 'the sharing economy: a pathway to sustainability or a nightmarish form of neoliberal capitalism?' (Martin 2016), to 'When the sharing economy becomes neoliberalism on steroids' (Murillo, Buckland & Val 2017). As revealed by this quick change in perspective, what was at first conceived – or at least marketed in the context of the 2008 systemic crisis – as an alternative solution to neoliberal markets, with many expectations regarding potential environmental, economic and social benefits, has turned out quite differently. 'Sharing economy' platforms have gradually challenged traditional sectors, public authorities and local communities. Studies have shown how platforms, such as Airbnb or Uber, are putting more pressure on already strained resources and infrastructures, (Cocola-Gant 2016), contributing to labour precariousness (Hill 2015) and being a further driver of inequality, such as perpetuating racial and gender biases (Ge et al. 2016; Edelman, Luca & Svirsky 2017; Schor et al. 2016; van Doorn 2017) or increasing earning inequalities within the 80% (Schor 2017).

To counteract this phenomenon and reconnect with some initial ideals of the collaborative economy, other models, such as platform cooperativism and open cooperativism, have emerged to put forth counter-hegemonic values and ways of doing. Platform cooperatives would combine collective ownership and decision-making, protection of workers, decent pay and security of income, transparency and portability of data (Scholz 2016). Workers would own, govern and operate such platforms. Open cooperativism promotes synergies between the commons-based peer production movement and the cooperative and solidarity economy movements, through multi-constituent governance, with active production of commons and a transnational orientation (Paizaitis et al. 2017).

Such movements have at times benefited from political support, leading to increased ressources to help foster emergent projects adhering to these values. At a local level, the city of Barcelona has been a prime example. The 2015 elections of Barcelona en Comú to the city hall propelled a new municipalist agenda of prefigurative politics (Rubio-Pueyo 2017; Russell 2019). This was reflected in its increased promotion of the social and solidarity economy (SSE) and the commons, both with a long tradition in Catalonia. This interest was extended to the collaborative economy and platforms, as the city was a battleground between residents, social movements and some platforms, such as Airbnb, Uber or Glovo. A co-creation process was designed that ultimately led to a series of commons-oriented collaborative economy policy recommendations (Fuster Morell & Senabre 2020). To study such models and make further recommendations, a local working group, BarCola, was created in 2016. It included academics, entrepreneurs and collectives from the SSE, the sharing economy or the commons and the local and regional public administration (Rodriguez Rivera & Fuster Morell 2018). Following on BarCola's activities, in March 2016 the city hosted Procomuns, the first encounter of the Commons Sharing Economies. 300 people gathered in 90 sessions and 30 talks to elaborate a Commons Declaration and 120 proposals for a commons-oriented sharing economy. The proposals were then posted on Decidim – a citizen participation platform – to craft the 2016 municipal action plan. Some of the proposals asked for training in socio-economic innovation and technological sovereignty for collaborative economy projects, through Barcelona Activa, the city's economic development agency. The "accelerator" training programme La Comunificadora was born.

Little is known about start-up training, notably accelerators, used by or dedicated to collaborative economy projects, despite their impact. Seed accelerators can be defined as 'a fixed-term, cohort-based program, including mentorship and educational components, that culminates in a public pitch event or demo-day' (Cohen & Hochberg 2014: 4). Airbnb is one of the most well-known alumni of Y Combinator, the prestigious start-up accelerator. Entrepreneurship training is a key step to understand how these projects are shaped in their early days and how this will mark their evolution. Accelerators aim at helping projects define their product, identify potential customers, secure resources and 'speed up market interactions in order to help nascent ventures adapt quickly and learn' (Cohen & Hochberg 2014: 10).

Beyond the mere access to resources, entrepreneurship training is also a site of producing ideals of entrepreneurship (Parkkari 2015), which reproduce and reinforce capital (Costa & Saraiva, 2012). For Parkkari (2015), accelerators socialize and discipline participants to perform entrepreneurship through pitching, to think big in terms of international projection and profitability, and to become lean tech start-ups. How then can entrepreneurship training, such as an accelerator, be the site of producing counter-hegemonic understandings of the economy and society? How can an accelerator such as La Comunificadora foster the emergence of collaborative economy projects adopting values and practices around empowerment, decentralization and social change and rejecting extractive practices? In this chapter, I will argue that the ideals and practices conveyed under the guise of entrepreneurship training depend on the values and framework adopted by the teaching team. Instead of reinforcing capitalocentric discourses, it can be the site of destabilization of the 'economy' by producing other understandings of what a diverse economy can be like (Gibson-Graham 2006), as can be seen through the case of La Comunificadora. Accelerators can thus play a key role in orientating projects towards specific framings of the collaborative economy over others.

La Comunificadora

I carried out this study while doing an ethnography of the third edition of La Comunificadora between November 2018 and April 2019. I did participant observation during the initial sessions of presentation and recruitment for the programme, the bi-weekly training sessions with the project holders and instructors and some sessions between project holders and their tutors. I had informal chats with project holders and instructors during the breaks, or before or after the sessions. This was complemented with 18 in-depth interviews with project holders from the first and second editions of the programme and the supervising team from Barcelona Activa. In an effort to triangulate multiple data sources, the interviews and fieldwork were combined with the analysis of notes and content produced by the participants in each session through Teixidora.net, a collaborative documentation tool.

Held in 2018–2019, the third edition of La Comunificadora gathered an initial cohort of 11 heterogeneous projects. The programme brought together a diversity of profiles, with varying degrees of familiarization with the framework of the SSE, the commons and collaborative economy. Projects too were heterogeneous, at different stages of their development – from idea to operating – and spanning sectors, which was actively sought after by the team. The heterogeneity in how familiar they are with these frameworks is related to how projects were informed of the programme. Some were oriented by advisors from *Barcelona Activa* towards the programme, and usually had less prior knowledge than those who heard of the programme directly from the teaching team. Projects were then selected through an application process, graded by the teaching team, Barcelona Activa's staff and some members from BarCola. The six-month programme offered bi-weekly classes and workshops. Each selected project was followed by a tutor and benefited from personalized mentorship to respond to the project's specific needs.

The teaching team is made of members of organizations directly involved in free/libre software, open and free knowledge and the SSE. Composed of members of femProcomuns and LabCoop, both cooperatives, the core of the organizing team, who won the public tender from Barcelona Activa, was part of the aforementioned BarCola group and Procomuns event. Their vision is directly informed by their professional and activist trajectory. Monica Garriga Miret and David Gómez Fontanills have co-founded femProcomuns. Monica is trained in law and communication, has been a foreign correspondent and developed several open knowledge projects. David has long been a digital commons activist, defending open knowledge notably in the Catalan Wikipedia chapter and in participatory art projects. He has also researched online collective creation. Wouter Tebbens, of the Free Knowledge Institute, is an industrial engineer with 20 years experience in free/libre software, open and free knowledge and commons-cooperative sustainability models. Guernica Facundo Vericat is trained as an economist and is a specialist of the social and solidarity economy; she co-founded LabCoop a cooperative of cooperatives dedicated to foster the creation of new cooperatives. Other instructors are members of Lab-Coop or come from other cooperatives, with complementary skills regarding emotions and communication or legal forms, for instance.

La Comunificadora presents several key differences from typical accelerators. First, it neither offers funding nor takes an equity stake. Second, the pace is much slower. It does not demand a seven-day-a-week commitment during its duration, with few assignments. Lastly, the day of final presentations leads to no award or reward. Projects arrive in La Comunificadora with a disposition to change and to produce change. Starting the programme means openness to the ideas and framework that will be developed. Nonetheless, it does not presume the actual effects. Participants do not see themselves as lacking; they are not characterized by hostility or powerlessness, as in the participants of Gibson-Graham's action research projects (2006), but are seen as having the capabilities to initiate an entrepreneurial project. Part of the work is already done when they arrive in the programme. Despite being receptive to change and connectedness, it is not a straightforward process. Language, subjectivity and collective action are all challenged and reconfigured during the length of the programme.

Building a Community Economy: A Politics of Language

To help foster counter-hegemonic projects, the teaching team develops a theoretical framework and sets of practice based on a reframing of the economy around the community. Gibson-Graham's *Post-Capitalist Politics* (2006) provides a useful framework to approach their work. The first step of such a project is to denaturalize the 'economy', as something that can be transformed instead of taken for granted. Imagining a different 'economy' takes into account the specific geographical contexts and historical path-dependencies shaping it rather than seeing it as something governing society (p. 53–54). This entails 'deconstructing the dominant capitalocentric discourse of economy' (p. 56) and 'dislocating the economy' to 'liberate these alternative languages [of economic difference] from their discursive subordination' (p. 57). Through a language politics that expands the economic vocabulary, it 'widen[s] the identity of the economy to include all of those practices excluded or marginalized by a strong theory of capitalism' (p. 60). To resocialize economic relations, Gibson-Graham points to a community economy to articulate economic interdependence, where 'economic decisions are made in the light of ethical discussions' (p. 80), on necessity, surplus, consumption and the commons as coordinates.

La Comunificadora attempts to liberate these languages of economic difference by denaturalizing the collaborative economy and the platform economy. It attempts to reframe values attached to them, resignify key notions such as community and the cooperative and introduce and normalize notions unfamiliar to many participants, such as commons and open knowledge. To do so, the teaching team elaborated their own situated framework drawing from international and Catalan academics and activist-scholars on the commons and the social market, putting the community at the centre.

The first session of the course is a three-hour session introducing the framework for the rest of the course around some key notions: the commons and the hybrid sustainability model around which they developed. It starts with a macro lens to denaturalize the economy: asking what the economy is for – to satisfy the needs of people – and who can fill this role – the state, the market and/or the commons, the most unfamiliar possibility for the participants. They then approach the commons from two perspectives. First the historical one of Elinor Ostrom (1990), of the resources shared by a community with a governance model of norms and regulations, situating it in the Catalan and Spanish context. Second, the one of digital commons, its replicability and unlimitedness and where relations are open and free, through the work of Yochai Benkler (2006). Its presentation of collaborative economies almost feels like reading a paper's state of the art on the topic: it traces its current understanding to the beginning of collaborative consumption and the work of Botsman & Rogers (2010) to popularize the notion. It then scales up through start-ups, unicorns and giants like Amazon, Airbnb, Uber or Deliveroo. They are not just presented as platforms but reframed as 'extractive' platforms pursuing the maximization of profits with the associated negative impacts on local economies or working rights, triggering the emergence of protests and social movements. This discursive destabilization provokes surprise and questioning, creating an affective disposition for participants to recognize what they took for granted: platforms either as neutral or as beneficial. They can then reframe them, taking into account a new paradigm allowing for a plurality of models:

> [the platforms of] ... like 'platform capitalism'. They say they are collaborative and all of a sudden we discover that, wait! They aren't all collaborative, far from it. There are the unicorns ... we learnt the nuances that exist, that is ... the differences [between models]. All that is sold as [collaborative] isn't collaborative, nor social. (Manuel, participant of the first edition)

The teaching team then presents possible answers. One is the revitalization of practices of community management, such as the urban commons or time-banks, and of the SSE and the social market. Other activists offer new notions, such as platform cooperativism (Scholz, 2016), centred for them on shared ownership and decision-making of the platform and protocols, or open coop-erativism (Bauwens & Kostakis 2014; Conaty & Bollier 2014), with a focus on the commons. They conclude on their own hybrid model between the commons and the social market they elaborated: that of 'commons sustainability'. At the centre is the community and its needs, around which are the pillars of governance, income and resources, modes of production and, last, knowledge sharing. Each pillar is then developed in following theoretical and practical sessions. Through this, participants are familiarized or reaffirmed with other ethical coordinates and normative values to guide their projects:

> There are the principles of the interests of a specific community or an association or a group of people that gather to cooperate, they create cooperatives, with the basic principles, with a governance. I learnt all of that more in detail in La Comunificadora. That its only purpose shouldn't be profit, although it can be influenced by it but there is a series of val-ues ... the sustainability, environmental and social aspects. And gender equality ... democracy, decision-making and the governance in those companies. And open knowledge and software, that is the data and the code understood as another instance of the common goods and services or resources of the entire community, right? It used to be water and land, well now it's also data. (Manuel, participant of the first edition)

The model they offer breaks from the most common conception of (digital) 'entrepreneurship' as something born by a visionary individual, centred on monetization and a business model. The centrality of community is derived from the adopted definition of the commons: that of a shared resource, around which a community is constituted to govern it. It is the collective, rather than the individual founder(s), that should decide what the initiative should be about and how to operationalize it around a model of sustainability rather than a business model, around different possibilities for labour, exchange and enterprise. Nonetheless, they find various challenges along the way regarding language. The notion of 'community' needs constant reframing during the pro-gramme, given the fuzziness of the term.

During a workshop session, projects were invited to reflect on their models of income, contributions and resources to share to be sustainable:

> Teacher: You have used the words 'client' and 'community', those are two different things.
>
> Participant 1: They are the same for me?
>
> Teacher: The client is not the community. Marketing makes us misuse concepts.

Participant 2: It's a subtle difference; you are a client of SomEnergia.

Teacher: Before being a client, you are a member, you need a 'godfather' [someone who can introduce you to the community]. A community is not a bunch of clients. It matters to know to what extent we are willing to hack the classical model of selling a service or use a community one, centred on the commons, where there's a shared resource. (La Comunificadora, 10 January 2019)

The teacher tries to signify the notion of community away from its capitalist co-optation as mere client. Gibson-Graham (2006) points to some of the problems of community as a notion. Its uses across the political spectrum, and specifically its neoliberal co-optation, give a sense of common being, that of unity, immediacy and mutual identification, and obscure difference, mediation, negotiation and becoming together, at the heart of a community. Gibson-Graham sees the community as an ethical space of decision, which transpires from the comment of the teacher in their idea of 'member', of an active participant who co-decides how to produce and sustain the commons.

The later sessions dedicated to each pillar allow some concepts to be normalized, notably to resignify the cooperative and to introduce open knowledge and licences. The sessions on governance present all possible legal forms the project can adopt in Catalonia. They dedicate a lot of attention to cooperatives, a model sometimes unknown or with bad connotations for participants:

I had a prejudice against the social and solidarity economy. This prejudice may have come from   because I have been living in Barcelona since 2010 and the three regions where I've lived are very different socially. So the solidarity economy in Andalucía, which is my previous reference, is very linked – and now I see it positively, before I didn't – to the agricultural world, to agricultural cooperativism, to some values that are against modernity   I know they are against capitalism, against neoliberalism but they are also very anti-modern depending on the cases ... it goes against my individual values. So what happened? When I got here [to La Comunificadora], the values of the social and solidarity economy, to which I didn't give a name, got more linked to civic values, which are more transversal than this difference between city and countryside ... That is fraternity, equality, etc. and if I consider how I feel as a cosmopolitan person ... they don't trigger, let's say, a cultural rejection like it did in Andalucía. (Juan, participant of the second edition)

The sessions allowed him to overcome his prejudice, by resignifying the values associated with cooperatives and more generally the SSE, thus making them compatible with his own ethical compass. Rather than being viewed as a rejection of modernity, the city, cooperatives are resignified positively, as promoting desirable values. Juan is not the only one who overcame his prejudices:

others acknowledged how their own lack of knowledge enabled them to project and generalize gossip, discrediting cooperatives. La Comunificadora allowed normalizing of cooperatives by presenting the possibilities and constraints of this legal form, on an equal footing with more familiar ones:

> Some ignorance, so, you only remember things you heard about some cooperatives ... about scams, frauds, and so on. Those things. So you think 'alright, it's a world ...' Basically like any other, because it's an obscure world if you don't know it. So, after seeing it [in the programme] you see that ultimately between a cooperative and a Ltd there is no difference. That is, both have a governance, both ... they have different ways [of doing so]. They are, like everything is very typified, very legalized, what you can do in both cases, right? It's not how it looks from the outside; it looks like everything is very hippie, like 'ah! Alright'. But ultimately it isn't really like that, right? So it's the ignorance of this world, both entrepreneurial and cooperative that I wasn't interested in. Because of La Comunificadora, well, you learn about the different forms that are out there. (Cesc, participant of the second edition)

Self-Transformation, Together: A Politics of the Subject

Another important step according to Gibson-Graham (2006) is building a politics of the subject, that is a process that goes beyond discourse to take into account the bodily experience and how the self and the world shape each other (p. 127). This process of self-transformation to 'reframe identities and capacities of individuals' (p. 144) is 'not an easy or sudden one. It is not so much about seeing and knowing as it is about feeling and doing' (p. 152). As we have seen previously, the discursive destabilization and ensuing resistance and non-recognition and the reframing of some notions are first steps in the process of self-transformation. The adoption of this new and resignified language of economic diversity can then lead to producing positive affect and creating spaces of identification and ethical openings to commonality. The cultivation of the self as subject of freedom entails 'self-believing in our economic capacities, [being] responsible to our political abilities, conscious of our potential to become something other than what we heretofore have "chosen" to be' (p. 169).

As seen previously, participants arrive at La Comunificadora with a disposition to change but much of the work is still ahead. This transformation is not only that of reframing economic notions and stopping seeing oneself as lacking, but also that of affirming one's vision and acting upon it. By accessing a new vocabulary or deepening one's understanding, participants can start naming things, giving them a sense of possible connection and relevance:

> We got empowered to speak of urban nature as a common good. We sensed it but didn't get there. (Mireia, participant of the second edition)

This self-transformation is also that of recognizing and acknowledging our interdependence, rather than just transforming into an enterprising self. It is less about responsibilization of one's employability, successes and failures and looking for constant self-optimization as can be taught in entrepreneurship programmes (Berglund 2013) and more about realizing one's agency, and one's need for and impact on the collective. During La Comunificadora they learn about many open source or local alternatives to dominant Silicon Valley platforms. They start realizing that through consumption, their choices affect others, by allocating demand, money or power towards companies whose values they may or not be aligned with. These decisions affect both what and whom they choose and do not choose. Are they helping to relocalize the economy? Are they impacting their health?, and so on. This leads to reassessing their consumption habits and making some adjustments, starting with the platforms they use:

> Instead of Google, we use Ecosia [for searching the web]. Well, those changes are not ... Well I did change phone companies, I got Som Connexió ... well, giving up on those big companies and seeing there are alternatives. That was also useful in La Comunificadora, to see that everything isn't La Caixa and Google. There are more options. But people don't know them. But they exist. (Carla, participant of the second edition)

This ethics of decision can start pervading all types of significant choices, and help assess who will be benefiting from them. Prioritizing certain types of enterprises, like cooperatives over large for-profit companies, can become a new norm.

> I took it into account for impactful decisions, at an individual level, a family level, a community level, at school. Things that I didn't use to value. If the school's kitchen could be run by a small cooperative rather than a big conglomerate producing 15,000 menus that have nothing to do with the territory. Situations in which I support these kinds of decisions, when other people question them. Five or six years ago, I wouldn't have done that. (Juan, participant of the second edition)

This acknowledgement of one's impact in the world is also the acknowledgement and affirmation of one's value, and the value of one's labour.

> Having it clear that you shouldn't work for free. That was something they told us at La Comunificadora ... It's not because you do something for the common good and let's say, something with ethical values and taking into account people, which it has to be free. That's a false concept that at times we had internalized, saying, 'If you do something for the community, it has to be for free'. No, it can also be a way of life, not a capitalist way of life looking to maximize profit, but to live with dignity. (Carla, participant of the second edition)

Ultimately La Comunificadora acts as a catalyst rather than a trigger of a larger process of redefinition of one's life choices. By affirming one's vision and value, by reintroducing an ethics of decision, participants become ready to make some significant professional changes.

> I have to say, when I started La Comunificadora, I was working as a freelancer in an architecture firm that was governed by a sexist, abusive architect. And participating also in La Comunificadora ... empowered me to say, 'I'm resigning from this job which doesn't satisfy me'; I realized I was a grey person, that I was living in automatic mode, that I was a grey professional basically. So I resigned and created my own business: 'Now I am going to do things the way I think they should be done and how I really decide', looking for this alignment with those values ... I said 'I will not feed this system anymore'. (Carla, participant of the second edition)

Rather than a goal achieved once and for all, such as becoming an active maker or being empowered to act, self-transformation should be seen as a permanent process, as a journey rather than a destination. It consists not only of reframing the existing, such as capabilities and skills, in a positive light, but also of allowing one to critically assess oneself and consider if one's many life choices reflect one's values.

This process of self-affirmation can sometimes be at odds with the adoption of the new framework and vocabulary. The teaching team can at times place this process of taking action above the fit of the work. During one session, participants, rather than the team, were invited to elaborate presentations and materials to teach some of their own skills to the other projects, while adapting them to the framework of the course. They covered social media skills, brand identity, facilitation, etc. Rather than adopting the participative workshop-like method of the programme, one presentation was a PowerPoint presentation explaining the basics of using social media without recalibrating with the tools and frames of the programme. After that session, one teacher told me: 'That presentation was really not a good fit, she didn't understand what we were aiming at, but what matters is that she got empowered, she got to present and speak to an audience.'

This transformation of the self, this acknowledgement of one's interdependency and affirmation of one's values, can then lead to the transformation of the projects. By giving examples of active projects from prior editions, such as Som Mobilitat[1] or Katuma,[2] the team shows it is feasible here and now, it is already being done. This can translate into changes of the projects. This shift is partially reflected in projects changing their name during the programme, either

---

[1] A Catalan electric car sharing platform cooperative.

[2] The Catalan version of open source platform Open Food network to connect food producers with consumer groups.

by clearly identifying them as a cooperative or to the SSE (by using 'coop', or 'ESS' in the name) or as part of a Catalan cooperative identity, emphasizing the collective (*som*, i.e. "we are"; *fem*, i.e. "we make"). It can translate into their legal status. SomAtents, a not-for-profit collective of journalists producing online media, had been considering becoming a cooperative and decided to effectively do so during La Comunificadora. They stopped viewing their readers only in monetary terms as customers–consumers. They started realizing instead the potential for participation, to view them as members of a community in which they can decide, be prescribers of the project. Adopting open licences can be more complicated. In a previous edition, the teaching team had many disagreements with a couriers' cooperative that did not want to adopt open software.

Transforming the World Together: A Politics of Collective Action

As Gibson-Graham (2006) put it, collective action aims at creating a community economy, based on what the collective will identify and debate as its needs, resources and skills.

> The community economy is an acknowledged space of social interdependency and self-formation. Anything but a blueprint, it is an unmapped and uncertain terrain that calls forth exploratory conversation and political/ethical acts of decision. (p. 166)

La Comunificadora is a site where, through self-transformation, the individual or organization can shift its priorities by acknowledging the role of the collective:

> A very strong feeling that things can be done collectively and that the world of economy isn't only 'free entrepreneurs'. But at times it's the creation of a community that really matters. (Quim, participant of the first edition)

Unlike conventional demands on entrepreneurship, this change can entail slowing the pace of the project. Project leaders can take a step backwards and reorient priorities to build a community and enable collective discussion and negotiation. This is reflected in the evolution of TextilESS, a project led by a foundation to help local seamstresses order larger amounts of materials. During the last session with their tutor and a worker from Barcelona Activa, to review their progress during the programme and map the next steps, the project team, made up of workers from a foundation, shared that they had stopped seeing themselves as an economic agent that wants to sell a project. On the contrary, they were finishing the training with the intention to foster a community around a product generated and sold collectively. They saw themselves no longer as the driving team of the project, but rather as facilitators, as another beneficiary.

Collective action is at the centre of the programme. Whether it is the initiative itself with collective rather than individual entrepreneurship, the group exercises, or the invitation for projects to think of ways of working together and the potential collaborations with projects of the social market, working with others is the norm. Initially the team tries to advocate for projects with a similar aim to merge, or at least build bridges, but the ideals behind the projects may not match despite an apparently similar end product. This happened with two projects of platforms to help parents build a support network in their neighbourhood. One project was meant only for single mothers, wanting to create a safe space for them and with some defiance of other family configurations, while the other one wanted to include any kind of family configuration, emphasizing the potential support over the type of family. The leader of the second project, Sara, ended up collaborating with a different project, that of an app to help families hire carers. The collaboration was built on sharing skills: Sara, a UX designer for apps, could help Ferran build the technical platform, and use this first experience for her own project. It was during the informal moments, the coffee breaks, that they got to know each other and slowly built the trust needed to volunteer to help the other.

Beyond the programme, collective action is also enacted through cooptation into the SSE sector in Barcelona and inter-cooperation. The project tutors and different experts helping orient the projects are key to find support after the end of the training and provide a safety net as trustworthy interlocutors:

> The first mentors we had in each area, like in communications, in finance and accounting, are the ones who, to this day, are still supporting us professionally in the project. Of course, bonds are somehow created that help you keep going and evolve your idea in the way you have been working it in La Comunificadora and this is really important. That you don't feel once the programme is over that you are alone again. (Laia, Participant of the second edition)

Nonetheless, collective action within La Comunificadora was constrained by precarious conditions of existence and limited resources granted by the public institution. Until its last edition in 2021, the contract was subjected to a yearly tender the team had to win again, with the date of publication changing. The teaching team was uncertain if the programme will be renewed and when it would be published every year. They had no budget to publicize it and usually had to rely in a short space of time on their personal network and social media contacts to help reach out to potential participants.

The programme had to face the expectations of the participants, which differ depending on their previous knowledge and the level of advancement of the project. The initial content was too theoretical and lacked practical aspects according to some projects, which expected a more classical accelerator programme. Given the limited time – three to six months depending on the edition – it may be too much content too quickly for those more unfamiliar with the concepts, while for others it was not enough. Finding a middle ground for the teaching team proves challenging and leads them to personalize the content more and more to fit each project.

Conclusion

We have seen in this chapter that La Comunificadora, a training programme for commons-oriented collaborative economy projects, can be a site for a diverse politics of economy. Rather than reinforcing capitalist understandings of the economy and a model of entrepreneurship tied to it, it enables a politics of language, of the subject and of collective action to be developed. The reframing process participants engage in allows them to resignify a series of notions away from a capitalocentric perspective and reappropriate them. This reframing process is also that of themselves: but not only that of their own narrative, to stop seeing themselves as subjugated and to be active makers. There is no end to this reframing. It is an ongoing process that is never over, that acknowledges their interdependence through their personal and professional choices and invites them to continuously assess them critically. Nonetheless, there are many resistances and non-recognitions of the framework presented, and the self-transformation of the participants and projects might not always go in the direction wanted by the instructors. The diverging expectations of participants, coupled to the precarious conditions of existence of the programme, limit the possibility of transformation of the individuals and of the projects. There is no singular outcome but rather a variety of paths taken.

One critical aspect that is not explored in this chapter but is worthy of attention is that of the tools and materials used during the programme. Many are similar, although at times tweaked, from usual accelerator programmes: canvases, elevator pitches, etc. The rationale is that participants must be familiarized with them, to be able to adapt and speak multiple languages depending on the context and who they will be interacting with. The values behind the process partially enable another outcome: that of creating 'entrepreneurs', with another set of values and ethical compass. But tools and processes are not neutral but performative, and shape people in certain ways rather than others. Further investigation into what this produces in such a context would enable us to better understand the tensions and limits of using such a format, that of entrepreneurial training, for a diverse politics of economy.

References

Acquier, A. Daudigeos, T. and Pinkse, J. 2017 'Promises and paradoxes of the sharing economy: An organizing framework.' *Technological Forecasting and Social Change* 125: –10.

Bauwens, M. and Kostakis, V. 2014 'From the Communism of Capital to Capital for the Commons: Towards an Open Co-operativism.' *TripleC: Communication, Capitalism & Critique* 12: 356–361.

Benkler, Y. 2006 *The Wealth of Networks: How Social Production Transforms Markets and Freedom.* New Haven: Yale University Press.

Berglund, K. 2013 'Fighting Against All Odds: Entrepreneurship Education as Employability Training.' *Ephemera* 13, no. 4: 717–735.

Botsman, R. and Rogers, R. 2010 *What's Mine Is Yours: The Rise of Collaborative Consumption.* New York, NY: Harper Business

Cocola-Gant, A. 2016 'Holiday Rentals : The New Gentrification Battlefront.' *Sociological Research Online* 21, no.3: 112–120.

Cohen, S. and Hochberg, Y. 2014 *Accelerating Start-ups: The Seed Accelerator Phenomenon.* Working paper. http://papers.ssrn.com/sol3/papers.cfm?abstract_id=2418000

Conaty, P. and Bollier, D. 2014 'Toward an Open-Cooperativism: A New Social Economy Based on Open Platforms, Co-operative Models and the Commons.' Commons Strategies Group Workshop.

Costa, A.S.M. and Saraiva, L.A.S. 2012 'Hegemonic Discourses on Entrepreneurship as an Ideological Mechanism for the Reproduction of Capital.' *Organization* 19, no. 5: 587–614.

Edelman B., Luca, M. and Svirsky, D. 2017 'Racial Discrimination in the Sharing Economy: Evidence from a Field Experiment.' *American Economic Journal: Applied Economics* 9, no. 2: 1–22.

Fuster Morell, M. and Senabre, E. 2020 'Co-creation Applied to Public Policies: A Case Study on Collaborative Policies for the Platform Economy in the City of Barcelona.' *CoDesign.*

Ge, Y., Knittel, C., Mackenzie, D. and Zoepf, S. 2016 *Racial and Gender Discrimination in Transportation Network Companies.* NBER Working Paper No 22776.

Gibson-Graham, J.K. 2006 *A Postcapitalist Politics.* Minneapolis, MN: University of Minnesota Press.

Heinrichs, H. 2013 'Sharing Economy: A Potential Pathway to Sustainability.' *Gaia* 22, no.4: 228–231.

Hill, S. 2015 *Raw Deal: How the 'Uber Economy' and Runaway Capitalism are Screwing American Workers.* New York: Martin's Press.

Malhotra, A. and Alstyne, M. 2014 'The Dark Side of the Sharing Economy and How to Lighten It.' *Viewpoints Communications of the ACM*, 57, no. 11 (November).

Martin, C.J. 2016 'The Sharing Economy: A Pathway to Sustainability or a Nightmarish Form of Neoliberal Capitalism?' *Ecol econ.* 121: 149–159.

Murillo, D., Buckland, H. and Val, E. 2017 'When the Sharing Economy Becomes Neoliberalism on Steroids: Unraveling the Controversies.' *Technological Forecasting and Social Change* 125: 66–76.

Ostrom, E. 1990 *Governing the Commons: The Evolution of Institutions for Collective Action*. Cambridge: Cambridge University Press.

Paizatis, A., Kostakis, V. and Bauwens, M. 2017 'Digital Economy and the Rise of Open Cooperativism: The Case of the Enspiral Network.' *Transfer: European Review of Labour and Research*.

Parkkari, P. 2015 'Problematizing Start-up Accelerator Programmes: Accelerating Ideals of Entrepreneurship?' Paper presented at *10th Critical Management Studies Conference, Leicester, UK*. https://www.researchgate.net/publication/308327098

Rubio-Pueyo, V. 2017 *Municipalism in Spain*. New York, NY: Rosa Luxemburg Stiftung.

Russell, B. 2019 'Beyond the Local Trap: New Municipalism and the Rise of the Fearless Cities.' *Antipode* 51, no.3: 989–1010.

Rodriguez Rivera, N. and Fuster Morell, M. 2018 'Public Innovation in Platform Economy Policies : Platforms, Policy Labs and Challenges.' In *Sharing Cities: A Worldwide Cities Overview on Platform Economy Policies With a Focus on Barcelona*, edited by Fuster Morell, M. Barcelona: Editorial UOC.

Scholz, T. 2016 *Platform Cooperativism: Challenging the Corporate Sharing Economy*. New York: Rosa Luxemburg Stiftung.

Schor, J.B. 2017 'Does the Sharing Economy Increase Inequality Within the Eighty Percent? Findings from a Qualitative Study of Platform Providers.' *Cambridge Journal of Regions, Economy and Society* 10, no.2: 263–279.

Schor, J.B., Fitzmaurice, C., Carfagna, L.B., Attwood-Charles, W. and Poteat, E.D. 2016 'Paradoxes of openness and distinction in the sharing economy.' *Poetics*, 54, 66–81.

Van Doorn, N. 2017 'Platform labor: On the gendered and racialized exploitation of low-income service work in the 'on-demand' economy.' *Information, Communication & Society*, 20, no.6: 898–914.

CHAPTER 7

Practising Solidarity and Developing Food Citizenship in Croatia: The Example of Croatian Community-Supported Agriculture

Olga Orlić

Institute for Anthropological Research, Zagreb,

Anita Čeh Časni and Kosjenka Dumančić

Faculty of Economics and Business, University of Zagreb

Abstract

Even though community-supported agriculture (CSA) has long been present at the margins of consumerist society all over the world, it has gained more transdisciplinary attention in the past 20–30 years. It has to do with raising awareness among various stakeholders about the need to change food politics, regarding not only securing enough amounts of food to feed the growing world population (food security) but also the most ethical means of achieving this goal (food sovereignty). This awareness resulted in small but growing changes of consumption practices of individuals and their growing interest in being

How to cite this book chapter:
Orlić, O., Čeh Časni, A. and Dumančić, K. 2022. Practising Solidarity and Developing Food Citizenship in Croatia: The Example of Croatian Community-Supported Agriculture. In: Travlou, P. and Ciolfi, L. (eds.) *Ethnographies of Collaborative Economies across Europe: Understanding Sharing and Caring*. Pp. 125–146. London: Ubiquity Press. DOI: https://doi.org/10.5334/bct.h. License: CC BY-NC-ND

actively engaged in co-creation of food politics, in processes of becoming food citizens. Policy makers, at least in the EU, appropriated some of these, once alternative, efforts into their programmes. In Croatia pioneers of a struggle for achieving food citizenship in the past decade have been initiators and other actors of CSA groups. This chapter provides a brief overview of CSA development in Croatia, especially within the wider context of food citizenship and solidarity economy concepts, aiming at changing dominant food politics or even the dominant economic mode.

Introduction: food security, food sovereignty and food citizenship

Food is a nexus for industry, rural urban relations, global trade relations, domestic and social life, biological health, social belonging, celebration of community, paid and unpaid work, expressions of care, abuse of power, hunger strikes, fasts and prayer. (Welsh & MacRae 1998: 242)

In past few decades, there has been a significant effort of various NGOs and grassroots movements advocating for reshaping power relations and rights in the food production–consumption chain (Patel 2009). This resulted in proliferation of various practices, such as community-supported agriculture, that are trying to reshape dominant food market system and impact food related policies on different levels. This struggle is accompanied by a rather new vocabulary, appropriated almost simultaneously by practitioners, scientists and policy makers.

Some terms, such as food security[1], were used even 50 years ago but the meaning has changed over the years, mostly by the influence and activities of NGOs like Via Campesina and various other advocates (Patel 2009: 665;

---

[1] The global agenda aiming at resolving hunger and poverty in the 20th century appeared within the framework of the League of Nations in the 1930s (Simon 2012: 10; Windfuhr & Jonsén 2005). This global agenda was named 'food security' at the 1974 United Nations World Food Conference held in Rome. Evolution of the definition over time reflects changes in perspectives towards resolving the problem (from original 1974 supply-oriented definition towards a more complex one that is more in line with the human security and human rights perspective of development (http://www.fao.org/3/y4671e/y4671e06.htm#fnB21). Scholars have identified over 200 definitions (Smith et al., 1993), but the most commonly accepted definition was approved by the 1996 World Food Summit (WFS). It states that 'Food security":? exists when all people, at all times, have physical, [social] and economic access to sufficient, safe and nutritious food which meets their

Gómez-Benito & Lozano, 2014: 145). Via Campesina introduced the term 'food sovereignty' at the World Food Summit in 1996, as a term opposing the food security concept (used primarily in the debate about the need to end world hunger and malnutrition). Windfuhr & Jonsén (2005) elaborated on the evolution of the food sovereignty concept and its potential, simultaneously pointing to the core problem of any serious hunger problem-solving effort – i.e., the unequal treatment of developing and industrialized countries. The first ones are forced by various treaties to open up their markets and to cut subsidies to their farmers; the same is not required from the industrialized countries. However, even in the industrialized countries subsidies rarely reach the small farmers and are intended for big agri-businesses (Windfuhr & Jonsén 2005:6–7). Precisely because of this, these authors argue that 'food sovereignty' is often used by developing countries and small farmers all over the world (Windfuhr & Jonsén 2005: 38). Together with the struggle of consumers for the right not only to know what they eat (labelling problem) but to choose what they eat, the most suitable definition of food sovereignty was offered by Patel – 'a call for peoples' rights to shape and craft food policy' (Patel 2009: 663).

However, despite the fact that food sovereignty was intended to represent a kind of opposition to food security, its creator, Via Campesina, recognized that the main aim of food sovereignty to achieve food security, only by using quite different approach and methods:

> Long-term food security depends on those who produce food and care for the natural environment. As the stewards of food producing resources we hold the following principles as the necessary foundation for achieving food security ... Food is a basic human right. This right can only be realized in a system where food sovereignty is guaranteed. Food sovereignty is the right of each nation to maintain and develop its own capacity to produce its basic foods respecting cultural and productive diversity. We have the right to produce our own food in our own territory. Food sovereignty is a precondition to genuine food security (Via Campesina 1996: 1–2).

The main difference between the concepts was found in power relations among various actors in the area of food politics – mentioned by Windfuhr & Jonsén (2005). However, Patel (2009: 666) revealed certain contradictions in a definition of food sovereignty, one of them being the fact that 'food producers' was quite a loose term, and that it could refer to transnational companies producing

---

dietary needs and food preferences for an active and healthy life' (http://www.fao.org/3/w3613e/w3613e00.htm).

food as well. The same author recognized that power relations within the food sovereignty concept were not quite clearly recognized. This referred e.g., to the relationship between farm owners and farm workers and to the fact that it would be difficult to reconcile the struggle for women's rights, simultaneously emphasizing the need to preserve family farms and neglecting the fact that family was, most often, the prime place for practising patriarchy.

Via Campesina has struggled for so-called natural (and not legal) food producers in the food production/consumption chain and their efforts have resulted by the adoption of the Declaration on the Rights of Peasants and Other People Working in Rural Areas[2] by the UN in 2018. All these efforts have forged a new concept – food citizenship – suitable to encompass all the various efforts aiming to alter dominant food politics.

Recognizing the proliferation and unsystematic use of the term in literature and in some food movements' websites, Gómez-Benito and Lozano proposed a definition of food citizen 'as the individual who has access to enough healthy, quality food or who mobilizes himself to achieve it' (Gómez-Benito and Lozano 2014: 152).

However, this citizen/consumer who would 'use their preferences as an expression of social agency' (De Tavernier 2012) would require not only food labelling information but information about the food production practices and the life cycle assessment of food products, as well (De Tavernier 2012: 905).

Lozano-Cabedo and Gómez-Benito considered the concept of food citizenship as closely related to appearance and development of civic food networks (see also Wilkins, 2005; Renting et al. 2012). They also thought this is the direction food movement practitioners should orient their objectives and activities. They propose a working theoretical model for food citizenship, structured into eight propositions:

> These propositions have as core ideas an extended concept of the right to food, the assumption of obligations, the combination of public and private behaviour, the individual and collective participation, the empowerment of all actors of the agri-food system, the promotion of justice, fairness and sustainability in food systems, and a cosmopolitan character of food Citizenship (Lozano-Cabedo and Gómez-Benito 2017: 2–3).

According to them, food citizenship could be perceived as an extension of the concept of ecological citizenship. The main difference between these two types of citizenship is that in food citizenship the rights come before obligations and duties (Lozano-Cabedo and Gómez-Benito 2017: 13).

---

[2] https://www.geneva-academy.ch/joomlatools-files/docman-files/UN %20Declaration%20on%20the%20rights%20of%20peasants.pdf

Community-Supported Agriculture (CSA) as a Cradle for Food Citizenship and Solidarity Economy

Recently various types of civic food networks have emerged and developed. The consumers/citizens play an active role in the initiation and operation of new forms of consumer–producer relations (Renting et al. 2012).

Community-supported agriculture is one of these civic food networks, and, one might add, not so new.[3] The movement was initiated in the 1960s in Japan (Kondoh 2014: 144; Parker 2005: 15) and a little later in Switzerland (Sahakian 2015: 145), independently. It was transferred, independently by two farmers, into the USA, where it developed under the name of CSA. The Italian groups, important for the introduction of the CSA movement into Croatia and named *Gruppi d' aquisto solidale*, were founded in 1994 in Ferrara (Randelli 2015: 19). Today the CSA are present in numerous countries all over the world under different names (for Europe, see for example Volz et al. 2016).

The CSA started as a bottom-up, grassroots movement based on mutual collaboration, partnership and solidarity between consumers and (in most cases organic[4] food producers). It could be perceived as an early attempt to practice food citizenship, even at the time the term did not exist. The incentive of a buyer from CSA groups was often the driving force of the groups.

The basic feature of the CSA's usual routine can be described as follows: a group of individuals interested in healthy food, environmental issues and support for small family farms and for the local economy, deciding to organize jointly their food provision by regular ordering a 'basket' of seasonally available products from farmer(s) living in proximity. The delivery is organized on a weekly basis and without middlemen. There are differences across CSA movements in

---

[3] The names for CSA or similar networks are different but similar: Alternative Food Network (AFN) (e.g. Grasseni 2013) or short food supply chains (SFSCs) and local food systems (LFS/SYAL. (Renting et al 2012:292). Although it can be perceived by some disciplines as a type of 'direct marketing' (Roque et al. 2008), Renting et al (2012) rightfully point to the fact that this is mainly not the case, since in AFNs usually it is the consumer who is the initiator (Renting et al 2012:290). The same authors consider that AFNs have not been useful any more, since today these networks no more emerge counter-hegemonic food networks like they used to do since the 1990s (ibid:292)

[4] By organic, we mean food that is produced by methods of organic farming that, according to Znaor et al., are 'sometimes also referred [to] as ecological, biological or alternative farming, [which] is an agricultural system that excludes agri-chemical inputs and genetic engineering and resorts to external inputs only where the system cannot be sustained by internal processes' (Znaor et al., 2014: 33).

different countries and even from one group to another, but the abovementioned routine can be identified as the basic feature of these groups, perceived as a kind of community of practice[5] (Orlić 2019: 12). Their mutual collaboration is manifested (in different variations across the globe) in continuous 'collective provisioning on the basis of solidarity principle' (Grasseni 2013: 5).

CSA has been recognized as one of the most prominent examples of global justice activism (Grasseni 2013: 3) oriented toward an alter-globalisation[6]

---

[5] Communities of practice is a concept stemming from the area of theory of learning. The concept was proposed by anthropologist Jean Lave and theories of practice scholar Etienne Wenger, first in relation to situated learning that takes place in groups with a master–apprentice relationship, i.e. in groups where the newcomers become the old-timers (Lave and Wenger, 1991). The members can be at the margins of the group as well as at the core. Elements of this concept can be found, according to Orlić (2019), in groups of CSAs because it is crucial their 'participation in the system of activities in which participants share understanding about what they are doing and what it means for their lives and their community' (Lave and Wenger 1991: 98).

[6] The movement was initiated in the mid-1990s by various protests against the negative consequences of globalisation. Therefore, at its initial phase the movement was labelled as an anti-globalisation movement, but this was soon proved to be inadequate (Pleyers, 2010: 6) and was replaced by the neologism 'alter-globalisation'. It was used for the first time in an interview with Arnauld Zacharie, one of the prominent actors of the movement in Belgium, published on 27 December 2001 in *La Libre Belgique*. The idea of 'another globalization' and the importance of constructing alternatives became widespread in francophone circles under this neologism, while in the English-speaking world the movement was first qualified as 'antiglobalization', then 'anti-corporate globalization' and eventually 'the global justice movement' (Pleyers, 2010: 6). It can be perceived as an umbrella movement (with World Social Forum as a core event providing a joint platform) that includes 'diverse and relatively autonomous actors and events' (Pleyers, 2010: 11) such as advocacy networks, citizens' networks like ATTAC or Global Trade Watch, Social Forums, trade unions, youth activists, indigenous peoples, human rights networks, green activists, third world solidarity networks, etc. (Pleyers, 2010). However, despite a quite diversified focus, the alter-globalisation or global justice movement can be perceived as a 'mature coherent ideological structure ("justice globalism") that provides conceptual and practical alternatives to the dominant paradigm of market globalism', as a qualitative morphological discourse analysis and quantitative content analysis of selected documents that World Social

movement (Šimleša, 2006) and relocalization towards boosting local autonomy in order to create resistance to the dominant system (Starr and Adams 2003). This boosting of local autonomy is extremely important within food sovereignty and the CSA seems to be a showcase for achieving it (Starr and Adams 2003). CSA is also an important building block of the solidarity economy, which refers to a set of very disparate initiatives and movements focused on creating and practising 'alternative ways of living, producing and consuming' (Bauhard 2014). These initiatives include practices such as communal living (e.g. Sargisson 2011; Hilder et al. 2018), community kitchens (e.g. Lenten 1993; Engler-Stringer and Berenbaum 2007; Gennari & Tornaghi 2020), Open Source initiatives (DiBona, Ockman & Stone 1999; Angelo 2010), workers' cooperatives (e.g. Vargas-Cetina 2005; Lima 2007; Breyer 2010; Pfeilstetter 2013), urban gardening (e.g. Biti and Blagaić Bergman 2014; Poljak Istenič 2016; Gulin Zrnić & Rubić 2015, 2018; Calvet-Mir & March 2019; Smith 2020), community-supported agriculture (Ostrom 2007; Schnell 2007; Feagan & Henderson 2009; Janssen 2010; Grasseni 2013, 2014; Sarjanović 2014; Orlić 2014, 2019; Slavuj Borčić 2020), ecovillages (Sargisson & Tower Sargent 2004; Sargisson 2007; Bokan 2012, 2014; Sherry & Ormsby 2016; Losardo 2016), ethical financing (Maurer 2005; Pitluck 2008), alternative currencies (Maurer 2005), LETS (Local Exchange Trading Systems) (Pacione 1997; Caldwell 2000; Cooper 2013), fair trade initiatives (Mober 2005; Besky 2008; Nichols 2010; Robbins 2013) and numerous others (see for example Simonič 2019). The basic goal of such economies and the initiatives they encompass is the attainment of the common good and their advocating for 'a set of practices that emphasizes environmental sustainability, cooperation, equity, and community well-being over profit' (van der Beck-Clark & Pyles 2012: 6). A key feature of such practices is that they have a socially innovative character, striving to redefine the existing economic space shaped by the negative consequences of the dominant capitalist system, such as growing economic and social inequalities and destruction of the environment and of natural resources.

The turning point for the proliferation of solidarity economy practices occurred after the start of the economic crisis in 2008, when a majority of people felt the cold insensitivity of the dominant economic system intensively (Ferguson & Gupta 2002; Kawano et al. 2009; Laville 2010; Simonič 2019). There are frequent deliberations over models that could lead to the creation of an alternative, or at least a corrective to capitalism. In this way, Wright (2015a) suggests a combination of the two approaches as the best strategy. On the

---

Forum-affiliated movements (45 movements) rely on has shown (Steger and Wilson, 2012: 440). These two authors have extracted seven common features of the ideological agenda of these movements and it is important to note that the food sovereignty is one of them.

one hand, he commits to 'taming capitalism' via political campaigns directed at actions of the institutional authorities ('from above'). On the other hand, he suggests 'corroding of capitalism', i.e., developing emancipatory, participative and egalitarian forms of economic activity ('from below'), which stimulate the development of social solidarity and collaboration (Wright 2005a). Hahnel and Wright also elaborated efforts to achieve transformations of the existing system as a combination of interstitial and symbiotic strategies (Hahnel and Wright 2014: 87–88). The 2008 crisis enabled a somewhat more intensive encounter between theoretical reflections and practices concerned with the necessity of change.

Development of CSA in Croatia

This chapter is a result of the joint analysis of the ethnographic research having been performed from 2013 until today in Zagreb and Istria by one of the authors (Orlić 2014, 2019). Methodologies used were qualitative ones, including participant observation, ethnographic observation and semi-structured in-depth interviews (n: 20) together with data received by informal conversation, i.e., with individuals who preferred not to be engaged in the interviewing process. (n: 6). The analysis of the macroeconomic situation that facilitated the appearance of CSA in Croatia is included as well, together with the analysis of a legal framework related to the process of organic products certification and the new Public Procurement Act that is, in a case of agricultural products, favourable towards short supply chains, such as CSA. The author first learned about the CSA movement in Zagreb in 2009 from a friend who decided to grow organic vegetables for her family usage, but also with the aim to sell the surpluses via this new and quite alternative network.

The aim of the author was not only directly support the small organic farmers but to study the emerging grassroots movement as well. She was able to supplement the information gathered from the growing body of scholarly and activist work and literature with the data gathered through semi-structured interviews carried out with various actors of the CSA movement. These included the so-called 'organizers', administrators, members and farmers. The initial contact with one of the initiators was made on the site of the weekly delivery of the basket to which the researcher subscribed. After that the snowball method enabled the researcher to trace and contact other actors/interlocutors. Since the CSA in 2012 started to function on a practical level, it was still quite fresh in the minds of the organizers and initiators (practical and ideological) and they were able to recall how CSA was brought to Croatia. In 2013 and 2014 this qualitative research was carried out in Zagreb and the surrounding area (Orlić 2014), and in 2017 with actors of CSA movement in Istria (for more detail see Orlić 2019). Participation in weekly deliveries of the products enabled the author to do ethnographic observation, even participant observation to some extent. Visits to farms were carried out as well, and deliveries for other group members.

The idea to introduce CSA in Croatia appeared in 2009 when one of the initiators of the movement in Croatia, Hrvoje,[7] met, during a permaculture course, Leo, a member of Italian GAS,[8] a man from Croatia (Pula) living in Italy. Leo organized a benefit dinner with members of 'his' GAS group and they collected money and invited people from Croatia and Bosnia and Herzegovina to visit their GAS in order to get introduced with the concept. After that, Hrvoje decided to support spreading of the movement in Croatia with help of ZMAG (Zelena mreža aktivističkih grupa – Green network of activist groups). Croatian CSA groups, as well as many other worldwide groups, relied on ten principles of *teikei*, formulated in 1971 by JOAA (Minamida 1995). However, the Croatian CSA emphasized three more general values to be followed as well: Transparency, Trust and Solidarity (Medić et al. 2013). In 2012, almost simultaneously, the groups in Zagreb and Istria started to function. In Istria the CSA developed under the influence of Neven, the founder and the president of the NGO Istrian Eco Product, which gathers certified organic producers in Istria. This fact strongly influenced the development of the Istrian CSA and caused the divergence of the movement in Croatia, related specifically to attitudes about the certification process.[9]

Unlike in Istria, CSA groups in Zagreb and surroundings actually did not trust the organic product certification process at all. Since most organizers had little or no trust in the state institutions, they assumed the process of certification would be somehow corrupted. Also, they mentioned that personal ties between consumers and producers can boost trust and solidarity, if the relationship was transparent. Therefore, most of them did not want "their" farmer to get "eco-certificate" at all. Visits to farms from organizers and consumers were considered to be enough. Then, in Zagreb numerous CSA groups by city districts were organized and they have been operating to the present day. However, the initial group, GSRijeda, was soon dismantled due to internal conflicts, but the farmer still supplies the individual supporters (their number grew from 10 to 40 families over the past decade). This support became important for

---

[7] Pseudonymous first names are used for all interlocutors in the text.
[8] GAS stands for the Italian *Gruppo d'aquisto Solidale*, meaning group for solidary purchase. GAS was organized in Italy in 1994 and its purchasing activity was not based solely on agricultural products.
[9] The certification of the organic agricultural products in Croatia is regulated by numerous acts. Act on the Implementation of Council Regulation (EC) 834/2007 on organic production and labelling of organic products (OJ 80/13, 14/2014), Ordinance on organic production (Official Gazette 86/2013), Ordinance on organic production of plants and animals (Official Gazette, 1/2013), Ordinance on organic agricultural production (Official Gazette, 19/2016). According to the law a farmer has to be registered as a trader to be allowed apply for the certification or to apply with any formal request.

them to survive after they became unemployed. However, the supporters also participated in actions like lending the money to the farmer for certain acquisitions. This kind of solidarity and collaboration is not an exception, since members of other CSA groups claim that they also pre-finance, e.g., the sowing for their farmer(s), so that s/he does not have to take loans from credit banks. This type of activity is considered almost as a conspiracy by some of the actors of the CSA, since it is aimed 'against' the banks and capitalist systems in general.

This conceptualization of the activity as a conspiracy leads us to the question of motivation of various actors. While this activist and advocacy element is quite visible among the initiators and organizers, a majority of them are quite aware that among most buyers it is not like that. In Istria, on the other hand, since their main organizer was already an eco-certified producer who strongly believed that this was the only valid way to protect both consumers and producers, this was the way groups were organized. In 2015, they even changed the name to Solidarne ekološke grupe (Solidary ecological group(s) or SEG) in order to distinguish themselves from non-certified groups. The Istrian groups did now include a lot of local fruit producing farmers, so they involved fruit producers from other parts of the country and became the tangible incentive for them to transfer to organic production.

Therefore, the Istrian CSA groups had a significant impact on transition to organic farming in general, especially since Neven persuaded the administrative bodies of the city of Pula and Istrian County to subsidize this 'transfer' (of local producers) by paying to producers in the transitional period (three years) part of expenses needed for a monitoring process. This is in line with the framework of the Rural Development Programme of the Republic of Croatia for the period 2014–2020, where there are some measures that ease the certification process. Besides, the members of the Istrian CSA groups also pay a yearly donation (instead of a membership fee) that can be used according to the needs and desires of groups. They can also donate it to some producers, as they did for Vera, a younger producer, who, after a burnout on the regular job, decided to go back to the family farm and to get an eco-certificate. Today she is a regular supplier of the Istrian CSA groups, and she claims that the importance of the CSA groups as regular consumers is huge.

According to the research and to the Croatian CSA actors, the structure of group members/buyers is represented mainly by younger families with (usually young) children. They tend to have a higher education and are environmentally aware at least to a certain level (Sarjanović 2014). For most of them, the trigger to join the CSA group was the care for the health of their new-born baby that later spread to the other family members. This is in accordance with previous research carried out among CSA groups, but one has to take into account also the fact that, according to some researchers, 'care' in this context may be perceived as quite self-oriented (or even selfish) (Brunori et al., 2010). The growing desire for organic healthy food is fuelled by mistrust of conventional agricultural practice (Yridoe et al. 2005). However, this is not the only motivation for this green consumption, since recently the market niche for organic products has been growing globally and in Croatia (Petljak 2010), resulting in the growing numbers related to organic production (Willer et al. 2018). Therefore, it is not so difficult to find organic products in shops and markets. However, it seems that this motivation related to environmental and health concerns is not entirely suited for buyers supporting alternative food networks such as CSA (Feagan 2008; Randelli 2015: 17), i.e. individuals who perceive themselves as food citizens, and not consumers.

According to the CBA data, in the period between 2007 and 2016 there was an upward trend in agricultural farms with organic farming. In 2016, the number of these farms was 1392 (representing in comparison to 2007 a growth of 97%). Organic food is much more expensive than conventional food, and therefore this type of consumption is considered to be a kind of elite consumerism. Most research of the CSA showed that it is also a highly gendered activity (Hatano 2008), and connected it with the 'caring consumption' of so-called eco-mums caring for health of the family and environment (Cone and Kakaliouras 1995; Abel et al. 1999; Cairns et al. 2014). Other members, not only organizers, perceive the CSA as an important way of struggle to achieve food sovereignty and to create some kind of alternative to the dominant neoliberal capitalist system.

However, it is also true that the CSA made significant economic impact enabling farmers to continue their work after the last economic crisis in 2008. The Great Recession of 2008 had an adverse effect on the Croatian economy, which ended up in a six-year recession that broadened further the income gap with respect to old (OMS) and new Member States (NMS) of the European Union (Čeh Časni et al. 2019). The crisis significantly influenced the purchasing power of a major part of Croatian citizens. Agricultural production in Croatia is on the decline since the end of World War II, due to intensive industrialization that happened during socialism. However, after the 1990s and the War of Independence (after which the political and economic systems changed), the neoliberal approach to market caused further difficulties, especially for small or private family farmers. Croatia has 1.3 million hectares of agricultural land and about 2.2 million hectares of forests. The country is self-sufficient in the production of wheat, corn, poultry, eggs, and wine, while still developing in the production of many other agricultural products. However, imports of agricultural and food products continue to grow. Although agriculture only contributes approximately 4 per cent to GDP, the importance of agricultural production is higher than its GDP share indicates. As far as Gross Value Added (GVA) contributions per component in OMS, NMS and Croatia are concerned, the contribution of agriculture to GVA growth in Croatia is negative, while in NMS and OMS it is positive. In addition, the primary sector (agriculture, forestry and fishing) accounted for only 1.5 per cent of GVA in 2015. (Čeh Časni et al. 2019)[10].

---

[10] The divergence of the Croatian economy has a long history that existed before the downfall of socialism and transition to the free market system.

The number of private family farms[11] in Croatia was largest in 2010, reaching 233 280, whereas by 2016 that number dropped by almost 58%, i.e., down to 134 459 private family farms. However, given the small average farm size and the fractured nature of the farms, restructuring policies in Croatia are of particular importance. At present, Croatian agriculture struggles with land ownership, the size of farms (which are small due to family inheritance laws) and outdated land registry books. The abovementioned economic reality, related to decline in the overall agricultural production and lower purchasing power of the citizens, in our opinion significantly fuelled the popularity of the CSA movement in Croatia. The movement enabled buyers from the disappearing stratum (at least in Croatia) of middle-income families to purchase organic food that would otherwise remain unaffordable to them, Therefore, researchers such as Grasseni (2013, 2014) and Rakopoulos (2016) are right to claim that these networks are not alternative anymore and that AFNs in Greece represent a material bridge for helping many citizens after the collapse of the state institutions that followed the crisis. Some interlocutors in Croatia also claim that it is a way of achieving autonomy, since the state institutions are no longer perceived as the ones that will take care of its citizens (regarding health etc.). The importance of collaboration, i.e. solidarity within the CSA, was considered to be more easily perceived from producers.

Yes, it was very important at the beginning. At the beginning it was GSR and it meant a lot – meaning, it was very important, before we put the milk vending machine we started to bring milk into GSR, where the market was, where this mountain society, we had a venue here and on Tuesdays we had exchange here, so, for me it meant a lot (milk and cheese producer from Istria).

Croatian GDP per capita had been converging in absolute terms from 1952 to the beginning of 1980s with OMS. In the early 1980s the divergence of Croatian GDP per capita from that of the OMS started, and by the end of the decade it had become obvious. After Croatia declared independence in 1990, the income divergence continued, encouraged by a deep transition recession. After a successful stabilization programme in late 1993, Croatian GDP per capita had started to grow again until the financial crisis of 2008.

[11]   A private family farm, according to the definition of CBA, is an economic unit of a household that is engaged in agricultural production, irrespective of its purpose, i.e. irrespective of whether it produces for sale on the market or for its own consumption. The concept 'private family farm' was introduced into the statistical system of agricultural statistics in 1998. Until that year the concepts 'private farmstead' and 'private producer' were used.

One meat producer noticed the difference towards the farmers and their dignity between 'regular' and the CSA buyers:

> You can see the difference between GSR buyers or buyers that are more aware about the food and buyers that consider a farmer to be some poor guy that works for them and has to be [grateful for doing so] (meat producer from Zagreb area).

Some of the buyers did raise the question about how exactly the producers are solidary with buyers (because usually the solidarity of buyers with farmers is more emphasized). Producers explain this at several levels. First and most important is the organic production itself – the producer has to produce organically and fairly and this is the most important feature, i.e., a prerequisite for solidarity of buyers with the producers. The prices also promote solidarity – they are lower than the same product would cost in the specialized store, and sometimes they are the same as or lower than on the farmers' markets.[12] This is not limited to small producers or organic producers exclusively – since the consumers are devoted to a particular producer he has to keep his prices affordable – after all, the middleman is cut in this chain and the producer receives enough money (more than via usual trading channels). Also, since he does not have to be concerned with (or at least devote a major part of the time to) marketing and distribution issues, he has more time to devote to production. Some Istrian SEG offer a possibility for buyers to earn their weekly basket by working at the farm and helping the farmer, in cases when the buyer has financial difficulties. In this way, both sides show solidarity and their collaboration continues.

Concluding remarks

The CSA in Croatia, as revealed by its leaflet, is based on three main principles that reflect its values and ethics: transparency, trust and solidarity (Medić et al. 2013). These principles have relied on 10 principles of *teikei* that were formulated in 1971 by JOAA[13] (Minamida 1995). Transparency is the key to achieving trust, and this is best described by a sentence from one of the

---

[12] Farmers' markets in the open space in Croatia have a long history, and were even considered, in appropriate situations, to be nominated for the national list of intangible cultural heritage (Vukušić, 2018). They are quite popular, not only as a place for provisioning local goods (although it is not entirely true), but also as a place of communication and meeting (Šarić Žic and Kocković Zaborski, 2016).

[13] Japan Organic Agriculture Association (https://directory.ifoam.bio/affiliates /724-japan-organic-agriculture-association).

ideological initiators of the movement: "I do not decide that I will have trust in you – You have to gain my trust and this is done by transparency". Transparency relates to both, members and farmers. Members in a search for a producer have to be clear about their wishes, and a farmer has to be transparent about the way of production. Visits to the farm(s) are a regular part of the CSA routine, but only more engaged members take part in this. In the case of Istrian SEG, the organic farmers, as regular group members, are skilled enough to protect the group and themselves from potential frauds. This kind of mutual transparency and trust finally builds the solidarity between the actors. This solidarity can be expressed in various ways – not only in supporting the producer by regular buying his products (Medić et al. 2013:6). Pre-financing of sowing, pre-financing of certain acquisitions are the usual ways in which members are showing solidarity with the farmer. However, it also included actions such as buying damaged apples for juice producing (by members), enabling a farmer in question to continue with organic production. The farmers in Istria offer the possibility to unemployed members to 'earn' their weekly basket by helping in fields. This is how their values and ethics are imagined and practised.

This ethics has become more popular worldwide especially after the 2008 economic crisis (Kawano et al. 2009). These collaborative practices between producers and consumers within the CSA for some producers mean a survival, and for families easier obtaining organic food at reasonable prices. Considering all factors mentioned above, we could conclude that in Croatia, the CSA is far from being the mode of elitist consumption or consumerism. This form of economy for producers, and especially small ones, is often the only way to survive in the hostile global economy. It is no surprise that the idea has been more widely accepted after the 2008 crisis, when a significant number of producers and consumers lost their jobs (or had to close production, in the case of farmers). The consumers pay less than for the same product in specialized stores, and producers are paid immediately upon delivery. They get far more for the same product than they would by using other distribution channels, i.e. both sides get a fair price. The producer can predict income and improve cash flow and has a regular and steady distribution channel. Within the CSA group producer does not have to deal with marketing and food distribution issues since the CSA group is a very reliable customer. Initially, a farmer or any other producer assists in the establishment of CSA, but in time, when they get to know each other, CSA group becomes organized in such a way to minimally disturb the agricultural work. Lack of a formal organization leads to different legal problems regarding the certification of products and potential activities of selling products to institutions like hospitals or kindergartens. However, this is also to be improved since the new Public Procurement Act (Official Gazette No. 120/2016, in effect since 1 July 2017) in Article 284 offers a possibility to favour short supply chains in the domain of agricultural production (i.e., if the product is more nutritious, locally produced). This relates to agricultural production in general, not to organic production exclusively. Therefore, it is unofficially called Green Public Procurement. It represents a significant step forward in national legislation, but it is not yet implemented fully. A recent study conducted by quantitative methods among farmers in Istria in order to analyse potential for institutional support for small family farmers and CSA farmers (Orlić 2021) showed that this is the case among Istrian CSA (SEG farmers). Not a single Istrian CSA farmer that participated in the study had tried to participate with his/her offer in the Green Public Procurement by the time the study was conducted (Orlić 2021:122). The reasons were different: most respondents never heard of it or did not know how to apply it (61.5%); 25% of them considered it too complicated even to try. Only a minority think that they do not have enough products quantities (5.8%). The same percentage thinks that the administration is too demanding, and 3.8% of them think that the prices they would have to offer are too low (Orlić 2021: 123).

This research directly supports the thesis that main problems relate to small size of family farms and small quantities they can produce, regarding Public Procurement of organic products. Croatian farmers individually do not have the strength to compete on Public Procurement. They have to act jointly if they want to profit from this legal change. The Rural Development Programme of the Ministry for Agriculture offered to finance the creation of farmers' cooperatives[14]. However, the majority of the respondents did not apply (91.2%). No Istrian SEG farmers applied. Most of them did not notice the call or did not have enough information. Others were aware of the impossibility to pre-finance the call or to find an adequate partner. They also think that they are not eligible (Orlić 2021: 125).

It remains to be seen whether CSA farmers will consider this as opportunity for them, or will they remain exclusively in the existing short supply chains.

The CSA in Croatia has been developing only for about 10 years. It really was an alternative food network at the beginning, but now it has been included in policy making at regional and local levels (e.g., the AGRISHORT short supply chain in the Međimurje region represents the first top-down initiative of the kind in Croatia (Bagarić 2021)). In Istria, bottom-up initiatives as SEG gained significant support from the local and regional administration. It seems that the food citizenship concept that was brought to Croatia with CSA groups has slowly taken root and become mainstream.

---

[14] The call was intended for funding of the 'production organizations', This odd term replaced the term *zadruga* (for various types of cooperatives), because of the negative connotations the term *zadruga* has from the socialist period when the forced collectivization in agricultural sector took place (Babić and Račić 2011)

References

Abel, J., Thomson, J. and Maretzki, A. 1999 Extension's Role with Farmers' Markets. Working with Farmers, Consumers, and Communities. *Journal of Extension*, 37(5). Retrieved from http://bit.ly/1Gsvyle

Angelo, A. 2010 Free/Libre Open Source Software, Liberalism, Conviviality and Private Property. An anthropological view of Zotero advocates, Thesis.

Babić, Z. and Račić, D. 2011 'Zadrugarstvo u Hrvatskoj. Trendovi, pokazatelji i perspektiva u europskom kontekstu'. *Sociologija i prostor* 49/3(191): 287–311

Bagarić, P. 2021 Kratki lanci opskrbe i projektno financiranje na primjeru Međimurja In: *Analiza institucionalne podrške prilikom osnivanja dvaju tipova kratkih lanaca opskrbe (model osnivanja odozdo i odozgo).* Bokan, N. (ed), pp. 50–83, Zagreb: Agronomski fakultet Sveučilišta u Zagrebu.

Bauhard, C. 2014 Solutions to the crisis? The Green New Deal, Degrowth, and the Solidarity Economy: Alternatives to the capitalist growth economy from an ecofeminist economics perspective. *Ecological Economics*, 102: 60–68.

Besky, S. 2008 Can a Plantation be Fair? Paradoxes and Possibilities in Fair Trade Darjeeling Tea Certification. *Anthropology of work review Vol XXIX, Number 1*

Biti, O. and Blagaić Bergman, M. 2014 Urbani vrtovi u Zagrebu – ulaganja i izloženost, inicijative i perspektive. *Sociologija i prostor*, 52(3(200)), 261–277. https://doi.org/10.5673/sip.52.3.2

Bokan, N. 2012. *Konceptualni pristupi ekološkim mikrosocijalnim zajednicama: studija slučaja u Hrvatskoj.* Ph.D. theisis, University of Zagreb

Bokan, N. 2016 Ekosela: subpolitični odgovor na neodrživost. *Sociologija i prostor*, 54, (204/1), 45–70.

Brunori, G., Rossi, A. and Malandrin, V. 2010 Co-producing Transition: Innovation Processes in Farms Adhering to Solidarity-based Purchase Groups (GAS) in Tuscany, Italy. *The International Journal of Sociology of Agriculture and Food* 18(1), 28–53.

Bryer, A. 2010 Beyond Bureaucracies? The Struggle for Social Responsibility in the Argentine Workers' Cooperatives, Critique of Anthropology, Vol 30(1) 41–61 [DOI: https://doi.org/10.1177/0308275X09345414]

Cairns, K., de Laat, K., Hohnston, J. and Bauman, S. 2014 The Caring, Committed Eco-mom. Consumption Ideals and Lived Realities of Toronto Mothers. In Barendregt B. and Rifke J. Eds. *Green consumption. The Global Rise of Eco-Chic*, (pp. 100–116). London, New Delhi, New York, Sidney: Bloomsbury.

Caldwell, C. 2000 Why Do People Join Local Exchange Trading Systems?*, *International Journal of Community Currency Research*, Volume 4, retrieved from http://www.uea.ac.uk/env/ijccr/abstracts/vol4(1)caldwell.html.

Calvet-Mir, L. and March, H. 2019 Crisis and post-crisis urbangardening initiatives from a Southern European perspective: The case of Barcelona, *European Urban and Regional Studies* Vol. 26(1) 97–112.

Časni, A.Č., Palić, P. and Vizek, M. 2019 Long-Term Trends in Croatian GDP Growth. In Petak Z., Kotarski K. (Eds.), Policy-Making at the European Periphery. *New Perspectives on South-East Europe* (pp. 127–145). Cham: Palgrave Macmillan.

Cone, C.A. and Kakaliouras, A. 1995 Community Supported Agriculture: Building Moral Community or an Alternative Consumer Choice. *Culture and Agriculture* 17, 28–31.

Cooper, D. 2013 Time against time: Normative temporalities and the failure of community labour in Local Exchange Trading Schemes, *Time & Society* 22(1) 31–54.

Declaration on the Rights of Peasants and Other People Working in Rural Areas. https://www.geneva-academy.ch/joomlatools-files/docman-files/UN %20Declaration%20on%20the%20rights%20of%20peasants.pdf

De Tavernier, J. 2012 Food Citizenship: Is There a Duty for Responsible Consumption?. *Journal of Agricultural and Environmental Ethics* 25, 895–907.

DiBona, C. Ockman, S. and Stone, M. 1999 *OPENSOURCES Voices from the Open Source Revolution*, O'Reilly & AssociatesEngler-Stringer, R., & Berenbaum, S. (2007). Exploring Food Security with Collective Kitchens Participants in Three Canadian Cities. Qualitative Health Research, 17(1), 75–84. DOI: https://doi.org/10.1177/1049732306296451

Feagan, R. 2008 'Direct Marketing. Towards Sustainable Local Food Systems?'. *Local Environment* 13/3: 161–167.

Feagan, R. and Henderson, A. 2009 'Devon Acres CSA. Local Struggles in a Global Food System'. *Agriculture and Human Values* 26/3: 203–217.

Ferguson, J. and Gupta, A. 2002 Spatializing States: Toward an Ethnography of Neoliberal Governmentality, *American Ethnologist*, 29(4), 981–1002.

Gennari, C. and Tornaghi, C. 2020 The transformative potential of community kitchens for an agroecological urbanism. Preliminary insights and a research agenda. In *Book of Proceedings of the 9th International Conference of the AESOP Sustainable food planning group*, Madrid, 2019. Granada: Universidad de Granada, 80–90.

Gómez-Benito, C. and Lozano, C. 2014 Constructing Food Citizenship: Theoretical Premises and Social Practices. *Italian Sociological Review*, 4(2), 135–156.

Grasseni, C. 2013 *Beyond Alternative Food Networks*. Bloomsbury. London, New Delhi, New York, Sydney. London: Bloomsbury.

Grasseni, C. 2014 Family Farmers between Re-localisation and Coproduction. *Anthropological Notebooks*, 20(3), 49–66.

Gulin, V. and Rubić, T. (Eds.). 2015 Vrtovi našega grada. Studije i zapisi o praksama urbanog vrtlarenja. Zagreb: Institut za etnologiju i folkloristiku, Hrvatsko etnološko društvo, Parkticipacija.

Gulin Zrnić, V. and Rubić, T. 2018 City-making through Urban Gardening: Public Space and Civic Engagement in Zagreb. *Narodna umjetnost*, 55(1), 159–179. https://doi.org/10.15176/vol55no109

Hahnel, R. and Wright, E.O. 2014 *Alternatives to Capitalism. Proposals for Democratic Economy*. Free e-book. Retrieved from https://www.ssc .wisc.edu/~wright/Published%20writing/Alternatives%20to%20Capital ism.pdf

Hatano, T. 2008 The Organic Agriculture Movement (Teikei) and Factors Leading to its Decline in Japan. *Journal of Rural and Food Economics*, 54(2) 21–34.

Hilder, J., Charles-Edwards, E., Sigler, T. and B-Metcalf 2018. Housemates, inmates and living mates: communal living in Australia, *Australian Planner*, 55:1, 12–27.

Janssen, B. 2010 "Local Food, Local Engagement- Community-Supported Agriculture in Eastern Iowa". Culture, Agriculture, Food and Environment 32(1): 4–16

Kawano, E., Masterson, T.N. and Teller-Elsberg, J. 2009 Introduction. In Kawano, E, Masterson, T. N., Teller-Elsberg, J. (Eds.), *Solidarity Economy I. Building Alternatives for People and Planets*. (pp. 1–7). Amherst: Centres for Popular Economics.

Kondoh, K. 2014 'The Alternative Food Movement in Japan. Challenges, Limits, and Resilience of the Teikei System'. Agriculture and Human Values 32/1:143–153

Lave, J. and Wenger, E. 1991 *Situated Learning. Legitimate Peripheral Participation*. Cambridge: Cambridge University Press.

Laville, J. 2010 The Solidarity Economy: An International Movement., *RCCS Annual Review*, 2(2), Retrieved from https://journals.openedition.org /rccsar/202

Lenten, R. 1993 *Cooking under the volcanoes: communal kitchens in the Southern Peruvian city of Arequipa*. Amsterdam: CEDLA.

Lima, J.C. 2007 Workers' Cooperatives in Brazil: Autonomy vs Precariousness *Economic and Industrial Democracy* 28: 589–621.

Losardo, M. 2016 'New Ways of Living, as Old as the World' Best Practices and Sustainability in the Example of the Italian Ecovillage Network. *Studia ethnologica Croatica*, 28(1), 47–70.

Lozano-Cabedo, C. and Gómez-Benito, C. 2017 A Theoretical Model of Food Citizenship for the Analysis of Social Praxis. *Journal of Agricultural and Environmental Ethics, 30*, 1–22.

Maurer, B. 2005 *Mutual life, limited: Islamic banking, alternative currencies, lateral reason*. Princeton, Oxford: Princeton University Press

Medić, A. et al. 2013 *Brošura GSR-a, Zelena mreža aktivističkih grupa*, Retrieved from http://www.grupasolidarnerazmjene.net/gsr-brosura/povi jestpokreta-ili-gsr-u-svijetu

Minamida, S. 1995 Teikei or Copartnership – A characteristic type of Producer-Consumer Relationship in the Organic Agriculture Movement in Japan. *Technical Bulletin of Faculty of Horticulture – Chiba University (Japan)*, 49, 189–199.

Moberg, M. 2005 Fair Trade and Eastern Caribbean Banana Farmers: Rhetoric and Reality in the AntiGlobalization Movement, *Human Organization*, Vol. 64(1) 4–15.

Nicholls, A. 2010 Fair Trade: Towards an Economics of Virtue. *J Bus Ethics* 92, 241–255.

Orlić, O. 2014 'Grupe solidarne razmjene. Počeci solidarne ekonomije u Hrvatskoj'. *Etnološka tribina* 37/44: 72–88.

Orlić, O. 2019 *Antropologija solidarnost: poljoprivreda potpomognuta u Hrvatskoj*. Zagreb: Hrvatsko etnološko društvo.

Orlić, O. 2021 Kratki lanci opskrbe i njihovo osnivanje odozdo na primjeru istarskih Solidarnih ekoloških grupa. In *Analiza institucionalne podrške prilikom osnivanja dvaju tipova kratkih lanaca opskrbe (model osnivanja odozdo i odozgo)* Bokan, N. (ed), pp. 84–146, Zagreb: Agronomski fakultet Sveučilišta u Zagrebu.

Ostrom, M. 2007 'Community Supported Agriculture as an Agent of Change. Is it Working?'. In *Remaking the North American Food System*. Clare Hinrichs and Tom Lyson, (Eds.). Lincoln: University of Nebraska Press, 99–120.

Pacione, M. 1997 Local Exchange Trading System s as a Response tothe Globalisation of Capitalism, *Urban Studies*, Vol. 34, No. 8, 1179–1199.

Parker, G. 2005 Sustainable food? Teikei, co-operatives and food citizenship in Japan and the UK. *Working Papers in Real Estate & Planning. 11/05*. Working Paper. University of Reading, Reading.

Patel, R. (Ed.). 2009 Food sovereignty, *The Journal of Peasant Studies*, 36:3, 663–706.

Petljak, K. 2010 Organic food category research among leading food retailers in Croatia/ Istraživanje kategorije ekoloških prehrambenih proizvoda među vodećim trgovcima hranom u Republici Hrvatskoj. *Market/Tržište: časopis za tržišnu teoriju i praksu*, 22(1), 93–112.

Pfeilstetter, R. 2013 Entrepreneurship and regional development in Europe: A comparative, socio-anthropological case study in Germany and Spain. *Anthropological Notebooks* 19(1): 45–57.

Pitluck, A.Z. 2008 Moral Behavior in Stock Markets: Islamic Finance and Socially Responsible Investment). In *Economics and morality: Anthropological approaches*, APPROACHES, K. E. Browne, B. L. Milgram, (Eds.), pp. 233–255, Lanham: AltaMira Press, Rowman & Littlefield Publishers,

Pleyers, G. 2010 *Alter-Globalization. Becoming Actors in the Global Age*, Cambridge: Polity Press.

Poljak Istenič, S. 2016 Reviving Public Spaces through Cycling and Gardening. Ljubljana – European Green Capital 2016. *Etnološka tribina*, 46(39), 157–175.

Rakopoulos, T. 2016 Solidarity: The egalitarian tensions of a bridge – concept. *Social Anthropology*, 24(2), 142–151.

Randelli, F. 2015 'The Role of Consumers in the Transition Towards a Sustainable Food Supply. The Case of Gruppi di acquisto solidale (Solidarity

Purchasing Groups) in Italy'. *International Journal of Food and Agricultural Economics* 3/4: 15–26.

Renting, H, Schermer, M. and Rossi, A. 2012 Building Food Democracy: Exploring Civic Food Networks and Newly Emerging Forms of Food Citizenship, *Int. Jrnl. of Soc. of Agr. & Food*, Vol. 19, No. 3, pp. 289–307.

Robbins, R.H. 2013 Coffee, Fair Trade, and the Commodification of Morality, *Reviews in Anthropology*, 42:4, 243–263.

Roque, O., Thévenod Mottet, E., Bourdin, D. and Barjolle, D. 2008 *Innovations in Direct Marketing in Agriculture in Switzerland* 1. General review 2. Case study: Community-supported Agriculture. Retrieved from http://bit.ly/1Leeipl

Rural Development Program of the Republic of Croatia for the Period 2014–2020. Retrieved from https://ruralnirazvoj.hr/files/documents/Programme_2014HR06RDNP001_5_3_en.pdf

Sahakian, M. 2015 'Getting Emotional. Historic and Current Changes in Food Consumption Practices Viewed Through the Lens of Cultural Theories'. In *Putting Sustainability into Practice. Applications and Advances in Research on Sustainable Consumption.* Emily H. Kennedy, Maurie J. Cohen and Naomi Krugman, (Eds.). London: Edward Elgar Publishing, 134–156.

Sargisson, L. 2007 Imperfect Utopias: Green Intentional Communities, *Ecopolitics Online Journal*, 1(1), 1–24.

Sargisson, L. 2011 'Cohousing Evolution in Scandinavia and the USA.' In *Cohousing in Brittan*, S. Bunker, C. Coates, M. Field, and J. How (Eds.), pp. 23–42. London: Diggers and Dreamers.

Sargisson, L. and Tower Sargent, L. 2004 *Living in Utopia: New Zealand's Intentional Communities.* Ashgate.

Šaric Žic, I. and Kockovič Zaborski, T. 2016 Tržnica – trbuh grada, catalogue of the exhibition, Rijeka and Pazin: Pomorski i povijesni muzej Hrvatskog primorja Rijeka i Etnografski muzej Istre.

Sarjanović, I. 2014 Uloga grupa solidarne razmjene u razvoju ekološke poljoprivrede u Hrvatskoj. *Geoadria*, 19(2), 1–25.

Schnell, S. 2007 'Food With a Farmer's Face. Community-supported Agriculture in the United States'. *Geographical Review* 97/4: 550–564.

Sherry, J. and Ormsby, A. 2016 'Sustainability in Practice: A Comparative Case Study Analysis of the Eco Village at Ithaca, Earthaven, and Sirius'. *Communal Societies* 36(2): 125–151.

Šimleša, D. 2006 *Četvrti svjetski rat. Globalni napad na život / Drugačiji svijet je moguć: globalni napad na život/priče iz našeg dvorišta.* Zagreb: Što čitaš.

Simon, G.A. 2012 *Food Security: Definition, Four dimensions, History.* Basic readings as an introduction to Food Security for students from the IPAD Master, SupAgro, Montpellier attending a joint training programme in Rome from 19th to 24th March 2012 (http://www.fao.org/fileadmin/templates/ERP/uni/F4D.pdf)

Simonič, P. 2019 *Anthropological perspectives of solidarity and reciprocity.* Ljubljana, Ljubljana Znanstvena založba Filozofske fakultete Univerze v Ljubljani.

Slavuj Borčić, L. 2020 Kratki opskrbni lanci u Hrvatskoj – perspektiva ekoloških poljoprivrednih proizvođača uključenih u grupe solidarne razmjene. Hrvatski geografski glasnik, 82(1), 5–33. https://doi.org/10.21861/HGG.2020.82.01.01

Smith, M., Pointing, J. and Maxwell, S. 1993 Household Food Security, concepts and Definitions: An annotated Bibliography. Brighton, Institute of Development Studies

Smith, R. 2020 An anthropological reflection on urban gardening through the lens of citizenship. In *Food Systems transformations: Social Movements, Local Economies, Collaborative Networks.* Cordula Kropp, Irene Antoni-Komar, Colin Sage (eds), London: Routledge.

Starr, A. and Adams, J. 2003 Anti-globalization: The Global Fight for Local Autonomy. *New Political Science*, 25/1, 19–42.

Steger, M. and Wilson, E. 2012 Anti-Globalization or Alter-Globalization? Mapping the Political Ideology of the Global Justice Movement, *International Studies Quarterly* 56, 439–454.

van den Berk-Clark, C. and Pyles, L. 2012 Deconstructing Neoliberal Community Development Approaches and a Case for the Solidarity Economy. *Journal of Progressive Human Services*, 23(1): 1–17.

Vargas-Cetina, G. 2005 Anthropology and Cooperatives: From the Community Paradigm to the Ephemeral Association in Chiapas, Mexico, Critique of Anthropology Vol 25(3) 229–251

Volz, P., Weckenbrock, P., Cressot, N. and Parot, J. (Eds.). 2016 Overview of Community Supported Agriculture in Europe. Retrieved from http://urgenci.net/wp-content/uploads/2016/05/Overview-of-Community-Supported-Agriculture-in-Europe-F.pdf

Vukušić, A. 2018 Farmers' Markets as Intangible Heritage. An Identity Resource and/or Renewable Economic Resource. *Etnološka tribina*, 48(41), 238–258. https://doi.org/10.15378/1848-9540.2018.41.09.

Welsh, J. and MacRae, R. 1998 Food Citizenship and Community Food Security: Lessons from Toronto, Canada, Canadian Journal of Development Studies/Revue canadienne d'études du développement, 19:4, 237–255.

Willer, H., Lernoud, J. and Kemper, L. 2018 The World of Organic Agriculture 2018. Summary, FiBL & IFOAM – Organics International. The World of Organic Agriculture. Frick and Bonn.

Williams, C.C., Aldridge, T., Lee, R.L., Leyshon, A., Thrift, N. and Tooke, J. 2001 Local Exchange and Trading Schemes (LETS): A tool for community renewal?, Community, Work & Family, 4:3, 355–361.

Windfuhr M. and Jonsén, J. 2005 Food Sovereignty. Towards Democracy in Localized Food Systems. FIAN. ITDG Publishing.

Wright, E.O. 2015 How to Be an Anticapitalist Today, *Jacobin*, 12.2.2015. Retrieved from https://www.jacobinmag.com/2015/12/erik-olin-wright-realutopias-anticapitalism-democracy.

Vía Campesina, La. 1996 'The Right to Produce and Access to Land'. Position of the Vía Campesina on Food Sovereignty presented at the World Food Summit. Rome. 13–17 November. http://safsc.org.za/wp-content/uploads/2015/09/1996-Declaration-of-Food-Sovereignty.pdf

Yridoe, E.K., Bonti-Ankomah, S. and Martin, R.C. 2005 'Comparison of Consumer Perceptions Toward Organic versus Conventionally Produced Foods. A Review and Update of the Literature'. Renewable Agriculture and Food Systems 20/4: 193–205.

Znaor, D., Landau, S., Karoglan, S., Mirecki, N., Mandić, S. and Nadlački, R. 2014 Unlocking the Future: Seeds of Change: Sustainable Agriculture as a Path to Prosperity for the Western Balkans. Zagreb: Heinrich Böll Stiftung

PART 3

Ethnographies of Co-designing Collaborative Economies

Building the Playground for Collective Imagination: Ethnography of a *Détournement* around Moneywork and Carework

Chiara Bassetti

Department of Sociology and Social Research, University of Trento, Italy;
and CNR, The Italian National Research Council, Italy

Abstract

The chapter presents a case study of a digital complementary currency – Santacoin (SC) – co-designed, implemented and deployed at a 10-day performing arts festival in Italy. SC allowed participants to create a parallel economy within the blurring boundaries of the festival, in a sort of 'serious game live': enacted in the wild, with money and bodies at stake. The case study was conducted through a team ethnography that analysed the engagement of festival attenders, artists and staff with the system and the artistic intervention at its root. Indeed, SC was conceived as the core of a performance co-designed by Macao art collective and a group of local caregivers and wellbeing practitioners

How to cite this book chapter:
Bassetti, C. 2022. Building the Playground for Collective Imagination: Ethnography of a
    Détournement around Moneywork and Carework. In: Travlou, P. and Ciolfi, L. (eds.)
    *Ethnographies of Collaborative Economies across Europe: Understanding Sharing and
    Caring.* Pp. 149–172. London: Ubiquity Press. DOI: https://doi.org/10.5334/bct.i.
    License: CC BY-NC-ND

who then provided their services in the public space. This was thought of as a radical and experimental performative action for leading people to imagine new forms of social production and reproduction within an alternative world, a 'citadel' where finance could be thematized and sociopolitical imaginaries practised. It was a localized experiment in community building and collective imagination around issues of inequality and social re/production. The chapter provides an ethnographic account of the collaborative intervention and its main results. In doing so, it reflects on two main dimensions: the intersection of 'moneywork' and caring practices as explicitly thematized in the public space, and the role social interaction, relationships and communities play in collective imagination experimentations.

Introduction

Monetary transactions 'support people in making connections, to other people, to their communities, to the places they move through, to their environment, and to what they consume' (Ferreira et al., 2015: 11). Money configures an interaction space where transactions are embedded in social relations (O'Neill et al., 2017) and their trustworthiness is socially constructed. The mechanisms and artefacts to conduct 'moneywork' influence collaborative interaction, which in turn shape relationships (Perry and Ferreira, 2018, see also 2014), and vice versa. It is within this framework that complementary currencies can contribute to counteract inequalities, as they allow experimenting with alternative systems (NEF, 2015) and provide opportunities for 'embodying design propositions about the future trajectories of economic exchange' (Carroll and Bellotti, 2015: 1507). However, how people may come to imagine such trajectories and new socio-economic models is more of an open question.

In this chapter, I reflect on how to foster collective imagination and on the role design and performing arts may play in that. I do so by discussing the case of Santacoin (SC), a digital complementary currency introduced as an artistic and action-research intervention at a 10-day, open-air performing arts festival in Italy – Santarcangelo Festival – in collaboration with the art collective Macao, based in Milan. Being also a means of payment for festival-related purchases, SC was conceived as the core of the artistic performance curated by Macao: CryptoRituals. Santacoin were accepted by local wellbeing practitioners, called Body&Soul Caregivers, who provided their services in the public plaza as part of CryptoRituals. It was a radical performative action for leading people to imagine and practise new forms of social re/production within an alternative world, a 'citadel' where socioeconomic relation could be thematized. It was an experiment in community building and collective imagination around inequality and mutual caring.

Part of an H2020 project and conducted as a team ethnography within a participatory action research and design framework characterizing the whole project, the intervention allowed observation of people confronted with a 'serious game live' – conducted 'in the wild', with money and bodies at stake. Mutual trust was thus fundamental, like the willingness to collectively experiment within the safe boundaries of the local, festival and artistic communities. How to provide for those boundaries? How to sustain and foster trust? Leveraging already existing social relations, in a context mixing diverse communities, revealed a critical success element. Design features of the Santacoin system also proved relevant, particularly in terms of 'moneywork interaction', i.e., social interaction in and around monetary transactions.

Related Work

Complementary currencies

A complementary currency (CC) is an agreement within a community to use something as a means of payment in parallel with official ones (Lietaer, 2001). Throughout history, CCs have been represented by heterogeneous materials, ranging from pieces of clay pots in Ancient Egypt to cigarettes in WWII to contemporary cryptocurrencies. These physical and digital artefacts have been used to facilitate trade in communities. Agreeing to accept them in exchange for goods and services gives a CC the status of money.

CCs can facilitate 'different types of relationships and behaviour, and they ask questions about how money could serve us' (Seyfang, 2009: 141) – i.e., they hold a transformative power. Manchester LETS, for instance, was conceived 'to bring about significant social change' by fostering decentralization and freedom of economic interaction, as users could set the value for each transaction (North, 1999, 2007). Faircoin is a digital CC for developing a fair global economy. Commoncoin is a collectively issued currency to reward individual contributions on the basis of both labour and political participation (De Paoli et al., 2017a, 2017b; cf. also further: subsection "Partners").

CCs can empower communities to counteract inequality by providing a parallel line of credit and increasing the local multiplier effect (Hughes, 2003). Further, as manifested also in time banking initiatives (Cahn, 2004; Carroll and Bellotti, 2015), CCs can be empowering and transformative by 'redefining work to include the unpaid "core economy" of work in the neighbourhood and community; nurturing reciprocity and exchange rather than dependency; growing social capital; encouraging learning and skills-sharing; involving people in decision-making' (Seyfang, 2009: 152). By promoting closed economic circles, moreover, communities can be insulated (vs isolated) from adverse dynamics of the mainstream business cycle. As a by-product of proximity trade, finally, CCs may reduce the ecological footprint (Seyfang and Longhurst, 2013).

Despite advantages, CCs face several challenges, particularly in scaling-up and infrastructuring. With few exceptions (Studer, 1998; Gelleri, 2009; Bendell and Greco, 2013), there is no normative framework to accommodate them. From a design perspective, the issue of 'standardization and interchangeability' is critical (Perry and Ferreira, 2018); as the 'one size fits all' approach may not always be desirable, interoperability becomes crucial between both digital and physical currencies and different types of digital ones (O'Neill et al., 2017). Overall, money configures a complex design space in which the cultural context (De Angeli et al., 2004) and issues of trust (Briggs et al., 2002; Vines et al., 2012), fairness and realness (Wang and Mainwaring, 2008), alongside usability (Coventry et al., 2003), are central. Therefore, CC design requires understanding the dynamics of cooperation and community building (O'Neill et al., 2017), as it offers possibilities to extend social interaction, make more local connections and derive value from them (Carrol and Bellotti, 2015).

Artistic practices and action research

Joint endeavours across the arts and ethnography – such as performance ethnography (Denzin, 2003; Alexander, 2005; Finely, 2005; Given, 2008) or arts-informed research (Cole et al., 2004; Irving, 2007) – and between the arts and action and/or participatory research (Kemmis and McTaggart, 2005; special issue edited by Brydon-Miller et al., 2011), including participatory arts-based research (PABR, see e.g. Nunn, 2020), are relatively recent. Yet they hold the promise of a more multifaceted understanding of social life and power relations, and of higher sociopolitical impact.

This resonates with action research (AR) 'emancipatory and transformational intentions' (Seeley, 2011: 85). Seeley proposes to consider action researchers as 'Artists of the Invisible' (Kaplan 2002: 86), working to create spaces that are transformative for ourselves, those we work with, and the systems of which we are intrinsic part. Performing arts seem particularly suited for such purposes. Beyes and Steyaert (2011) consider neo-avant-garde performative practices and highlight their politico-aesthetic power to interfere with social assemblages and to change what is visible, sayable and doable.

This posits AR 'as a creative and potentially political practice of world-making [where] research, politics, and aesthetics are interwoven' (Beyes and Steyaert, 2011: 104).

With a stronger political accent, and addressing marginalized populations, Tofteng and Husted (2011: 27) argue for theatre-based AR to open 'new ways to communicate and make visible knowledges and experiences from below'. They connect to critical utopian AR, and theatrical traditions like Brecht's and Boal's, to emphasise how criticism must be combined with envisioning alternative pathways, and how non-traditional drama forms underpin societal learning. Erel and colleagues (2017: 307–308), looking at participatory theatre, similarly point out the importance 'to embed forum theatre in a critical and emancipatory discourse of social transformation that highlights a range of different power relations' and underline that the 'process is transformational in that it allows participants to see the social world as one that can be changed' (Erel et al., 2017: 310). If the Theatre of the Oppressed (Boal, 1974, 2009) requires a certain commitment by the spect-actors involved, as much as PABR projects do with their recurring encounters – a condition shared by CryptoRituals Caregivers – in some cases, such as the one considered here, it is *also* the attention of the passers-by that one may want to attract and that a playful performative action may provide.

In this respect, two concepts may prove fruitful: on the one hand, the Debordian (1967 [1994]) *détournement*, intended as the dialectical inversion of the existing relations among concepts (thesis 206), which allows a critique of mainstream cultural representations together with a critique of extant social and power relations. Displacing body care practices in the public plaza (*piazza*, in Italian, with all its cultural underpinnings[1]) like CryptoRituals did, can be considered a performative inversion of this kind. On the other hand, it is worth noticing that (design) games, and play more generally, in co-design have been found useful for 'promoting a creative and explorative attitude' in participants and for 'facilitating the players in envisioning and enacting' (Vaajakallio and Mattelmäki, 2014: 66). A 'fantasy aesthetic' (Zhang and Zurlo, 2021) can be helpful for 'transporting participants into another world – a magic circle as physical and ideal playground' (Vaajakallio and Mattelmäki, 2014: 65; see also Zhang and Zurlo, 2021: 1752). 'Ideally, the magic circle invites participants to think beyond the ordinary'; it is a place 'where consequences of different decisions can be played out in safe circumstances' (Vaajakallio and Mattelmäki, 2014: 67), 'a sphere of engagement "freed from the usual constraints" [and r]emoved from everyday life – though informing and informed by it' (Nunn, 2020: 5). As the 'circle' or the 'citadel' is also a physical space, the importance of the setting and location for the

---

[1] The *piazza* is the public place *par excellence* in Italy (e.g., Garau, 2016).

performance has been highlighted (e.g. Agger Eriksen, 2012: 399, cited in Vaajakallio and Mattelmäki, 2014).

Case Study

The intervention was the outcome of a long-lasting collaboration among the H2020 PIE News / Commonfare project (2016–2019), grounded in participatory action research and design; the Macao collective, involved in the project since its start and characterized by an engagement with both the arts and action research; and the Santarcangelo Festival, with which Macao has collaborated for years, based on a common interest in performing arts, community building and sociopolitical transformation.

Partners

Commonfare's objective was to promote the Welfare of the Common as an alternative and sustainable socioeconomic model based on collaboration, solidarity and caring (Fumagalli, 2015; General Intellect, 2018). We co-designed a digital space, commonfare.net, together with people and communities in three countries (Bassetti et al., 2018, 2019). It allows sharing information about collaborative economy initiatives and supports experimentation via the Social Wallet API (Roio and Beneti, 2017), which easily creates CCs. It was used to implement Commoncoin – commonfare.net built-in CC – and several Group Currencies by and for communities. Santacoin experience was instrumental to develop, test and refine this tool.

Macao is a collective that emerged in Milan in 2012 in response to the precarious conditions of cultural workers. It defines itself as an 'independent centre for arts, culture and research'. It provides co-working spaces, events, art exhibitions and a variety of workshops to fellow citizens. As mentioned, Macao has been involved in the Commonfare project since the beginning, experimenting with Commoncoin as it was prototyped. 'In a nutshell, Macao conceived of Commoncoin as an internal digital complementary currency and basic income provisioning system in Euros for financing and remunerating biopolitical production, while discouraging hoarding and speculative practices' (Bassetti and Sachy, 2019).

Held in a small but renowned medieval city in Italy, Santarcangelo Festival is the biggest of its kind in the country, and an international reference. During the 2017 edition, various CCs including Commoncoin and Faircoin were presented to the municipality and festival organizers. This increased their interest in experimenting with money(work) between art and socioeconomic innovation. The vision was then enacted in 2018, with Santacoin allowing participants to create a parallel economy within the blurring festival boundaries.

Figure 8.1: CryptoRituals at Santarcangelo Festival: overviews (a, d); details (b, c).

CryptoRituals

CryptoRituals was a performance enacted by crossing caring practices and economics, while focusing on care and love of oneself, the other and festival participants as a community. A group of 30 local caregivers – yoga practitioners, masseurs, hairdressers, Ayurveda professionals, etc. – were involved by Macao months before to co-design the performance, and they provided their services in the public space in the evenings (7pm–1am) of the two festival weekends, accepting payment in SC only (Figure 8.1). This was complemented by performative readings by Macao members, bringing attention to finance and carework.

Practising care in the plaza was configured as an interference with social order, performed by caregivers together with their audience, who actively participated by bringing in the power of their exposed bodies. The CC was used to make visible, hence rethinkable, the power money holds in structuring social relations. Overall, CryptoRituals is to be thought of as a community building and social innovation artistic project supported by a digital complementary currency and proposing caring as a key political element of social life.

Figure 8.2: Talisman with QRCode encoding the digital wallet.

Santacoin

SC was designed in collaboration by the Commonfare team, Macao and the festival organization. It was intended to be bought at an exchange rate at par with euro. Visitors could pay for merchandising, tickets, food and beverages. SC were issued through the Social Wallet API implemented in commonfare.net as a social-purpose, open-source digital wallet (Roio and Beneti, 2017). To give visitors a sense of belonging and a tangible artefact, a Talisman (Figure 8.2) was designed to interface the API. It portrayed a QRCode sticker on a recuperated, biodegradable plastic plate, wearable as a necklace. By scanning the QRCode, the holder could access commonfare.net and register, thereby creating a digital wallet (optional), where balance and transactions could be checked, supporting liquidity awareness (Perry and Ferreira, 2018).

The buyer would show the talisman or digital QRCode to the merchant, who would scan it with a smartphone, fill in the amount and ask the payer to click the 'Confirm' button on the interface, thereby improving transactional visibility (Perry and Ferreira, 2018) and embedding a mechanism for sharing transaction responsibility (Figure 8.3).

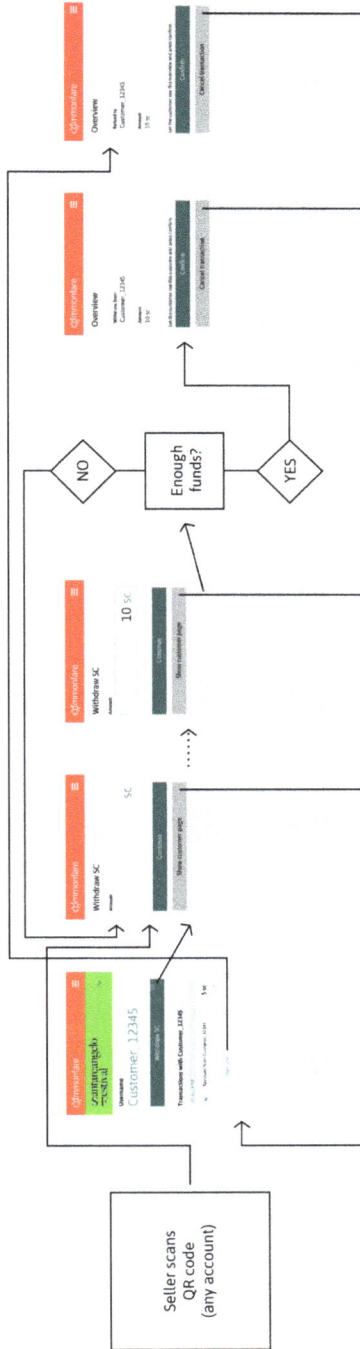

Figure 8.3: Payment process in SC.

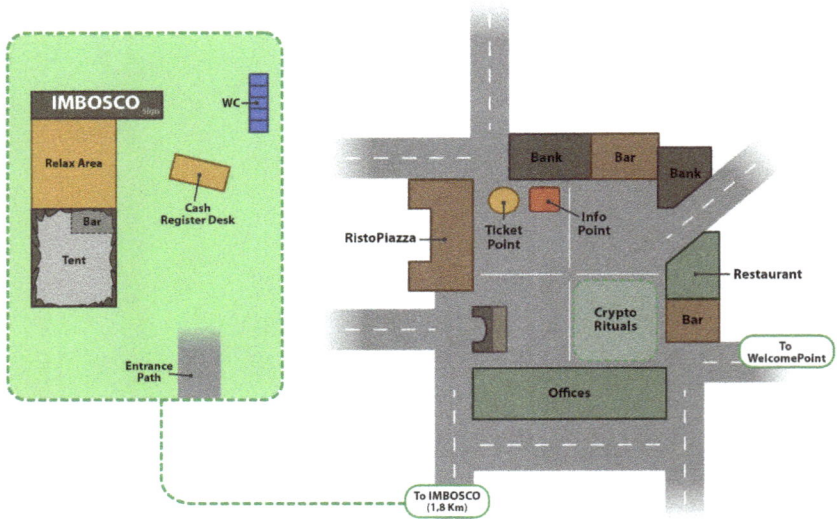

Figure 8.4: Map of SF main locations.

Locations and staff

SC were managed at six locations during the festival (Figures 8.4 and 8.5):

- InfoPoint, where information on the programme and SC were provided, talismans managed, and merchandising sold;
- TicketPoint, where tickets bought online were collected, and seldom bought;
- RistoPiazza, where dinner was served under the Municipality colonnade;
- Imbosco clubbing venue, featuring since the second day a SC-only register;
- WelcomePoint for artists, journalists and critics, where empty talismans were given to guests with the welcome kit;
- CryptoRituals area, also managing talismans since the second evening.

The cashiers at RistoPiazza and Imbosco were local women aged 25 to 50; the WelcomePoint staff too included local women, more connected to the arts; InfoPoint and TicketPoint operators were university students in their twenties with an interest in art management, and nonlocal. All operators had been working for the festival organisation for months, and most of them were staff members also in previous editions.

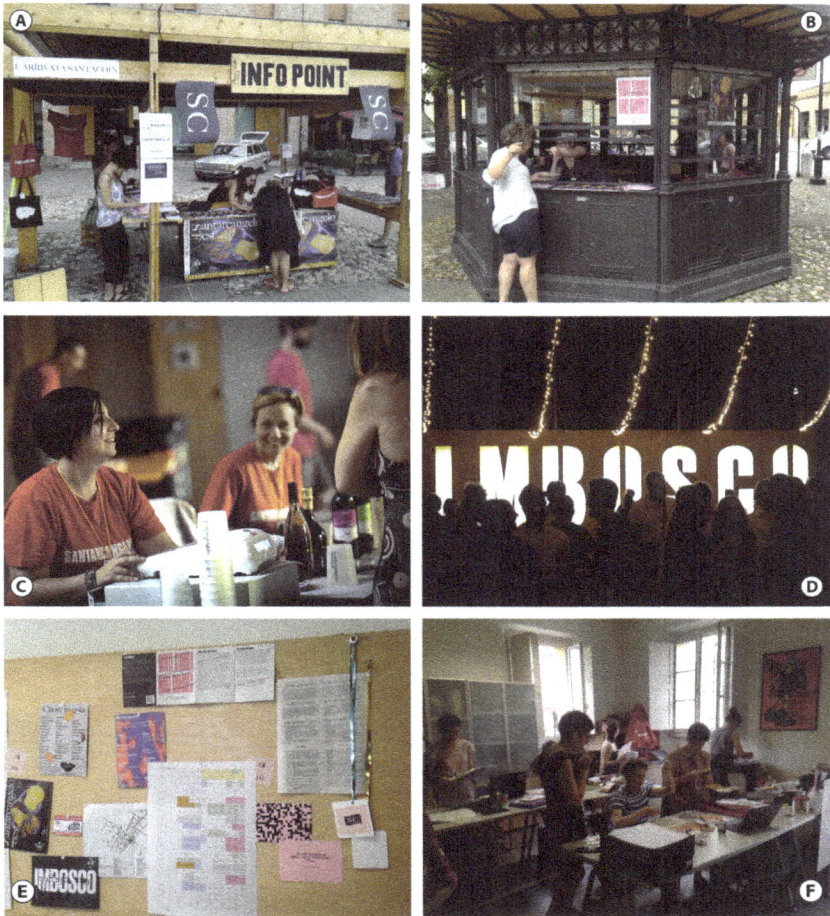

Figure 8.5: Santarcangelo Festival locations: (a) InfoPoint, (b) TicketPoint, (c) RistoPiazza, (d) Imbosco, (e, f) WelcomePoint.

Figures

Santarcangelo Festival 2018 saw 11,324 tickets sold, >12,000 attendants and 200 performances. 8,908.88 SC were exchanged (cash-in, top-up, cash-out). Out of this, around 30% was converted back to euro. The remainder (6,078.40) was spent (Figure 8.6): CryptoRituals accounted for almost half of the income – confirming the motivating effect of the artistic intervention – followed by RistoPiazza and Imbosco, the sociability location *par excellence*.

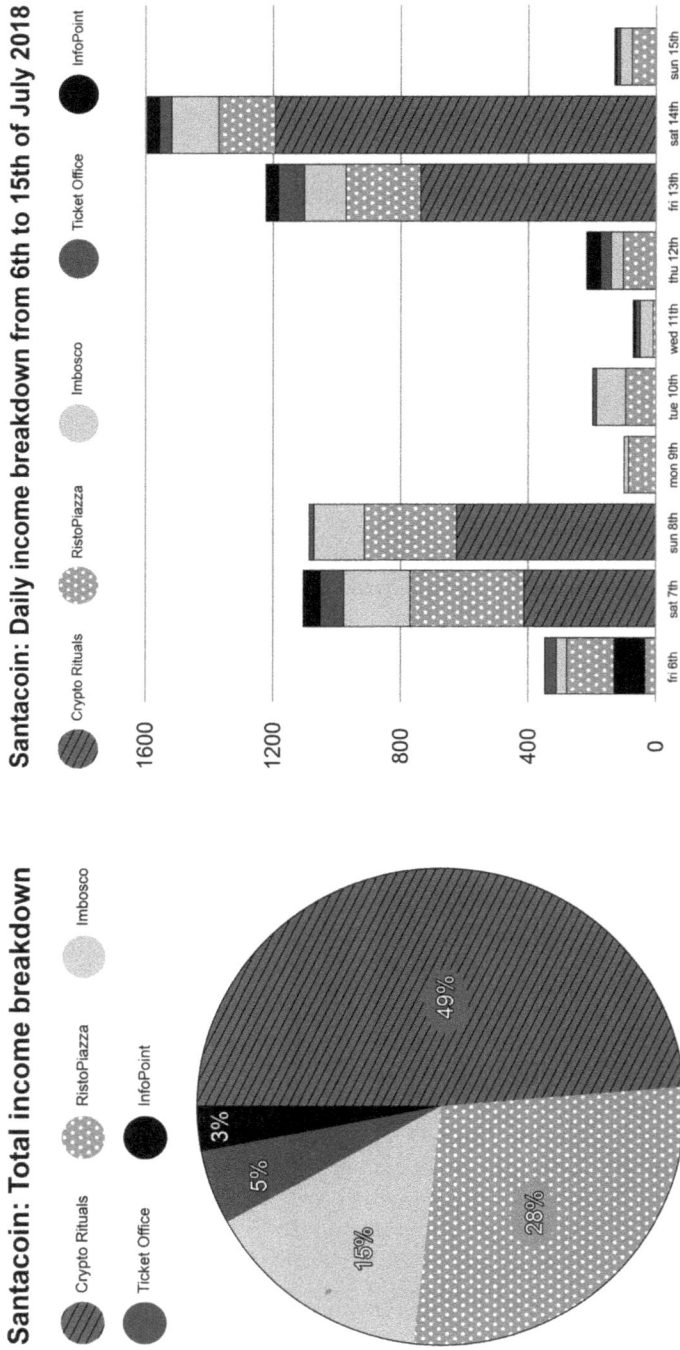

Figure 8.6: SC (a) total and (b) daily income breakdown.

Team Ethnography

During the festival, a group of researchers conducted team ethnography, provided technical support, and contributed to dissemination – all in close cooperation with Macao members. Additionally, the team together with Macao networked with local authorities and associations with a view to extending SC potential benefits beyond the festival. We held meetings and shared knowledge with the city Mayor and representatives of local businesses and associations, who were by then intrigued about the opportunities offered by CCs, and we explored possibilities for future development also with a local group that provides legal and CC-related support to cooperatives and communities nationwide, but whose relationship with the municipality and other actors in the territory was minimal at the time, and was reinforced by the considered action research activities.

Led by the author, the ethnographic team consisted of eight researchers in total. The daily group ranged from four to six people (more at the weekends), with two researchers – the author and the CC expert who also worked with Macao at piloting Commoncoin – covering the whole duration. The schedule was such that all day periods (10am–3am) were covered. The ethnographers alternated in different times and weekdays in the different locations, to share observations and develop a common understanding. We favoured shared immersion across sites (Creese et al., 2008) over the 'divide and conquer' approach (Easterby-Smith and Malina, 1999). Debriefing sessions were held once or twice per day. A fieldwork plan was prepared in advance alongside common research tools including guides for observation, informal interviews and semi-structured interviews with staff.

Data include daily fieldnotes by individual ethnographers, six semi-structured interviews and several informal ethnographic interviews, photos and videos. In parallel, we collected log-data on SC transactions and commonfare. net usage. The chapter is based on a thematic, abductive (Peirce, 1995; see Tavory and Timmermans, 2014) analysis of fieldnotes and interviews.

World-Makings

The making of a citadel

As the festival itself temporarily transforms the town, the intervention was aimed both at supporting such a transformation via a devoted currency and at creating a further qualified place – a citadel within the festival space-time – where socioeconomic relations could take centre stage and be collectively reimagined.

The overall successful engagement with SC of attendants, artists and staff that we observed relates not only to the convenience of the system (see next sub-section), but also to the enthusiasm for a devoted currency, an identitarian object marking the community boundaries. The issue of such boundaries and the community they mark – or create – is crucial. In this respect, most participants held a common expectation: once they understood what SC was, they took for granted that the whole city was involved.

> He is in his mid-fifties, not Italian. Mary presents SC … 'I'm not sure I understand. This badge is a sort of money, right?' … He asks how he can recognise shops dealing in SC. Mary does not understand the question … By taking for granted that during the festival the whole city or so deals in SC, he repeats his question: 'How do I know who's taking SC? Is there a sticker with QRCode or something?' [6 July 2018, WelcomePoint]

> 'So, at the moment you can only pay festival-related stuff, not yet the whole city, right?' Mary confirms. He: 'Alright, then I take the 20-SC one [talisman].' [6 July 2018, WelcomePoint]

> She regrets SC is useless in local shops and bars. She wishes for an extended coverage in 2019. [7 July 2018, InfoPoint]

As soon as the status of money is bestowed on an artefact – on clay tiles, metal coins, plastic talismans or digital QRCodes – the 'model of use' is available to participants, and the artefact becomes an object of talk, discourse and practice – of social interaction – based on a tacit mutual agreement grounded in a shared imaginary. Social interaction, in turn, is nothing but where collective imaginaries are practised and (re)produced (e.g. Fine, 2012). As space is tightly bound to practice – thereby marking a place – the question about its boundaries is pivotal, as it marks the boundaries of both the community and the experience itself. Participants wished for a city–festival community, for a complete overlap between the city('s) and the festival('s borders). The dialectic between the city-place and the temporary festival-place lies at the bottom of unmet expectations. Behind the existence itself of a *place* to experience lies instead a common imaginary.

The CryptoRituals place was more self-contained, and further qualified than the city/festival one. Located in one quarter of the large *piazza* (see Figure 8.4), the area was characterized by scenographic and proxemic arrangements delineating boundaries. Although porous ones, their relevance was evident. Originally, the area was intended for caring services only, with people having to reach the InfoPoint to take the talisman to pay caregivers. This proved less than satisfactory, hence a desk managing talismans was added at the centre of the area on the second evening, resulting in almost doubled participation. A caregiver – a schoolteacher in her forties with the hobby of Tarot reading – elaborated on the issues as follows:

> She says it is a matter of 'context', to which she repeatedly refers as a 'citadel'. 'Once inside the citadel, people didn't want to exit to reach the InfoPoint, they didn't want to cross the thresholds between the two

worlds so quickly'. She insists that it was not a matter of distance (less than 50 meters), but of atmosphere and experience. It was neither that people were bothered by the impossibility to pay in euro, she repeats nobody complained about that. She adds that years ago in Brisighella there was a medieval festival … 'where you paid everything with the Brisighello, the local currency in medieval times. So, it was already more than 10 years ago, and none was even dreaming of complaining. The idea was precisely to enter to have an experience, knowing you're crossing the thresholds of a new world, so to speak.' She interprets CryptoRituals in the same way. [14 July 2018, CryptoRituals]

Not going to InfoPoint once within CryptoRituals and desiring the festival to completely overlap with city life are grounded, I believe, in the very same desire for immersive experience, one in which you forget you are playing, you lose yourself in the action, an 'optimal experience' (Csikszentmihalyi, 1990).

Not only proxemics and artefacts as diverse as the scenography and the currency (physical and digital infrastructure) contributed to citadel-making, but also activities and their location. The wall-less citadel being located in the public space, caring practices were dislocated from their usual private space to the public sphere, that of political action. This qualified as a significant disruption of the everyday interaction order (Goffman, 1983) and social order* (Garfinkel, 1967) at large (see also Tavory and Fine, 2020). First, half-naked bodies, or bodies in (usually regarded as) embarrassing positions/conditions, were staged in the plaza, apparently unconcerned with their face (Goffman, 1955, 1959); second, (usually regarded as) mundane bodily maintenance activities and 'reflexive body techniques' (Crossley, 2005) were publicly performed not for disruption per se, but to bring socio-political issues to public debate.

Finance was made mundane and malleable, differently imaginable, reconnected to people's lives and the life of their community. For a caregiver in her seventies:

I think it's important, and it's good that certain new activities are experimented in small communities, because the small community can easily change and practically work. Otherwise, we only hear all those discourses from the big finance and … and imagine who knows what. People are wary. People are afraid especially in a climate, like today, where we are in an economic recession … And instead in small communities, perhaps, the sense of self is taken back, the sense of having something in common. [Gigliola, 14 July 2018]

In parallel, CryptoRituals made visible neglected activities deserving appreciation: caring practices as the concrete work of maintenance of the community, with affective, ethical and political implications (Puig de la Bellacasa, 2017).

Here the body as both (a) the locus of subjectivity – as it is often conceived in Western societies – and, at the same time and more importantly, (b) where intersubjectivity takes substance and is experienced (Bassetti, 2021: 177–192) was the crucial technology.

The making of a currency

A surprising result concerns festival staff, as they were not involved in CryptoRituals nor in the currency co-design, and as routine workers are generally disadvantaged by technological innovation (Ehn, 1988; Grudin, 1988; Agre, 1995; Card and DiNardo, 2005; Bassetti, 2012). Instead, operators – local cashiers especially – found Santacoin convenient.

> Roberta turns the smartphone towards me to allow me to press 'Confirm' … While clicking, I ask: 'Is it easy to use, rather than open the register, calculate the change…?' – 'Oh my goodness! Look, it's truly truly soooo much easier, really.' [8 July 2018, RistoPiazza]

Whereas initially Roberta was supposed to be the only cashier managing SC payments at the RistoPiazza, with the days passing by, the confidence in the system increasing and Santacoin spreading among festival participants, also the second cashier working at the venue started to manage payments in SC, until the two colleagues ended up playfully fighting over the only SC-devoted smartphone:

> 22.50, at the dinner cash desk, Roberta says to her colleague: 'C'mon, do you stop stealing the phone?' – 'Eh, my dear, they gave us just one …' – '[…] C'mon, give me that thingumabob.' She picks up the SC-devoted smartphone and scans my digital QR code while we all laugh. [13 July 2018, RistoPiazza]

The system seamlessly integrated with the ordinary working practices of the cashiers, both in *cognitive* and *interactional* terms. Attentional resources being freed from the tedious and critical task of checking the change, they could turn on the customer. Transaction time was not affected; cashiers invested the time saved to engage in social interaction, fulfilling one of their work tasks and more importantly, a rewarding one. This was embedded by design with the 'Confirm' button, contributing to transactional visibility (Perry and Ferreira, 2018), and allowing responsibility to be shared while also offering a conversational opportunity. The interactional gain proved critical, especially as cashiers were operating in a context where existing social relationships with local customers were also at stake.

Further evidence of local cashiers' enthusiasm – in terms of both convenience (cognitive efficiency, interactional reward and shared responsibility) and the desire for an identitarian element strengthening the temporary community – concerns the Imbosco SC-devoted cash register (and queue). When we arrived in Santarcangelo the day before the festival opening, we had an aperitif with Macao members and other artists. The latter pointed out 'how cool it would be to have a SC-devoted cash register at the Imbosco'. The evening after, I spotted the General Director and Roberta, the RistoPiazza cashier, at the Imbosco cash desk.[2] I approached them to discuss the opportunity of an additional cash register at the Imbosco, accepting SC only.

> I start by talking primarily to him (gaze), but I immediately realise that Roberta … has already fallen in love with SC. Therefore, I do my part to provide her with conversational space, and indeed she supports my 'peroratio' in an amazing (and/as unexpected) manner. [6 July 2018, Imbosco]

The Santacoin team was not thinking of a devoted register in the first place, but a group of artists made us do so. Then we tried to actualize the idea, and, in the absence of practical need for a further register, having local people (Roberta was not the only one) sharing the related imaginary and proactively acting accordingly was crucial. The visible presence of Santacoin at the Imbosco has been an act of collective imagination and action.

Art-student operators too favoured transactions in SC, to the point that they were at times annoyed by having to perform 'normal' transactions.

> An operator asks a tourist: 'Do you pay in Euro or Santacoin?'. The tourist replies 'Euro'. The operator grimaces with disappointment. [13 July 2018, InfoPoint]

However, when working at the euro–SC interface and acting as accountants, they witnessed the difficulties related to the lack of a legal framework:

> The top-up proceeds as smooth as silk with Anna. At the same time, Paolo is topping-up 20 for a man who has arrived just after me, and has addressed Paolo with 'Hi, I would like to top-up' – 'Sure, how much?' – 'Twenty' – 'Ok, just wait until I also prepare the receipt for you'. The 'problem', the dull, long, bureaucratic, tedious thing is precisely the handwritten, carbon-copied receipt. On the contrary, the top-up takes an instant, it is (presented as) non-problematic. [10 July 2018, InfoPoint]

---

[2] Roberta can be considered as the informal local cashiers' coordinator: once the RistoPiazza was closed, she was checking everything was in order at the Imbosco.

They also regretted the under-exploitation of the system:

> I believe SC is super handy. Also bookkeeping is done automatically. On the contrary, doing double accounting as we are doing is stupid. [Edoardo, InfoPoint]

> Giulio asks me about filtering opportunities for SC transaction data, as he is thinking to the potential advantages in terms of administration and bookkeeping. [8 July 2018, InfoPoint]

And they envisioned adopting SC internally to the festival organisation, to manage food and accommodation costs of artists and operators.

Conclusion

Overall, people's enthusiasm and imagination superseded our expectations. Art-student operators envisioned digital bookkeeping and internal costs management. It was a group of artists that proposed the Imbosco SC-only register, and cashiers that pushed for it with festival management. Within the festival community at large, many expected a full coverage scenario. Here, the festival as a frame for experimentation, as enabling the engagement of imaginaries, is quite relevant. And such a frame consists of conceiving the festival as a space-time of extra-ordinary experience, of immersion, of belonging. Artefacts such as complementary currencies can contribute to that.

Social relations within and among communities were central to engagement. Initially, people's trust was towards not Commonfare or Macao but the organisation of a renown festival (by artists, art operators and non-local audience), and local fellows belonging to such an organisation (by local attendants).[3] Participation by local and nearby inhabitants with limited interest in the arts was mostly due to their relationship with local festival staff or caregivers. Many had dinner at the RistoPiazza; the cash register was the second fulcrum of social interaction besides tables. Similarly, the register desk was a conversational point at the Imbosco. In both, we observed sustained interaction around the talisman and the SC smartphone.

CryptoRituals further succeeded in creating a citadel wherein usual social order and 'relations in public' (Goffman, 1971, 1983) were subverted, hence re-imaginable. This was supported by the currency, but also and more specifically by the 'détournement power' of bodies and of the literal staging, representation and performance of the centrality of caring practices. Moreover, CryptoRituals

---

[3] Initially, they are cautious with respect to my questions. They loosen up when I say I am with the festival organisation. [6 July 2018, InfoPoint]

played a crucial role in engaging people belonging to different communities. Extant relationships were pivotal also for participation in CryptoRituals. Local caregivers' involvement and the characteristics of the performance itself allowed for a participating audience made both of 'lay' people and art experts. This is crucial for the development of *narratives of alternatives* shared across individuals and communities, which is fundamental to empowerment (Carr, 2003; Freire, 2005).

This all enlightens the relevance of communities – local and not – in creating the opportunities for social ties to further develop, mutual trust to increase, and hence *citadels of experimentation and imagination* to exist. There is where people are provided with a context to interact, thereby developing a common cultural terrain allowing them, in turn, to imagine together, to share visions and narratives, which is central to infrastructuring (Neumann and Star, 1996; Kow and Lustig, 2018). The thematization of the monetary dimension of living together – brought down to earth rather than framed as theoretical debate – allowed for a temporary place where people felt comfortable in experimenting with alternative forms of interaction, living together and sociopolitical envisioning. A place for cultivating a different culture rooted in care has been sustained through an artistic and AR intervention where technology was used to make visible hence rethinkable the power of money in structuring social relations. It is worth mentioning that the Mayor of Santarcangelo met with the Santacoin team by her request and based on her interest in the experiment. She was considering both to extend Santacoin to the whole city in the 2019 festival edition and, more importantly, to employ SC to increase the purchasing power of the poorest strata of the population, homeless people in particular, through a city-issued currency accepted by local businesses (whose interest in the complementary currency was reported by the Mayor) and repeatedly recirculated in the local economy.[4] In short, a process of collective imagination and envisioning had set in.

Acknowledgements

I am grateful to the former Mayor and the Municipality of Santarcangelo di Romagna, the organisers of the Santarcangelo Festival, and Macao for their hospitality, willingness and efforts to experiment with Santacoin. My gratitude also goes to the festival staff and the CryptoRituals caregivers, whose commitment has been invaluable for the successful outcome of the experimentation. Special recognition goes to the Commonfare researchers for their dedication to co-designing and implementing Santacoin, and observing and evaluating the intervention during the festival.

---

[4] This was not actualised as, with the coming election in Autumn 2018, the mentioned Mayor was not re-elected.

Funding Acknowledgements

The PIE News / Commonfare project was funded by the European Commission under the H2020 programme (Grant Agreement No. 687922).

References

Agre, P. 1995 Conceptions of the user in computer systems design. In P. Thomas, ed., *The social and interactional dimensions of human – computer interfaces*, 1st ed. Cambridge / New York: Cambridge University Press, pp. 67–106.

Alexander, B.K. 2005 Performance ethnography. The re-enacting and inciting of culture. In N.K. Denzin and Y.S. Lincoln, eds., *Handbook of Qualitative Inquiry*, 3rd ed. Thousand Oaks, CA: Sage, pp. 411–441.

Bassetti, C. 2012 IS-related organizational change and the necessity of techno-organizational co- design(-in-use). An experience with ethnomethodo-logically oriented ethnography. In G. Viscusi, G.M.Campagnolo and Y. Curzi, eds., *Phenomenology, Organizational Politics, and IT Design: The Social Study of Information Systems*. Hershey, Penn.: IGI Global, pp. 289–310.

Bassetti, C. 2021 *Corpo, apprendimento e identità. Sé e intersoggettività nella danza*. Verona: OmbreCorte.

Bassetti, C., Botto, F. and Teli, M. 2018 The Commonfare Project. Designing to Support Grassroots Welfare Initiatives. *Digitcult – Scientific Journal on Digital Cultures*, vol. 3(1): 31–40.

Bassetti, C., Sciannamblo, M., Lyle, P., Teli, M., De Paoli, S. and De Angeli, A. 2019 Co-designing for common values: creating hybrid spaces to nurture autonomous cooperation, *CoDesign*, vol. 15(3): 256–271.

Bassetti, C. and Sachy, M. 2019 Macao independent centre for arts, culture and research: Working with Commonfare for the "Money of the Common". Sharing and Caring Case Studies, http://sharingandcaring.eu/node/400.

Bendell, J. and Greco, T.H. 2013 Currencies of transition: transforming money to unleash sustainability. In: M. McIntosh, ed., *The necessary transition: the journey towards the sustainable enterprise economy*. Sheffield, UK: Greenleaf Publishing, pp. 221–242.

Beyes, T. and Steyaert, C. 2011 The ontological politics of artistic interventions: Implications for performing action research. *Action Research*, vol. 9(1): 100–115.

Boal, A. 1974 *Teatro do Oprimido*. Rio de Janeiro, Civilização Brasileira.

Boal, A. 2009 *A Estética do Oprimido*. Rio de Janeiro, Garamond.

Brydon-Miller, M., Berthoin Antal, A., Friedman, V. and Gayá Wicks, P. 2011 The changing landscape of arts and action research. *Action Research*, 9(1), pp. 3–11.

Briggs, P., Burford, B., De Angeli, A. and Lynch, P. 2002 Trust in Online Advice. *Social Science Computer Review*, 20(3), pp. 321–332.

Cahn, E. 2004 *No More Thrown Away People*. Washington, DC: Essential Books.

Card, D. and DiNardo, J.E. 2005 The Impact of Technological Change on Low Wage Workers: A Review. *National Poverty Center Working Paper Series*, #05–28. University of Michigan, pp. 1–39.

Carr, E.S. 2003 Rethinking Empowerment Theory Using a Feminist Lens: The Importance of Process. *Affilia*, 18(1), pp. 8–20.

Carroll, J.M. and Bellotti, V. 2015 Creating Value Together: The Emerging Design Space of Peer-to-Peer Currency and Exchange. In: *Proceedings of the 18th ACM Conference on Computer Supported Cooperative Work & Social Computing*. New York: ACM, pp. 1500–1510.

Clerke, T. and Hopwood, N. 2014 *Doing Ethnography in Teams*. New York: Springer.

Cole, A., Neilsen, L., Knowles, J.G. and Luciani, T. (eds) 2004 *Provoked by Art: Theorizing Arts-informed Research*. Toronto: Backalong Books & Centre for Arts Informed Research.

Coventry, L., De Angeli, A. and Johnson, G.I. 2003 Usability and Biometric Verification at the ATM Interface. In: *Proceedings of the Conference on Human Factors in Computing Systems*. New York: ACM, pp. 153–160.

Creese, A., Bhatt, A., Bhojani, N. and Martin, P. 2008 Fieldnotes in team ethnography: Researching complementary schools. *Qualitative Research*, 8(2), pp. 197–215.

Crossley, N. 2005 Mapping Reflexive Body Techniques: On Body Modification and Maintenance. *Body & Society*, 11(1), pp. 1–35.

Csikszentmihalyi, M. 1990 Flow: The Psychology of Optimal Experience, New York: Harper-Perenniel.

De Angeli, A., Athavankar, U., Joshi, A., Coventry, L. and Johnson, G.I. 2004 Introducing ATMs in India: a contextual inquiry. *Interacting with Computers*, 16(1), pp. 29–44.

Debord, G. 1967[1994] *The Society of the Spectacle*. New York: Zone Books.

Denzin, N.K. 2003 *Performance ethnography: Critical pedagogy and the politics of culture*. Thousand Oaks, CA: Sage.

De Paoli, S., Wilson, A., Sachy, M., De Pellegrini, F. and Ottaviano, S. 2017a *Reputation Mechanics, Digital Currency Model and Network Dynamics and Algorithms*. [online] Available at: http://pieproject.eu/wp-content/uploads /2017/10/PIE_D3.2_FIN.pdf [Accessed 30 Sept. 2018].

De Paoli, S., Wilson, A., Sachy, M. and De Pellegrini, F. 2017b *User Research Report and Scenarios*. Available at: http://pieproject.eu/wp-content/uploads /2017/07/PIE_D3.1_FIN.pdf [Accessed 30 Sept. 2018].

Easterby-Smith, M. and Malina, D. 1999 Cross-Cultural Collaborative Research: Toward Reflexivity. *Academy of Management Journal*, 42(1), pp. 76–86.

Ehn, P. 1988 *Work-oriented design of computer artifacts.* Institutionen for Informationsbehandling Umeå Universitet.

Ferreira, J., Perry, M. and Subramanian, S. 2015 Spending Time with Money: From Shared Values to Social Connectivity. In: *Proceedings of the 18th ACM Conference on Computer Supported Cooperative Work & Social Computing.* New York: ACM, pp. 1222–1234.

Ferreira, J. and Perry, M. 2014 Building an alternative social currency: dematerialising and rematerialising digital money across media. In: *Proceedings of HCI Korea.* Seoul: Hanbit Media Inc., pp. 122–131.

Fine, G.A. 2012 *Tiny Publics: A Theory of Group Action and Culture.* New York: Russell Sage Foundation.

Finley, S. 2005 Arts-based inquiry: Performing revolutionary pedagogy. In: N.K. Denzin and Y.S. Lincoln, eds., *Handbook of Qualitative Inquiry,* 3rd ed. Thousand Oaks, CA: Sage, pp. 681–694.

Freire, P. 2005 *The Pedagogy of the Oppressed.* New York: Continuum.

Fumagalli, A. 2015 Commonwealth, Commonfare and Money of the Common: the challenge to fight life subsumption. In M. Bak Jorgensen and O. Garcìa Agustìn, eds., *Politics of Dissent,* 1st ed. Frankfurt: Peter Lange, pp. 157–179.

Garau, P. 2016 Measuring the Magic of Public Space. Le Piazze di Roma. *The Journal of Public Space,* 1(1), pp. 17–24.

Gelleri, C. 2009 Chiemgauer Regiomoney: Theory and Practice of a Local Currency. *International Journal of Community Currency Research,* 13(2), pp. 61–75.

General Intellect. 2018 Commonfare or the Welfare of the Commonwealth. In: *MoneyLabReader #2: Overcoming the Hype.* Amsterdam: Institute of Net Cultures, pp. 243–51.

Given, L.M. 2008 Performance Ethnography. In: *The sage encyclopedia of qualitative research methods,* vol. 0. Thousand Oaks, CA: Sage. https://doi.org/10.4135/9781412963909 [Accessed 20 Jul. 2019].

Goffman, E. 1955 On Face-Work. *Psychiatry,* 18(3), pp. 213–231.

Goffman, E. 1959 *The presentation of self in everyday life.* New York: Anchor Books.

Goffman, E. 1971 *Relations in Public. Microstudies of the Public Order.* New York: Basic Books.

Goffman, E. 1983 The Interaction Order: American Sociological Association, 1982 Presidential Address. *American Sociological Review,* 48(1), 1–17.

Grudin, J. 1988 Why CSCW applications fail: problems in the design and evaluation of Organisational Interfaces. In: *Proceedings of the 1988 ACM Conference on Computer Supported Cooperative Work.* Portland, Oregon: ACM, pp. 85–93.

Hughes, D.W. 2003 Policy Uses of Economic Multiplier and Impact Analysis. *Choices,* 18(2), pp. 25–29.

Irving, A. 2007 Ethnography, art, and death. *Journal of the Royal Anthropological Institute,* 13, pp. 185–208.

Kemmis, S. and McTaggart, R. 2005 Participatory action research: Communicative action and the public sphere. In N.K. Denzin and Y.S. Lincoln, eds., *Handbook of Qualitative Inquiry*, 3rd ed. Thousand Oaks, CA: Sage, pp. 559–603.

Kennedy, M., Lietaer, B. and Rogers, J. 2012 *People's Money – the promise of regional currencies*. Triarchy Press.

Kow, Y.M. and Lustig, C. 2018 Imaginaries and Crystallization Processes in Bitcoin Infrastructuring. *Computer Supported Cooperative Work*, 27(2), pp. 209–232.

Lietaer, B. 2001 *The Future of Money*, London and New York: Randomhouse.

New Economics Foundation (2015). *People Powered Money – designing, developing and delivering community currencies*, London: New Economics Foundation.

Neumann, L.J. and Star, S.L. 1996 Making Infrastructure: The Dream of a CommonLanguage. In: *Proceedings of the Participatory Design Conference, Cambridge, MA, USA, 13–16 November 1996*. Palo Alto, CA: Computer Professionals for Social Responsibility, pp. 231–240.

North, P.J. 2007 *Money and Liberation: The Micropolitics of Alternative Currency Movements*. Minneapolis: University of Minnesota Press.

North, P.J. 1999 Explorations in Heterotopia: LETS and the micropolitics of money and livelihood. *Environment and Planning D: Society and Space*, 17(1), pp. 69–86.

Nunn, C. 2020 The participatory arts-based research project as an exceptional sphere of belonging. *Qualitative Research*, https://doi.org/10.1177/1468794120980971

O'Neill, J., Dhareshwar, A. and Muralidhar, S.H. 2017 Working Digital Money into a Cash Economy: The Collaborative Work of Loan Payment. *Computer Supported Cooperative Work*, 26(4–6), pp. 733–768.

Peirce, C.S. 1955 *Philosophical writings of Peirce* (Ed. by Justus Buchler). New York: Dover.

Perry, M. and Ferreira, J. 2018 Moneywork: Practices of Use and Social Interaction around Digital and Analog Money. *ACM Transactions on Computer-Human Interaction*, 24(6), art. 41.

Puig de la Bellacasa, M. 2017 *Matters of Care. Speculative Ethics in More Than Human Worlds*. Londres: University of Minnesota Press.

Roio, D. and Beneti, A. 2017 *Reputation, Digital Currency and Network Dynamics. PIE News Project Deliverable 4.2*. http://pieproject.eu/wp-content/uploads/2018/01/PIE_D4.2_FIN.pdf. Accessed 30 September 2018.

Seeley, C. 2011 Uncharted territory: Imagining a stronger relationship between the arts and action research. *Action Research*, 9(1), pp. 83–99.

Seyfang, G. and Longhurst, N. 2013 Growing green money? Mapping community currencies for sustainable development. *Ecological Economics*, 86, pp. 65–77.

Seyfang, G. 2009 *The New Economics of Sustainable Consumption – Seeds of Change.*

Tavory, I. and Timmermans, S. 2014 *Abductive Analysis: Theorizing Qualitative Research.* Chicago: University of Chicago Press.

Tavory, I. and Fine, G. 2020 Disruption and the theory of the interaction order. *Theory and Society*, 49, pp. 365–385.

Tofteng, D. and Husted, M. 2011 Theatre and action research: How drama can empower action research processes in the field of unemployment. *Action Research*, 9(1), pp. 27–41.

Vaajakallio, K. and Mattelmäki, T. 2014 Design games in codesign: as a tool, a mindset and a structure. *CoDesign*, 10(1), pp. 63–77.

Vines J., Dunphy, P., Blythe, M., Lindsay, S., Monk, A. and Oliver, P. 2012 The joy of cheques: trust, paper and eighty somethings. In: *Proceedings of the ACM 2012 conference on Computer Supported Cooperative Work.* New York: ACM, pp. 147–156.

Wang, Y. and Mainwaring, S.D. 2008 Human-Currency Interaction: learning from virtual currency use in China. In: *Proceedings of the SIGCHI Conference on Human Factors in Computing Systems.* New York: ACM, pp. 25–28.

Zhang, Z. and Zurlo, F. 2021 How Game and Game Principles Facilitate the Co-Design Processes: Reflections on Two Case Studies. In: *Proceedings of the International Conference on Engineering Design* (ICED21). Gothenburg, Sweden, 16–20 August 2021.

CHAPTER 9

Reflective Ethnographic Design of Collaborative Economy Business Models Using Annotated Portfolios

Justin Larner

University of Cumbria, UK

Abstract

As the collaborative platform economy develops, network effects tend to create one dominant platform within each domain such as transport, reducing the power of workers to find alternatives. The research problem is to find a specific methodology that could enable researchers to draw on the experience of participants as workers and their wish to create ways of working that offer them greater power in the collaborative economy. Ethnographic studies can enable researchers to discover how workers make sense of their involvement in the collaborative platform economy and provide valuable data on how current business models and platforms can affect worker power. However, a wish to promote worker power implies a participatory form of research that aims to break down power relations between researchers and participants. This chapter reflects on the methodological challenges of studying the collaborative

How to cite this book chapter:
Larner, J. 2022. Reflective Ethnographic Design of Collaborative Economy Business Models Using Annotated Portfolios. In: Travlou, P. and Ciolfi, L. (eds.) *Ethnographies of Collaborative Economies across Europe: Understanding Sharing and Caring.* Pp. 173–191. London: Ubiquity Press. DOI: https://doi.org/10.5334/bct.j. License: CC BY-NC-ND

economy ethnographically in order to develop new business models and platforms. Annotated portfolios, a technique used in human-computer interaction, offers the potential to enable worker experience to inform new business model designs. Researchers can use annotated portfolios to articulate latent designs in ethnographic data gathered from engagement with workers in the collaborative economy. In bringing these designs into existence, researchers can then contribute their perspective to a co-design process with these workers. Annotated portfolio techniques can thus help both researchers and workers to use ethnographic data to design new business models in the collaborative economy.

Introduction

This chapter proposes an ethnographic methodology for designing new business models in the collaborative economy, where the starting point is engagement by researchers with workers through online forums or a similar medium to gather data on not only their current situation but also their future wishes and desires. Annotated portfolio analysis within a narrative framework can then enable researchers to articulate latent business model designs in this ethnographic data. This section briefly introduces the context of worker power in the collaborative platform economy, then the next section considers the potential for new business models. The following sections explore ethnography as a business model design technique, introduce a narrative framework, then present annotated portfolios as a business model design methodology. The chapter concludes by offering an ethnographic methodology that can enable co-design of business models with workers in the collaborative economy using narrative and annotated portfolio techniques.

The collaborative or sharing economy has been defined as 'using internet technologies to connect distributed groups of people to make better use of goods, skills and other useful things' (Stokes et al., 2014: 10). Since its inception in the mid-1990s, the collaborative economy has become increasingly monetized, and by the mid-2000s companies such as iStockphoto, InnoCentive and Amazon Mechanical Turk were formed to coordinate the work of amateurs, but this crowdsourcing became a problem for professionals, who found their livelihoods being undermined by these new platforms (Howe, 2006). The term 'platform' was originally adopted by industrial economists to describe a system or institution that mediates transactions between agents (Baldwin and Woodard, 2009). Several writers have since used the term 'platform economy' to distinguish the growing trend towards monetization of the digital platforms that people use to communicate and increasingly to gain employment (Fuchs, 2014; Kenney & Zysman, 2016; De Groen et al., 2016). This monetization has created a new class of digital labourers, or precariats (Bradley, 2014; Pignot, 2021). Kenney & Zysman (2016: 61) define platforms as 'multisided digital frameworks that shape the terms on which participants interact with one another'.

In the platform economy, the main actors are the companies that own the platforms, such as Uber, Airbnb or Deliveroo; customers, who receive goods or services via the platform; and freelance workers who provide the goods or services on offer (De Groen et al., 2016). Digital platforms can facilitate social media such as Facebook or Twitter, enable marketplaces such as Ebay or create new forms of business such as Uber.

Uber is an example of where the platform algorithmically manages independent workers according to customer demand (Pignot, 2021). When goods or services are provided on a paid basis, employers hold far greater market power than workers, including unilaterally setting wages for each task (Kingsley et al., 2015). The issue of how platform firms can exert power over workers is an increasing problem for policy, as a platform can potentially replace entire industries or services, such as with Uber and the taxi industry (Pignot, 2021). In the context of software production, the lock-in effect has been noted, whereby if a piece of software can gain enough market share, it gains further customers and complementary applications and eventually dominates the market (Bonaccorsi & Rossi, 2003). In the collaborative platform economy, these network effects have enabled one platform to become dominant in each domain, reducing the power of workers to find alternatives (Kenney & Zysman, 2016).

Although the Organisation for Economic Co-operation and Development reported that the platform economy is less than 1% of the total economy (OECD, 2017), that proportion is growing rapidly. This trend is a concern, as workers don't benefit from regular employment: they take on tasks as and when they are given them, responding to temporary offers of work via an app (De Groen et al., 2016). These platforms benefit customers as they can find the lowest price for products and services worldwide, but workers do not have the job security, opportunities for collective action or benefits that workers in more traditional organizations have (Scholz, 2016). Collective action in the collaborative economy is currently largely expressed by workers creating internet-based forums to share knowledge and experience (Fabo et al., 2017). For example, workers have started to create online forums to share experience and problems (Ride Share Drivers United, 2022), and in some cases researchers have set up forums (Irani and Siberman, 2013) that are now run by their worker community, who 'watch out for each other' (Turkopticon, 2022). These forums can benefit workers who use them, but don't directly change power relations between those workers and platform operators.

Another way for workers to deal with these economic changes is through organized strikes, such as when Deliveroo workers went on strike in 2016. The strike started with workers meeting and self-organizing at points that had been algorithmically determined by the platform (Woodcock and Graham, 2020). Collective action has now broadened to platform economy workers aligning with unions, creating guild-like organizations and worker-led platform cooperatives (Vandaele, 2018), which have had some success in niche markets (Scholz, 2016).

These initiatives highlight wider issues in the collaborative economy, which is shaped by political, economic, social and technological factors, including worker power (Woodcock & Graham, 2020). One means of exerting power is through ownership: Kenney & Zysman (2016: 66) ask the questions, 'Who owns or controls the platform?', 'How is value created?' and 'Who captures the value?'. Business models are framed in terms of creating and capturing value (Zott et al., 2011), hence they are a useful concept to frame power relations in the collaborative economy. It is thus important to find business models that can offer more of a balance of power between workers and firms, where the issue of worker power is the context for designing new collaborative economy business models.

Worker-led forums have been a source of online ethnographic data for researchers, contrasting the perspectives of workers and the platform firm (Pignot, 2021; Irani & Siberman, 2013). The experience of these workers, in particular their reflection on working in a particular domain (Lee et al., 2015), could inform the development of new business models in the collaborative economy. Ethnography can enable gaining a deep understanding of the experience of workers in the collaborative economy, but further steps will be needed for ethnographic data to inform new business models. A narrative framework enables analysis of ethnographic data from engagement with collaborative economy workers not only on their current situation, but on their wishes and desires for the future. Considering how wishes and desires for the future could be fulfilled through new business models implies a design process, of 'creating something that does not yet exist' (Nelson & Stolterman, 2012: 28). Annotated portfolios are a design technique introduced in the context of human–computer interaction by Gaver & Bowers (2012) that can bring together a number of artefacts and identify the aspects that are common to them. These artefacts could include textual as well as material objects.

This chapter explains how narratives of engagement with collaborative economy workers can be annotated as a portfolio of business models that can potentially be used to create new ways of working in the collaborative economy. The next section introduces the potential for worker-led business models in the collaborative platform economy.

The Potential for Worker-Led Business Models in the Collaborative Economy

Although the concept of business models was first mentioned in the 1950s (Bellman et al., 1957), the use of the term was not widespread until the early 2000s, in the context of the internet and e-business (DaSilva & Trkman, 2014). Thus the business model as a concept and the digital platform economy have co-evolved. Business models are generally defined in terms of value creation and capture, for example that a business model 'describes the rationale of how an organization creates, delivers, and captures value' (Osterwalder & Pigneur, 2010: 14), and that a 'business model articulates the logic, the data and other evidence that support a value proposition for the customer, and a viable structure of revenues and costs for the enterprise delivering that value' (Teece, 2010: 179). Business models have also been defined in terms of boundary spanning: Zott et al. (2011: 1020) highlight that 'the business model is a new unit of analysis that is distinct from the product, firm, industry, or network; it is centered on a focal firm, but its boundaries are wider than those of the firm'.

In the collaborative platform economy, innovation can extend from products and services to business models (George & Bock, 2011). In particular, firms have adopted two-sided business models that deliver a value proposition to customers, who benefit from services such as transport at a reduced cost (Kenney & Zysman, 2016). These firms use the resources afforded by the Internet to create software platforms that link customers with freelance workers who provide these services. These workers are a vital resource to the platform firm, but are viewed as independent contractors, with an uncertain income as a result. The UK Good Work report (Taylor, 2017) challenges the notion of independent contractors in relation to platform firms, proposing that the term 'dependent contractor' is more appropriate. The Frankfurt Paper on Platform-Based Work notes, from a European perspective, that workers as independent contractors in the digital platform economy are 'typically excluded from the legal and social protections established for employees over the last hundred years' (Frankfurt Paper, 2016: 2), and that 'worker organizing has for decades been correlated with the economic well-being of working people' (p. 6), calling for a 'co-operative turn', 'in which workers, clients, platform operators, investors, policy makers, and worker organizations work together to improve outcomes for all stakeholders' (p. 3).

Considering how research can contribute to creating new worker-owned business models in the collaborative economy implies adopting participatory methods that aim to change the situation of workers. The problem that this chapter explores is to find a specific methodology that can draw directly on the experience of participants as workers, and their wish to create ways of working that can offer them greater power in the collaborative platform economy. Ethnography is a technique that can enable researchers to gain valuable data on how workers both participate in and make sense of the collaborative economy, but the challenge is then how to bridge the gap between data and action. The next section introduces how ethnography and action research can be combined to enable business model design in the collaborative economy.

Ethnography as a Business Model Design Technique

Ethnography is generally described as a research methodology that aims to gain a deep understanding of the experience of individuals and groups in their context through techniques such as participant observation (e.g. Silverman, 2007). Gaining a deep understanding of the experience of workers in the collaborative economy can then be a starting point for making change with those workers.

Action research has been described as a 'broadly interventionist approach to change and improvement that enables individuals, groups and organizations to use reflection on action in a problematic situation as a basis for the creation of new actions and knowledge' (Ellis & Kiely, 2000: 83). Through enabling researchers and participants to reflect on their current situation, ethnography can contribute to reflection that leads to action (Cassell & Johnson, 2006).

Bringing about change implies that the researcher takes an epistemological position of critical theory, where they engage in a dialogue with research participants in order to understand both how structures in society have gained their own reality independent of their creators and how these structures could be changed (Guba & Lincoln, 1994). In the context of workers who wish to gain power in the collaborative economy, changing the situation of these workers from an existing to a desired state implies a design process. Action research has been linked with participatory design, as both methodologies encourage participation by stakeholders to make real-world change (Foth & Axup, 2006). Design is about an 'inquiry into the ideal' focusing on what is desirable but 'not-yet-real' (Nelson & Stolterman, 2012: 35), and is 'concerned with how things ought to be, with devising artefacts to attain goals' (Simon, 1969: 59).

Taking an epistemological position of critical theory in the context of design leads to critical design, introduced by Dunne & Raby (2001) and developed further by Bowen (2007: 1) as 'critical design practices' that can enable 'stakeholders to engage with novel situations and consequently engage in creative thinking about future possibilities'. In this case, the stakeholders are workers in the collaborative economy, and the future possibilities are new business models. Critical design practices include speculative design (Dunne & Raby, 2013), co-design and participatory design. The last of these links with participatory action research, which in turn can be informed by ethnography (Cassell & Johnson, 2006). In the situation of seeking to design new business models in the collaborative economy, a critical design approach can be helpful, which can offer insight into existing social structures by creating new ones that promote 'social change, from the present to a hoped-for future that is attainable but not immediately within reach' (Bardzell & Bardzell, 2013: 3304).

Building on critical design, critical design ethnography was introduced by Barab et al. (2004: 254) as 'a process that sits at the intersection of participatory action research, critical ethnography, and socially responsive instructional design'. Implementing critical design ethnography starts with understanding cultural context through rich description, as with other forms of ethnography, then making commitments to social change that are expressed in a design for potential action, which can be generalized beyond the original ethnographic context (Barab et al., 2004). In the context of the collaborative economy, ethnographic data from engagement with workers can offer a rich description not only of their current situation but also of their hoped-for future, including a future where they as workers gain greater power. Taking a critical design perspective, the research process is thus about articulating these wishes and hopes as designs for new worker-led business models. In this respect, the design pro-cess functions in the way suggested by Zimmerman & Forlizzi (2008: 44), where designers can create an artefact that 'functions as a specific instantiation of a model – a theory – linking the current state to the proposed, preferred state', in this case modelling desires for their future that are expressed by workers in the collaborative economy in online forums or similar media. These desires for the future can be expressed as narratives, where a narrative framework can enable ethnographic data to become part of a design process.

The methodology described in this chapter builds on critical design ethnog-raphy to elicit business model designs from ethnographic study of workers in the collaborative platform economy through the use of annotated portfolio techniques within a narrative framework. The next section presents a narrative framework for analysis of ethnographic data in a business model context.

A Narrative Framework for Ethnographic Data Analysis as a Design Process

Narratives are a form of discourse that can be a 'form not only of representing but of constituting reality' (Bruner, 1991: 5), more specifically in constituting social reality (Ricoeur, 1979). Building on the perspective that narratives can create a potential reality, Rosner (2018) highlights the potential of 'fabulations' as a form of narrative that blends the real and the imaginary, where the latter can be an imagined future. Narratives as a form of discourse can exist not only as text, but also as actions, images, mime or material objects (Hawkins & Saleem, 2012). Narratives can be 'viewed as the cognitive framework that guides an individual in making sense of experiences' (Hawkins & Saleem, 2012: 208), and can go beyond individual sense-making to 'also frame policies for subse-quent action and interpretation' (Flory & Iglesias, 2010: 116–117). Narratives can thus both communicate and help create potential futures, which makes them a helpful tool in design. Narratives could thus be helpful in the design of business models in the collaborative economy through making sense of ethno-graphic data.

A narrative has the elements of plot (events in a chronological order) and theme (an overarching meaning), and takes place in a setting or context (Solouki, 2017). Narratives can exist not only on the individual level, but also on group and societal levels (Gabriel, 2004), including organizational narratives (Hawkins & Saleem, 2012), potentially including business models. Business models have been viewed as narratives by several authors; for example, Margetta (2002: 4) saw business models as 'stories that explain how enterprises work. A good business model answers Peter Drucker's age-old questions: Who is the customer? And what does the customer value?', while Doganova & Eyquem-Renault (2009) framed the business model in terms of narrative devices that are co-created with stakeholders to enable a shared understanding. Going beyond understanding, Araujo & Easton (2012: 316) claimed that a narrative 'begins to perform the world it narrates with every successful iteration'. Organisations can thus be viewed as narratives in a 'constant state of becoming' (Ropo & Höykinpuro, 2017: 358), and this perspective extends to business models, as 'a text that re-describes and re-constructs reality' (Perkmann & Spicer, 2010: 5). The performative, constructive aspect of business models expressed as narratives links with a design perspective, where the business model can be seen as an artefact embodying the wishes and desires of those who create it. Building on the work of Solouki and other authors, Larner (2019: 63) offers a useful definition of narratives that was developed in the context of business model design:

> A narrative expresses and enacts the purposeful intent of human or other actors who have an agency and inner life. Narratives have a plot, that depicts particular incidents or events occurring in a causal sequence. A narrative expresses an initial point of view within a specific context or frame of reference, but then offers a new point of view. Narratives express a consistent meaning that can both reflect reality and create it. They can become institutionalized through enactment of narrative structures.

Ethnographic data can be analysed in a narrative frame (Burke, 1945), where the definition offered above can become a framework:

1. The narrative expresses and enacts the purposeful intent of human or other actors.
2. The narrative is enacted by human or other actors who have an agency and inner life.
3. The narrative depicts particular incidents or events.
4. The depicted incidents or events occur in a causal sequence.
5. The depicted incidents or events are set within an accepted context or frame of reference.
6. The depicted incidents or events express a specific point of view on the context or frame of reference.
7. The depicted incidents or events then offer a new point of view on this context or frame of reference.
8. The narrative expresses a consistent meaning that can both reflect reality and create it.
9. The narrative can become institutionalized as structures.

Metaphors, analogies and narratives 'often seem to play a similar role in qualitative research as quantitative models', and these

> artefacts, re-presentations of, on the one hand empirical 'reality', and, on the other hand, theory, should then be considered as entities in their

own right, irreducible to and potentially more important to the research process than either of these two, yet playing a mediating role between them. (Alvesson & Sköldberg, 2009: 23)

This perspective implies that, in mediating between ethnographic data and developing theory, narratives can act as a model. In the research context of business models in the collaborative economy, a narrative derived from ethnographic data on workers can potentially act as one or more business models. However, a further stage of analysis will be needed to focus specifically on potential business models by eliciting latent designs from the data. Annotated portfolios, a technique used in human–computer interaction, offer the potential to enable ethnographic data on the experience of workers in the collaborative economy to inform new business model designs within a narrative framework. The next section introduces annotated portfolios as a design technique, then offers a narrative framework for designing business models.

Annotated Portfolios within a Narrative Framework as a Business Model Design Methodology

Annotated portfolios were originally developed in the context of classroom assessment (Yancey, 1992) as a narrative frame (Burke, 1945) that enabled students and teachers to collaborate more effectively and gain transformative insights. Beyond the classroom, annotated portfolios were first used in the context of mental health to evaluate the design of clinical treatment strategies (Lavori & Dawson, 1998). Annotated portfolios were then reintroduced in the context of human-computer interaction as a method that could bring together a number of artefacts and identify the aspects that were common among them through text annotations (Gaver, 2012; Bowers, 2012; Gaver & Bowers, 2012). Annotated portfolios can be seen as an example of intermediate-level knowledge (Löwgren, 2013), a level of abstraction between the 'ultimate particular' (Nelson & Stolterman, 2012) of each artefact and a more generalizable level of theory. The technique thus offers a way to build on the narrative framework offered in the previous section to focus more specifically on potential business models.

Annotated portfolios can contribute to producing knowledge of 'what ought to be' (Gaver & Bowers, 2012: 42), or a desired change in the future, rather than documenting what already exists. In this respect, annotated portfolios can contribute to design, by bridging the gap between research and design, where the 'essence of research is to produce knowledge, and the essence of design is to produce artifacts' (Löwgren, 2013: 30). Annotated portfolios are not limited to material artefacts: Bowers (2012: 71) highlights that any 'material form can be considered for an annotated portfolio including an illustrated monograph, a scientific paper, a curated exhibition and so forth', implying that ethnographic data can be annotated as a portfolio. The technique could thus be applicable to the design of business models in the collaborative economy, where the artefacts are ethnographic data from online engagement with workers, annotated as a portfolio that can then reveal potential business model designs.

A starting point for annotation is the categories of choices that influence the design of an artefact offered by Gaver & Bowers (2012: 43):

- functionality
- aesthetics
- practicalities
- motivation for designing
- identities and capabilities of the people for whom it is intended
- culture.

In identifying business model design elements of an annotated portfolio, a helpful perspective is that a business model can be considered 'as a material object, as a scale model of the new venture' (Doganova & Eyquem-Renault, 2009: 1568). Taking this perspective, a business model design will need to contain all the components that would be found in the business itself. A business model is essentially about for whom the business creates value, what the business is competent at, the scope of the business, its position in the market, where it will find resources and how it gains revenue (Morris et al., 2005) in a particular context (Downing, 2005). In drawing up a business model, the entrepreneur needs to consider the activities the business will undertake, and how those activities will create additional value for customers that the business can capture as profit (Al-debei & Avison, 2010; Chesbrough, 2006; Amit & Zott, 2001).

The business model can be viewed as being created 'through the performative practices (i.e. actions, constructions) of actors' (Wieland et al., 2017: 926), where personal and investor factors are key (Morris et al., 2005). As the business develops, its business model defines its boundaries as a 'focal actor' (Zott & Amit, 2010), enabling the business to explore opportunities across organizational boundaries (Jensen, 2013). Shafer et al. (2005: 202) point out that a business model 'helps articulate and make explicit key assumptions about cause-and-effect relationships and the internal consistency of strategic choices', while the business model can also play 'an important sense-making and sense-creating role for various stakeholders, despite their individual approaches and understandings of the term' (Jensen, 2013: 62). As this sense-making process progresses, the business model can then create institutional norms and beliefs (Vargo & Lusch, 2016), which then become formalized into 'the design of organizational structures to enact a commercial opportunity' (George & Bock 2011: 99).

The components of a business model can thus be identified as:

- personal factors
- resources

- opportunities
- stakeholders
- value creation and capture
- strategy
- boundaries
- structure
- activities
- customers
- revenue and costs
- profit.

Business model design can also contribute to organizational design, where Stanford (2007: 5) offers the relevant parameters of:

- culture
- systems
- structure
- people
- performance measures and processes
- products and services
- operating context.

The elements of design choices, business model components and organizational design parameters can then be combined as business model design elements:

- activities
- aesthetics
- boundaries
- culture
- customers
- functionality
- identities and capabilities of the people for whom it is intended
- motivation for designing
- operating context
- opportunities
- performance measures and processes
- personal factors
- practicalities
- products and services
- profit
- resources
- revenue and costs
- stakeholders

- strategy
- structure
- systems
- value creation and capture.

The elements can then be set within the narrative framework to create a business model narrative framework as shown in Table 9.1.

The next section explores how the business model narrative framework can be used to create an annotated portfolio of potential business model designs from the ethnographic data. The ethnographic data can be gathered through engagement with existing online forums that workers use to share experience and knowledge, or new forums created by researchers.

Table 9.1: Business model narrative framework

Narrative framework element	Business model design elements
The narrative expresses and enacts the purposeful intent of human or other actors	Culture Motivation for designing
The narrative is enacted by human or other actors who have an agency and inner life	Aesthetics Identities and capabilities of the people for whom it is intended Personal factors
The narrative depicts particular incidents or events	Functionality Customers
The depicted incidents or events occur in a causal sequence	Revenues and costs Value creation and capture Profit
The depicted incidents or events are set within an accepted context or frame of reference	Resources Opportunities Operating context
The depicted incidents or events express a specific point of view on the context or frame of reference	Practicalities Stakeholders
The depicted incidents or events then offer a new point of view on this context or frame of reference	Activities Products and services
The narrative expresses a consistent meaning that can both reflect reality and create it	Strategy Performance measures and processes
The narrative can become institutionalized as structures	Systems Boundaries Structure

Using Annotated Portfolios within a Narrative Framework
to Co-design Business Models in the Collaborative Economy

As well as sharing experience and knowledge through online forums, workers have created their own platforms in the collaborative economy. For example, ZicXoc Rides (2022) is an 'app-based booking system, designed to connect drivers with riders directly, enabling drivers to run a truly independent business, while offering passengers a better service for better value'. This alternative platform offers rideshare drivers greater power in the platform economy to create their identity as an individual driver-led business rather than take on the identity of an existing platform. Such alternative platforms could thus help to overcome the network effects that enable existing platform firms such as Uber to become dominant in a specific domain, in this case transport. This and other alternative platforms suggest that there is potential to create niche worker-led business models in the collaborative platform economy.

Business models are in themselves a representation of how an organization strategically manages value creation and capture, and particularly in the collaborative economy are implemented as computing systems. The design process developed in this chapter can thus be a starting point for implementing new business models in the collaborative platform economy. The design process can take place in these steps:

1. Identify a domain in the collaborative economy where a dominant platform reduces worker power (such as in transport).
2. Identify existing forums or other mechanisms that workers use to exchange knowledge and experience about working for that platform.
3. If there is not an existing forum to share experience, researchers can create one and encourage workers to join.
4. With the consent of participants, both their experiences as collaborative economy workers and their hopes for the future can be collected as ethnographic data.
5. This data is then annotated as a portfolio of potential business model designs using the business model narrative framework in Table 9.1.
6. These business model designs can then be offered to workers through the forum for discussion and further development.
7. Researchers could also offer in-person workshops to enable other participatory design methods to be used.
8. When a feasible new business model has emerged from this co-design process, researchers can then collaborate with workers and with software designers to code a new platform to implement the model.

The design process outlined above can contribute to ethnographic fieldwork research practice through offering a data gathering and analysis framework that focuses on how the experiences and hopes for the future of collaborative economy participants can be articulated as business models.

This chapter has developed an ethnographic design methodology that builds on critical design ethnography (Barab et al., 2004) to enable ethnographic data on workers in the collaborative platform economy to be a starting point for the design of new business models as an action research process. Action research aims to promote and document a change process (Checkland & Howell, 1998; Ellis & Kiely, 2000), linking with design research in its aim of bringing about a changed future (Foth & Axup, 2006; Dunne & Raby, 2013). In the collaborative platform economy, the potential changed future is one where worker-led business models can compete with existing dominant platforms through enabling collective action. An example of how this can happen is Ride Share Drivers United (2022), which started as a forum for ride share drivers on platforms such as Uber or Lyft to share experience and problems. Ride Share Drivers United then built on the experience of their members to establish its own ZicXoc Rides platform (2022) to provide a driver-led alternative business model. Another example is how drivers for Indonesia's Gojek ride sharing platform are using existing motorcycle base camps share experience and to take collective action, both in hacking the platform and influencing its development (Hao & Freischlad, 2022).

The ethnographic design methodology proposed in this chapter can enable ethnographic researchers to facilitate an action research / design process with collaborative economy workers. By eliciting new business models from analysis of ethnographic data on their experiences and wishes, researchers can then review potential new business model designs with workers in a process of performative practice (Wieland et al., 2017) to establish new platform business models.

As presented here, the methodology has the limitation of trying to derive new business models from ethnographic data on the problems workers have with existing collaborative platforms. Researchers will need to find ways of encouraging participants not only to focus on their present problems, but to consider creatively what their future in the collaborative platform economy could look like. Building on the methodology presented in this chapter to design potential futures through ethnography in the collaborative economy could be an area for future study.

Conclusion

This chapter first introduced the issue of worker power in the collaborative platform economy, where network effects have resulted in a tendency towards one dominant platform in each domain. These network effects reduce worker power in relation to platform firms, as they then cannot bargain with the firm by withdrawing their labour. Platform workers in the collaborative economy are using online forums to share issues that they experience, a form of collaboration that enables them to gain some collective power. A further development in gaining collective power is where workers have created alternative worker-led business models such as platform cooperatives that enable them to gain greater power in niche markets. However, most workers in the collaborative economy continue to gain their employment through dominant platform firms.

There is thus potential for researchers to create new business models through engagement with workers on existing platforms in the collaborative economy. An ethnographic methodology can enable researchers to use online forums or a collaborative platform to engage with these workers to not only find out about their existing situation but also discover their wishes and desires for the future. Design is about bringing about a desired future, implying a design methodology. This chapter proposes a design methodology for designing new business models in the collaborative economy, where annotated portfolio techniques and a business model narrative framework can enable researchers to articulate latent business model designs in ethnographic data. This articulation can then be a starting point for a business model co-design process with workers that builds on their particular expertise or geographical knowledge in challenging dominant platforms in niche areas of the collaborative economy.

Acknowledgements

This chapter is developed from a presentation to the Ethnographies of Collaborative Economi(es) Conference, Edinburgh, October 2019. I wish to acknowledge the helpful comments of two anonymous reviewers on the conference paper which helped strengthen the arguments made. The research that underpins this chapter was funded by the UK Engineering and Physical Sciences Research Council through the Digital Economy Programme (RCUK Grant EP/G037582/1), which supports the HighWire Centre for Doctoral Training.

References

Al-Debei, M.M. and Avison, D. 2010. 'Developing a unified framework of the business model concept.' *European Journal of Information Systems* 19(3): 359–376.

Alvesson, M. and Sköldberg, K. 2009 *Reflexive Methodology (Second Edition)*. London: SAGE.

Amit, R. and Zott, C. 2001. 'Value creation in e-business.' *Strategic Management Journal* 22(6–7): 493–520.

Araujo, L. and Easton, G. 2012 'Temporality in business networks: The role of narratives and management technologies.' *Industrial Marketing Management* 41(2): 312–318.

Baldwin, C.Y. and Woodard, C.J. 2009 'The architecture of platforms: A unified view.' *Platforms, Markets and Innovation*: 19–44. Cheltenham: Edward Elgar.

Barab, S.A., Thomas, M.K., Dodge, T., Squire, K. and Newell, M. 2004 'Critical design ethnography: Designing for change.' *Anthropology & Education Quarterly* 35(2): 254–268.

Bardzell, J. and Bardzell, S. 2013. 'What is 'critical' about critical design?.' In *Proceedings of the SIGCHI Conference on Human Factors in Computing Systems*, pp. 3297–3306.

Bellman, R., Clark, C.E. Malcolm, D.G., Craft, C.J. and Ricciardi, F.M. 1957 'On the construction of a multi-stage, multi-person business game.' *Operations Research* 5(4): 469–503.

Bonaccorsi, A. and Rossi, C. 2003 'Why open source software can succeed.' *Research Policy* 32(7): 1243–1258.

Bowen, S.J. 2007 'Crazy ideas or creative probes?: Presenting critical artefacts to stakeholders to develop innovative product ideas'. In *Proceedings of EAD07: Dancing with Disorder: Design, Discourse and Disaster.*

Bowers, J. 2012 'The logic of annotated portfolios: communicating the value of research through design.' In *Proceedings of the Designing Interactive Systems Conference*, pp. 68–77.

Bradley, G. 2014 'Social informatics and ethics: towards the good information and communication society.' *Critique, Social Media and the Information Society*, pp. 91–107.

Bruner, J. 1991 'The narrative construction of reality.' *Critical Inquiry* 18(1): 1–21.

Burke, K. 1945 *A Grammar of Motives.* (1945). New York: Prentice-Hall.

Cassell, C. and Johnson, P. 2006 'Action research: Explaining the diversity.' *Human Relations* 59(6): 783–814.

Checkland, P. and Howell, S. 1998 'Action Research: Its Nature and Validity.' Systemic Practice and Action Research 11(1): 9–21.

Chesbrough, H.W. 2006 *Open innovation: The new imperative for creating and profiting from technology.* Boston: Harvard Business Press.

DaSilva, C.M. and Trkman, P. 2014 'Business model: What it is and what it is not.' *Long Range Planning* 47(6): 379–389.

Doganova, L. and Eyquem-Renault, M. 2009 'What do business models do?: Innovation devices in technology entrepreneurship.' *Research Policy* 38(10): 1559–1570.

Downing, S. 2005 'The social construction of entrepreneurship: Narrative and dramatic processes in the coproduction of organizations and identities.' *Entrepreneurship Theory and Practice* 29(2): 185–204.

Dunne, A. and Raby, F. 2001 *Design Noir: The Secret Life of Electronic Objects.* (2001). Princeton Architectural Press.

Dunne, A. and Raby, F. 2013 *Speculative Everything: Design, Fiction, and Social Dreaming.* London: MIT Press.

Ellis, J.H.M. and Kiely, J.A. 2000 'Action inquiry strategies: taking stock and moving forward.' *Journal of Applied Management Studies* 9(1): 83–94.

Fabo, B., Karanovic, J. and Dukova, K. 2017 'In search of an adequate European policy response to the platform economy.' *Transfer: European Review of Labour and Research* 23(2): 163–175.

Flory, M. and Iglesias, O. 2010 'Once upon a time: The role of rhetoric and narratives in management research and practice.' *Journal of Organizational Change Management* 23(2): 113–119.

Foth, M. and Axup, J. 2006 'Participatory design and action research: Identical twins or synergetic pair?.' In *Expanding Boundaries in Design: Proceedings Ninth Participatory Design Conference (Vol 2)*, pp. 93–96.

Frankfurt Paper. 2016 *Frankfurt Paper on Platform-Based Work.* Retrieved 28 April 2022, from https://www.igmetall.de/download/docs_20161214 _Frankfurt_Paper_on_Platform_Based_Work_EN_b939ef89f7e5f3a639cd6a 1a930feffd8f55cecb.pdf

Fuchs, C. 2014 'Critique of the Political Economy of Informational Capitalism and Social Media.' *Critique, Social Media and the Information Society*, pp. 51–65.

Gabriel, Y. 2004 'The narrative veil: Truth and untruths in storytelling.' *Myths, Stories and Organizations: Premodern narratives for our times*, pp. 17–31.

Gaver, W. 2012 'What should we expect from research through design?.' In *Proceedings of the SIGCHI Conference on Human Factors in Computing Systems*, pp. 937–946.

Gaver, B. and Bowers, J. 2012 'Annotated Portfolios.' *Interactions* 19(4): 40–49.

George, G. and Bock, A.J. 2011 'The Business Model in Practice and its Implications for Entrepreneurship Research.' *Entrepreneurship Theory and Practice* 35(1): 83–111.

De Groen, W., Maselli, I. and Fabo, B. 2016 'The Digital Market for Local Services: A one-night stand for workers? An example from the on-demand economy.' *CEPS Special Report 133.* Retrieved 28 April 2022, from https:// www.ceps.eu/publications/digital-market-local-services-one-night-stand -workers-example-demand-economy

Guba, E.G. and Lincoln, Y.S. 1994 'Competing Paradigms in Qualitative Research.' *Handbook of Qualitative Research*, pp. 105–111. Thousand Oaks: Sage.

Hao, K. and Freischlad, N. 2022 'The gig workers fighting back against the algorithms' MIT Technology Review. Retrieved 24 April 2022 from https://www.technologyreview.com/2022/04/21/1050381/the-gig-workers -fighting-back-against-the-algorithms/

Hawkins, M.A. and Saleem, F.Z. 2012 'The omnipresent personal narrative: story formulation and the interplay among narratives.' *Journal of Organizational Change Management* 25(2): 204–219.

Howe, J. 2006 'The rise of crowdsourcing.' *Wired Magazine* 14, no. 6.

Irani, L.C. and Six Silberman, M. 2013 'Turkopticon: Interrupting Worker Invisibility in Amazon Mechanical Turk.' In *Proceedings of the SIGCHI Conference on Human Factors in Computing Systems*, pp. 611–620.

Jensen, A.B. 2013 'Do we need one business model definition?.' *Journal of Business Models* 1(1): 61–84.

Kenney, M. and Zysman, J. 2016 'The Rise of the Platform Economy.' *Issues in Science and Technology* 32(3): 61–69.

Kingsley, S.C., Gray, M.L. and Suri, S. 2019 'Accounting for Market Frictions and Power Asymmetries in Online Labor Markets.' *Policy & Internet* 7(4): 383–400.

Larner, J. 2019 *The Entrepreneur as System Architect: Designing narrative forms of open source business model.* PhD thesis, Lancaster University.

Lavori, P.W. and Dawson, D. 1998 'Developing and Comparing Treatment Strategies: An Annotated Portfolio of Designs.' *Psychopharmacology Bulletin* 34(1): 13–18.

Lee, M.K., Kusbit, D., Metsky, E. and Dabbish, L. 2015 'Working with machines: The impact of algorithmic and data-driven management on human workers.' In *Proceedings of the SIGCHI Conference on Human Factors in Computing Systems*, pp. 1603–1612.

Löwgren, J. 2013 'Annotated portfolios and other forms of intermediate-level knowledge.' *Interactions* 20(1): 30–34.

Magretta, J. 2002 'Why Business Models Matter.' *Harvard Business Review* May 2002: 86–92.

Morris, M.H., Schindehutte, M., Walton, J. and Allen, J. 2002 'The Ethical Context of Entrepreneurship: Proposing and Testing a Developmental Framework.' *Journal of Business Ethics* 40(4): 331–361.

Nelson, H.G. and Stolterman, E. 2014 *The Design Way.* London: MIT Press.

OECD. *OECD Employment Outlook 2017.* 2017 Paris: Organisation for Economic Co-operation and Development.

Osterwalder, A. and Pigneur, Y. 2010 *Business Model Generation.* Hoboken: John Wiley & Sons.

Perkmann, M. and Spicer, A. 2010 What are business models? Developing a theory of performative representations. *Research in the Sociology of Organization* 29: 265–275.

Pignot, E. 2021 'Who is pulling the strings in the platform economy? Accounting for the dark and unexpected sides of algorithmic control.' *Organization* 28(1): 208–235.

Ricoeur, P. 1979 'The function of fiction in shaping reality.' *Man and World* 12(2): 123–141.

Ride Share Drivers United. 2022 *Mission Statement.* Retrieved 28 April 2022 from https://ridesharedriversunited.com/mission-statement.

Ropo, A. and Höykinpuro, R. 2017 'Narrating organizational spaces.' *Journal of Organizational Change Management* 30(3): 357–366.

Rosner, D.K. 2018 *Critical Fabulations: Reworking the Methods and Margins of Design.* London: MIT Press.

Scholz, T. 2016 *Platform cooperativism: Challenging the corporate sharing economy.* New York: Rosa Luxemburg Foundation.

Shafer, S.M., Smith, J.H. and Linder, J.C. 2005 'The power of business models.' *Business Horizons* 48(3): 199–207.

Silverman, D. 2007 *A Very Short, Fairly Interesting and Reasonably Cheap Book about Qualitative Research.* London: Sage.

Simon, H.A. 1969 *The Sciences of the Artificial.* Cambridge, MA: MIT Press.

Solouki, Z. 2017 'The road not taken: narratives of action and organizational change.' *Journal of Organizational Change Management* 30(3): 334–343.

Stanford, N. 2007 *Guide to Organisation Design: Creating High-performing and Adaptable Enterprises.* London: Profile Books.

Stokes, K., Clarence, E Anderson, L., and Rinne, A. 2014 *Making Sense of the UK Collaborative Economy.* London: Nesta.

Taylor, M., Marsh, G., Nicol, D. and Broadbent, P. 2017 *Good work: The Taylor review of modern working practices.* London: Department for Business, Energy & Industrial Strategy.

Teece, D.J. 2010 'Business Models, Business Strategy and Innovation.' *Long Range Planning* 43(2–3): 172–194.

Turkopticon. 2022 *About.* Retrieved 28 April 2022 from https://turkopticon.net/

Vandaele, K. 2018 *Will trade unions survive in the platform economy.* Emerging patterns of platform workers' collective voice and representation in Europe Working Paper 2018.05. Brussels: European Trade Union Institute.

Vargo, S.L. and Lusch, R.F. 2016 'Institutions and axioms: an extension and update of service-dominant logic.' *Journal of the Academy of Marketing Science* 44(1): 15–23.

Wieland, H., Hartmann, N.N. and Vargo, S.L. 2017 'Business models as service strategy.' *Journal of the Academy of Marketing Science* 45(6): 925–943.

Woodcock, J. and Graham, M. 2020 *The Gig Economy: A Critical Introduction.* London: Polity Press.

Yancey, K.B. 1992 *Portfolios in the Writing Classroom: An Introduction.* Urbana, IL: National Council of Teachers of English.

ZicXoc Rides. 2022 *Welcome driver!* Retrieved 28 April 2022 from https://zicxoc.com/portal

Zimmerman, J. and Forlizzi, J. 2008 'The role of design artifacts in design theory construction.' *Artifact: Journal of Design Practice* 2(1): 41–45.

Zott, C. and Amit, R. 2010 'Business model design: An activity system perspective.' *Long Range Planning* 43(2–3): 216–226.

Zott, C., Amit, R. and Massa, L. 2011 'The Business Model: Recent Developments and Future Research.' *Journal of Management* 37(4): 1019–1042.

CHAPTER 10

Co-designing Collaborative Care Work through Ethnography

Mariacristina Sciannamblo
Sapienza University of Rome, Italy

Roberto Cibin
Institute of Sociology of the Czech Academy of Sciences
& Masaryk University, Czech Republic

Maurizio Teli
Aalborg University, Denmark

Abstract

This chapter focuses on instances of ethnographically informed design of collaborative systems as they emerge from two European projects aimed at developing sociotechnical infrastructures based on more just collaborative practices. We outline and discuss a number of issues related to the importance of language, the relationship between digital and physical public engagement, the caring role of community gatekeepers, and the reconfiguration of sociotechnical infrastructures during the Covid-19 pandemic. Our contribution aims to uncover how ethnographically informed design can support caring-based practices of social collaboration in different contexts.

How to cite this book chapter:
Sciannamblo, M., Cibin, R. and Teli, M. 2022. Co-designing Collaborative Care Work through Ethnography. In: Travlou, P. and Ciolfi, L. (eds.) *Ethnographies of Collaborative Economies across Europe: Understanding Sharing and Caring.* Pp. 193–209. London: Ubiquity Press. DOI: https://doi.org/10.5334/bct.k. License: CC BY-NC-ND

Introduction

The term 'sharing economy' has been used in recent years to label a variety of initiatives, business models, and forms of work and governance that have sparked increasing attention. Critical views are questioning some of the discourses that have characterized the promotion of commercial platforms – such as the rhetoric of socially driven initiatives – in order to unveil the mechanisms through which they reproduce forms of exploitation (Huws, 2015). In this respect, an increasing number of researchers and practitioners have called into question the rhetoric of 'sharing economy' in order to unpack the mechanisms by which such platforms exploit social collaboration (Avram et al., 2017). Such an approach has been inflected into several shapes and fields of social life: as digital platforms designed to foster autonomous social cooperation (e.g. Bassetti et al., 2019), as sustainable societal relations beyond the immediate design of objects or services (e.g. Light and Akama, 2014) or as technologies supporting workers in their daily conflicts with employers (e.g. Dombrowski et al., 2016; Irani & Silberman, 2013).

A common thread running through these examples is the adoption of a caring-based sharing approach (Belk, 2017) that relies on 'relational assets', rather than financial rewards, which, in turn, offer an ecology of situated mutually supportive systems. Light & Miskelly (2019) have recently explored this issue through the concept of 'meshing', that is the layering of local sharing initiatives, developing and maintaining local collective agency through their aggregation. The interesting aspect conveyed by the idea of 'meshing' is a commitment to designing beyond the sharing economy, in order to promote a different economic mechanism from trade as it focuses on generating caring interpersonal ties and a sense of community (Puig de la Bellacasa, 2017).

Communities have been located at the 'core of collaborative consumption' (Albinsson & Yasanthi Perera, 2012: 305) and, in general, communities are increasingly relevant characters in participatory design endeavours (DiSalvo et al., 2012). Cibin and colleagues (2019) underlined the complexity of this social construct and proposed the use of the concept of 'grassroots community' to overcome the distinction between 'communities of place' and 'communities of interest/practice'. In their perspective, grassroots communities are defined through their relation to other social actors – such as existing institutions or corporate actors – and they integrate various configurations of physical relations, shared interests and common practices.

Against this backdrop, this chapter focuses on instances of ethnographically informed design of collaborative systems as they emerge from two European projects that aim to develop sociotechnical infrastructures based on more livable collaborative practices. The first project, Commonfare, aimed at the co-design of a digital platform to respond to societal challenges relating to precariousness, low income, poverty, and unemployment. The second, Grassroots Radio, focused on the development and testing of a platform supporting the creation of community radios for media pluralism and community deliberation. We compare these two case studies to unpack the ways whereby the co-design of collaborative systems through ethnography can support grassroots communities in (1) elaborating and spreading forms of social collaboration starting from local needs and desires, and (2) constructing spaces for informed reflection and public deliberation within small and isolated areas. In doing so, we ask: what kind of issues emerge from the formation of collaborative subjects through ethnographically informed design interventions? How can ethnographically informed and caring-based design of platforms co-produce collaborative subjects?

By putting these two case studies in conversation with each other, in this chapter we will outline key issues that emerged from such ethnographically informed design interventions related to: (1) the importance of language, (2) the relationship between digital and physical public engagement, (3) the caring role of community gatekeepers, and (4) the reconfiguration of sociotechnical infrastructures during the Covid-19 pandemic. In this way, our contribution aims to uncover how ethnographically informed design can support caring-based practices of social collaboration in different contexts.

The chapter is organised as follows: section 2 provides a discussion of the concept of 'community' and the emergence of the notion of 'grassroots' community; section 3 gives an overview of the relationship between ethnography and participatory design (PD); section 4 offers a description of the two case studies alongside the illustration of ethnographic data; and section 5 delivers a discussion of the issues emerged related to language, the relationship between digital and physical commitment, the role of community gatekeepers and the impact of the Covid-19 pandemic.

Defining communities

The concept of 'community', real or imagined (Anderson, 2006), and its interaction with technology (Tufekci, 2014) is increasingly central in the debate about the design of collaborative systems (DiSalvo et al., 2012). The literature outlines two main kinds of this social construct. From one side, the *geographical community* or *community of place* (Cabitza et al., 2015; Fernback, 2007) describes a group of people defined by the sharing of physical boundaries. On the other side, the bonds connecting people in a *community of interests* concern the pursuit of a shared process or goal. These definitions of community are not exclusive; indeed, in many collaborative systems they may overlap, as in the case of a local section of an online marketplace, or the 'missed connections' category in Craigslist. A particular specification of community of interest is the concept of *community of practice* (Lave & Wenger, 1991): in this context, people not necessarily belonging to the same organization share similar activities in a framework that allows their evolution from peripheral participation to full membership.

Cibin and colleagues (2019) show how in the design of community-based technology for social innovation it is necessary to re-discuss the above mentioned 'space vs interest dichotomy': the groups of people engaged in these processes cannot be described merely as pure geographical communities or communities of practice, but are the result of the continuous interaction between these two aspects of their common life. To stress the analytical relevance of this interconnection, the concept of 'grassroots community', outlined by Kuznetsov and colleagues (2011), has been advanced as an 'often spontaneous, non-hierarchical and volunteer-driven' group of people engaged in shaping the context in which social activism takes place, often in contrast with 'the power structures implemented by traditional top-down organizations' (Kuznetsov et al., 2011: 2). For this reason, grassroots communities 'face unique challenges, risks and constraints, which shape designs and appropriations of interactive systems' (Kuznetsov et al., 2011: 2).

The adaptability of the concept of 'grassroots community' and its connection with the formation of collaborative subjects will become more evident in the next sections through the comparison of two European projects, one aimed to support communities beginning with their shared interests, and the other one involving communities starting with their geographical place.

(Re)positioning Ethnography within Participatory Design

As mentioned, the participatory design projects illustrated here have been navigated through ethnographic methods and sensibilities in order to map issues, outline diverse concerns and support the design-in-use processes. As Blomberg & Karasti (2013) point out, the relationship between ethnography and PD has been a topic of debate since anthropologically trained social scientists entered the field of design of information systems at the end of the 1980s (e.g., Suchman, 1987). All the different positions concerning the relationship between ethnography and PD point to the sensibilities, commitments and requirements of the two fields, which share practical limits and philosophical synergies. As Blomberg and colleagues (1993) suggest, the guiding principles of ethnography include studying phenomena in their everyday settings, developing a holistic view, providing a descriptive understanding, and assuming a members' perspective; on the other hand, PD's commitments start from mutual respect for the knowledge of different members (typically users and designers), the need to create opportunities for mutual learning, a joint negotiation of project goals, and the development of tools and processes to facilitate participation.

While early influential research programmes exploring the connections between ethnography and PD proposed a set of strategies to integrate the two agendas (i.e. by outlining their reflexive relation, by treating ethnography as a component of PD's methodology as well as to inform design requirements), more recent approaches suggest seeing ethnography as more than a method, and to embed ethnographic accounts in the design process itself. One of the latter approaches has been defined as 'co-realization' (Blomberg & Karasti 2013), which assumes that the full implications of a new sociotechnical system cannot be grasped by studying the context in the moment of the observation, but will only be revealed in and through the system's subsequent use. Such an assumption generates a reconfiguration of ethnography within design, which responds to a long-term and direct engagement between designers and users, as well as to the establishment of the locus of design activities in the site of use. Accordingly, the aim of co-realization is to erase the boundaries between design and use, and to engage researchers/designers in the site of use, for them to become members of the local setting as well as to get familiar with local members' knowledge and mundane competencies. This is even more relevant in multi-sited, longitudinal research projects such as Commonfare and Grassroots Radio, the two projects here analysed, which entailed both temporal and spatial scaling, thus an understanding and a practice of ethnography and design as ongoing achievements of participants over time and space.

The methods whereby such a practice of ethnography took shape in the two projects were design workshops organised with local members of the communities involved, associated with qualitative research techniques such as focus groups, interviews, participant observations and informal meetings and conversations. Moreover, these research activities have been actively shaped by pilot partners and intermediary organisations as part of the project consortium. In this chapter, we refer to such an arrangement of ethnographic activities in a design project as *ethnographically informed design*, a set of practices and activities organised in order to respond not only to the need of collecting useful inputs and requirements for design, but also (and mainly) to explore with local populations the meanings associated to the technologies at stake (a digital platform and a radio), as well as participants' experience and understanding of the social issues implicated in the projects (i.e. precariousness, poverty, media pluralism, community deliberation). In this respect, as Blomberg & Karasti (2013) argue, ethnography brings an important reflexive stance into design processes, 'for researchers and designers ... to be able to reflect upon not only activities in the design process, but also upon the multiple intentions and interpretations that build the analytic lens of the research or design project' (Mörtberg et al., 2010: 107).

Commonfare and Grassroots Radio

The case studies treated in this chapter pertain to two European projects – named Commonfare and Grassroots Radio – based on the collaborative design of ICT technologies for emancipatory aims.

The Commonfare project (2016–2019) was a European participatory design project seeking to respond to societal challenges within the European Union relating to precariousness, low income, poverty, and unemployment (Bassetti et al., 2018; Sciannamblo, Lyle & Teli, 2018). The project has been piloted in three countries – Croatia, Italy, The Netherlands – with people in precarious employment, freelancers, non-Western migrants, and unemployed youth. The goal of the project is to support communities beginning with their shared values (Bassetti et al., 2019) and interests on the improvement of accessibility of welfare state provisions as well as on grassroots welfare and care practices (Sciannamblo et al., 2021). The designed platform, called commonfare.net, includes storytelling, digital currency (Teli et al., 2018) and trust representation tools (Rough et al., 2019), and it is now managed by an association including some researchers belonging to the initial consortium.

Grassroots Radio (2017–2020) was a European civic innovation project. It was based on the use and development of RootIO (Csíkszentmihályi and Mukundane, 2015, 2016), a free/open hardware and software platform that supports the creation of a low-budget and low-power FM radio station (Dunbar-Hester, 2014), without the need for a studio. The aim of the project was the creation of local community radio stations to support citizen collective action (Cibin et al., 2020), community deliberation, media pluralism and the free flow of information in rural geographic communities across Europe, starting from the pilot countries of Ireland, Romania and Portugal (Robinson et al., 2021).

In what follows we address a number of issues emerging from research activities consisting of focus groups, semi-structured interviews, public meetings, informal conversations and participant observation, whose transcripts and elaborations have been collected in documents both internal and public. These issues pertain to the crucial role of language, physical interactions and commonality and the caring role of community gatekeepers, along with the reconfiguration of project activities due to the pandemic. These themes are relevant to the research questions investigated here in that they play a significant role in the articulation of the process of *meshing*, thus in the creation of caring interpersonal ties and a sense of community (Light & Miskelly, 2019; Belk, 2017) beyond the 'space vs interest' binarism (Cibin et al., 2019; Kuznetsov et al., 2011).

Handling sensitive issues: the importance of language

The Commonfare project aims at involving different populations – such as those in precarious employment, freelancers, non-Western migrants, unemployed youth – located in European countries – Croatia, Italy, The Netherlands – that present several differences, but also unexpected similarities, in terms of political and cultural history and economic and labour policies (Fumagalli et al., 2017). Institutional agencies usually define these individuals 'the poor' or people at risk of poverty or social exclusion (Eurostat, 2019). Such labelling reflects their subalternity and is often associated with a 'lack of' a fundamental property (such as human or financial capital), or a 'dependency on' something else (such as welfare provisions) (Bassetti et al., 2019; Sciannamblo & Teli, 2017). The use of such language informed the initial project research activities, including the distribution of a survey, interviews and focus groups with research participants, as well as self-reflexive exercises within consortium partners.

A key moment of these initial research activities was the self-evaluation focus group conducted with pilot partners in order to discuss their experience with the empirical research and, more generally, about the project. During this activity, many partners, as well as Croatian participants in a parallel focus group, expressed their dissatisfaction with the language used until then to describe the project, a vocabulary deeply marked by the rhetoric typical of institutional funding agencies like the EC. In particular, the preliminary results of the empirical work conducted in the pilot sites suggested that the participants were refusing the labels of 'poor' or 'socially excluded' employed by official statistics (Sciannamblo & Teli, 2017). Indeed, such a language turned out to be experienced as a form of stigma by participants. In early focus groups most people defined themselves *neither poor nor rich*, despite their economic difficulties (Bassetti et al., 2017). What emerged, indeed, is that the target populations refuse to feel themselves excluded, even if it is financially impossible for them to address unexpected expenses of a few hundred euros. Moreover, rather than passively accepting what was perceived as a paternalistic definition, several research participants responded by recognizing values such as social relations and wealth of time and knowledge, outside the capitalist logic of labour-wage.

These findings led the whole consortium to engage in significant discussions regarding the role of language in building sociotechnical projects, and to the consequent redefinition of the project communication, starting from its initial name: PIE News (see Figure 10.1). The consortium used the 'PIE' acronym pointing to the three social issues confronted (Poverty, lack of Income, and unEmployment), but participants rejected the word 'poverty' as a stigmatising

COMMONFARE AND PIE NEWS: TWO NAMES FOR ONE RESEARCH AND CO-DESIGN STORY

by pienews | Feb 21, 2017 | News

In mid January we, the Commonfare consortium, met in Zagreb to discuss what we did so far and to organize the next phases of participatory design activities. There, we worked with Croatian participants on the design of the platform and we engaged in collective discussions about the research activities that pilot partners are carrying out in Croatia, Italy, and The Netherlands. A pressing issue arising in several contexts concerned the language we adopt to describe the project, its goals, and its ethical and political aspirations.

Figure 10.1: News on the change of the name of the project on the project website.

label. As a result, the consortium decided to change the name of the project to 'Commonfare', which refers to the 'welfare of the Common' (Fumagalli & Lucarelli, 2015) as a concept inspiring the whole project since the very beginning (Sciannamblo et al., 2018).

The decision to change the name to Commonfare was aimed at emphasising the positive aspects of the project: chiefly, doing things together. This orientation has also informed the name of the platform – commonfare.net – as well as the claim it displays: 'We have so much in Common'.

The relationship between online and offline relations

The issue of language articulated in the previous paragraph can be considered an example of *meshing* (Light and Miskelly, 2019), namely an effort to build mutual commitment within communities located in different spaces by developing and maintaining local collective agency. Another issue in this regard concerns the need to generate participation towards the commonfare.net platform, one of the main objectives of the consortium since the beginning. To reach this goal, the consortium focused on the organisation of a significant number of events not only in the pilot countries, but also in neighbouring countries. This strategy has served to pursue both dissemination and design goals since the beginning of the project, as specified in the grant agreement: '24 PIE News Networking Events will be organised, to present the project's results (even preliminary ones) to invited stakeholders in order to keep on adapting PIE News focus and stay fixed on the most important challenges for the specific stakeholders' community, based on their feedback'. More specifically, these types of events pursue three main goals: (a) to promote the long-term sustainability of commonfare.net by strengthening the relationship with supporting organisations; (b) to generate content for and attract a diverse and Europe-wide group of participants to commonfare.net, and (c) to promote the concept of Commonfare and create spaces for networking among Commonfare good practices, thus informing and inspiring future actions that promote the idea of Commonfare.

The arrangement of 24 'networking events' was managed by pilot partners through a subcontracting formula, to directly engage like-minded organisations in the activities of the project and promote the formation of a variety of publics around the platform. Moreover, the organisation of these events has been linked to the articulation of the co-design activities in order to make the project itself a 'matter of concern'.

The organisation of networking events in different geographical areas has proved to be a successful strategy able to aggregate and meet different needs. This has been exemplified in the final report dedicated to the account of the events.

> As we progressed through our research and design phase through a participatory approach, it became clear that certain communities, those most affected by the 'PIE conditions' of poverty, lack of income and

unemployment, were often least informed and least mobilised to act. For example, in Croatia, a country with one of the highest rates of youth precarity, PIE focus groups uncovered that the majority of youth were not even familiar with the concept of 'precarity', and few had heard of a 'universal basic income'. As a result, our target audiences grew ever larger over the project, as the unmet need for informing, organising and mobilising collective action to preserve the commons is an effort for all citizens. (Pleic et al., 2019)

Indeed, in pursuing this activity pilot partners recognized that their respective countries and regions, and their own unique identities as organisations, required different strategies. The Basic Income Network in Italy decided to foster an early and continuous dialogue with institutional actors. The Center for Peace Studies in Croatia pursued collaboration with NGOs, bottom-up citizen initiatives and movements committed to addressing systemic problems of poverty, inequality and insecurity through bottom-up actions. Museu da Crise in The Netherlands decided to focus more heavily on the individuals directly affected by precariousness via artistic provocation. Dyne organised events focused on Commoncoin and commonfare.net to raise awareness of alternative ways of economic and social organisation. Through the interactive game 'Le Grand Jeu', Dyne involved communities in thinking about how democracy, money and self-organisation are intertwined. In all those cases, the goal was to start conversations and to break the mould of social habits and norms.

Grassroots care work through ethnography

One of the Grassroots Radio project's primary goals was the creation of community radio stations that could represent the voice of all the communities' members, and also of those groups of people usually marginalised. The involvement of a sufficient number of volunteers to take over the activities related to the management of the radio stations and creating content was one of the main challenges of the project. Initially, this activity turned out to be quite difficult for the project partners when dealing with the inhabitants of a small rural village in Romania. The first encounters with members of this community seemed to indicate a lack of interest in the project due to, among other things, a loss of confidence in voluntary work after the forced experiences during the communist regime. The involvement of Anna, a nurse and community assistant who offers health and social support by meeting people in the village, going house to house, represented the turning point in this situation. After participating in an interview for the station, she expressed interest in the project and quickly started to produce contents, as this account from one of the partners working in the field describes:

So I went there, and I showed how we work on WhatsApp with the volunteers in [the other radio station], and we chose a recording software, and we chose this from Google Play. She [Anna] put it on her phone, I left, and within one hour she was already sending some announcements, and then everything blew up, everything went from there. She kept on sending interviews. It is like she was born to do radio work. (project partner)

Soon, Anna became one of the radio station's points of reference for the community, doing activities that have many similarities with those practised by ethnographers. The possibility of meeting different people every day allowed her to collect memories, old songs, greetings, cooking recipes and announcements to be broadcast by the station. In addition, Anna asked the interviewees, often older people, to share old photos they kept in their drawers.

I receive messages asking me to find out if a certain person in an old photo on display is not their grandmother or father because they have no picture with them, others ask me to send them a certain picture in the message because there is a relative in it, and they have no picture with that person, many thanks for seeing dear people who are no more here today or send me photos with the request to display them in the memory of the relative who was originally from the village. (Anna)

Together with images of the community's places, these photographs have become part of the content published on the Facebook page of the radio station, also created by Anna. These contents soon became the stimulus to unite the past with the present of the community and the people living in the village with the numerous emigrants. They have found on the Facebook page a meeting point with their roots. It is interesting to note that while the village has about 600 inhabitants, the Facebook page has almost 3000 followers.

At the same time, Anna took advantage of the radio station to face issues concerning her work, as when the Covid-19 pandemic created restrictions on visiting people's homes:

For me, as a community nurse, radio was the means by which I could continue health education actions for the community, broadcasting Health Pills [the name of her radio programme] in the context of the pandemic when I am not allowed to carry out such actions with people gathering indoors. (Anna)

Anna's ongoing networking within the community has also enabled her to engage new volunteers for the station among residents and diaspora members.

Care in a time of pandemic: the role of community radio

Living in a geographically remote island can be very problematic in times of emergency, when people need medical support and most daily activities are disrupted. This was the case during the Covid-19 pandemic, which arrived at the beginning of 2020, when the Grassroots Radio was approaching its last year of project activities. The outbreak of SARS-COV-2 inevitably affected the activities of the radio stations and their relationships with community members. In Ireland, public health guidelines ruled that only permanent residents could stay on an island, and restrictions were in place for travelling to the island. This resulted in a number of regular radio presenters and collaborators from the mainland not being able to travel to the islands to provide technical and content-making support. In Romania, the restrictions imposed by the pandemic forced community organisations to reduce their travel to the project sites.

Against this backdrop, the community radio stations showed a remarkable, and sometimes unexpected, capacity to provide organisational, informational and psychological support. For example, the community of the Irish Island was quite careful about adopting measures and behaviours to protect local inhabitants, especially the most vulnerable. Besides reinforcing distancing measures, the Irish island community used the radio to lift the spirit of residents and helped to supplement daily activities. For example, the radio has been used to broadcast the Sunday Mass as the local priest, who is over 70, was forced to cocoon for safety reasons. He agreed to record the mass from home via his phone and the radio was able to broadcast this online and on FM. This allowed those unable to attend the church service due to distance, illness or old age to participate in this community activity. The hospital in the Irish island ensures patients can listen to mass each Sunday on the local community stations. One respondent to a recent listener feedback survey stated, 'Mass during Covid-19 was like a godsend' and another stated that they listened to the radio to get mass but ended up listening to the whole Sunday programme.

Moreover, the radio has been used to support educational activities. Schools in Ireland were shut down on 12 March 2020. The Irish Island's school principal approached the local community radio for support to broadcast to the student body and to help maintain momentum for students who could no longer attend school, and were being taught via internet packages. School assemblies took place at 8.55 every day during this period and the intention was to reinforce the school motto 'Ní Neart go Cur le Chéile' (Strength in Unity), to help keep everyone together, support all the students and help parents through these challenging times. The principal reported that having the assembly online helped motivate students, providing structure before daily online instruction during the pandemic.

In Romania, Radio Civic, the community radio built through the project, organised several initiatives related to Covid-19. Among these was an information campaign to keep the two local communities involved in the project informed with reliable and official sources. The local radio has also devoted efforts to provide the communities with reliable medical advice shared by doctors and nurses in the 'Health Pills' (*masuri de preventie*) programmes. Moreover, as the level of negative news was rising, Radio Civic attempted to also communicate positive information as much as possible. It therefore created a news programme called 'Vesti Bune' (Good News), where an actor volunteered to read good news. The local radio also kept bringing the voices of the locals in the programmes, so that they could tell their stories of coping with the isolation and pandemic restrictions.

Another relevant aspect that emerged from the deployment of the radio during the lockdown restrictions was the need to cope with isolation and social distancing from people living away, as one of the Irish listeners told in an online survey:

> During the lockdown, I looked forward to tuning in every Sunday. It gave me a great sense of comfort hearing my own people, their accents and easy chatter and talking about the Beara community and its diaspora. I felt included in such strange times. I really appreciate all their efforts.

The deployment and use of the radio during the first weeks of the pandemic in geographically remote sites proved that getting reliable information and maintaining and reinforcing collective and educational activities – such as school and the mass – are important elements to consider to maintain and repair caring interpersonal ties and a sense of community. This was all the more true when the geographical isolation was exacerbated by physical and social distancing as a consequence of the pandemic. In this situation, the presence of a community radio can alleviate the void and isolation, as the expatriate listener pointed out.

Discussion

We started this chapter by raising two related research questions – concerning issues emerging from the formation of collaborative subjects through ethnographically informed design interventions, and how caring-based design of platforms can co-produce collaborative subjects. We have discussed examples related to two projects, Commonfare and Grassroots Radio, that – although addressing communities beginning with their interests (Commonfare) or their location (Grassroots Radio) – both show how communities can be thought as integrating interests and place, being therefore definable as grassroots communities.

Although the projects shared a similar perspective and organisation of work, they differed substantially, not only in terms of goals, locations, target populations and technologies, but also in terms of the relation with the grassroots communities involved. If in Commonfare the goal had been to co-design and implement technologies supporting already existing grassroots communities engaging in caring practices in their mutual recognition and in building networks, in Grassroots Radio the aim was to favour the formation of bonds and ties in geographical communities through the design process. In this way, we can see how the different communities involved approached the issue of *language*: in the case of Commonfare, already existing collaborative subjects rejected the label imposed on them by the project and by the official statistical label, forcing the designers to reshape the language; in Grassroots Radio the use of spoken language in the radio programme triggered a process of bonding, entailing also the visual language of old pictures and the telling of stories about the ancestors of the actual residents. Equally, the dimension of *physical interaction* is different: in Commonfare physical events and interactions were crucial for the adoption and use of digital technologies; in Grassroots Radio the limitation of physical interactions related to the diffusion of SARS-COV-2 showed how the radio stations could be an infrastructure to maintain a sense of community and collective ownership of a shared heritage (Bidwell, 2016).

Finally, the issue of *commonality* can be stressed: how does one foster a sense of collective ownership and communal resource? In Commonfare, the refusal of the initial project name suggested a further step to undertake in order to achieve a sense of commonality; in Grassroots Radio, commonality has been built by active intermediaries, from Anna to the local priest, who have turned the design project into daily life experiences that are familiar to the members of the community and that have contributed to strengthening the bonds between people, even for those no longer living within geographical boundaries. These relational assets are the basis for the emergence and stabilisation of a grassroots community.

These emerging issues – *language, physical interaction*, and *commonality* – let us reflect on how design can contribute to the emergence of collaborative subjects, that is to trigger and recognize potential controversies (such as the potential stigmatisation in Commonfare), and to support the emergence of dense interactions, face to face or remotely, allowing people to tackle these potential controversies. Moreover, the networking events in Commonfare and the use of radios during the Covid-related lockdowns in Grassroots Radio, together with the relations cultivated in both cases, suggest that platform design not only should aim at designing the digital platform, but also should focus on *meshing* the physical infrastructure for the creation of caring interpersonal ties and a sense of community (Light & Miskelly, 2019; Belk, 2017).

Conclusion

In this chapter, we have focused on instances of ethnographically informed design of collaborative systems as they emerge from two European projects that aim to develop sociotechnical infrastructures based on more than just collaborative practices. In particular, as we referred to ethnographically informed design as a set of practices and activities organised in order to respond to the need not only to collect useful inputs and requirements for design, but also (and mainly) to explore with local populations the meanings associated with the technologies at stake, as well as participants' experience and understanding of the social issues implicated in the different design projects, we could see the importance of language, the relationship between digital and physical public engagement, the caring role of community gatekeepers, and the reconfiguration of sociotechnical infrastructures during the Covid-19 pandemic.

More specifically, when engaging with language, physical interactions and commonality, designers could benefit from considering ethnographically informed design interventions supporting practices and ethics of care (Belk, 2017; Puig de la Bellacasa, 2017), not so much as means to collect inputs to be translated into programming languages, but rather as ways of creating the conditions of *meshing* (that is, layering local interactions and agency) based on discussions about taken-for-granted labels, controversies and local interests. That opens up a set of new research directions, which extend beyond the projects we have presented. For example, Commonfare and Grassroots Radio have highlighted the importance of having flexibility and being reflexive, one of the key elements of ethnography, which pose questions when one is planning a design project. Is flexibility accommodated? Is reflexivity an explicit part of the approach?

Another example comes from the concept of 'meshing', as it questions design projects in relation to their capacity to fit the existing relational assets and to position design activities and outputs in relation to the different layers. How can projects be planned and conducted in a way that relates meaningfully to the existing, and evolving, layers of local interactions and agency? In summary, we think our projects have reiterated the importance of organising design projects around ethnography and meshing and that, with the focus on language, physical interaction and commonality, they have highlighted where to begin in structuring an approach to organise meshing-oriented design projects.

References

Albinsson, P.A. and Yasanthi Perera, B. 2012. 'Alternative Marketplaces in the 21st Century: Building Community through Sharing Events.' *Journal of Consumer Behaviour* 11(4): 303–15.

Anderson, B. 2006 *Imagined Communities: Reflections on the Origin and Spread of Nationalism*. Revised edition. London ; New York: Verso Books.

Atkinson, P. 2007 *Ethnography : Principles in Practice*. Routledge. https://doi.org/10.4324/9780203944769.

Avram, G., Hee-jeong Choi, J., De Paoli, S., Light, A., Lyle, P. and Teli, M. 2017 'Collaborative Economies: From Sharing to Caring.' In *Proceedings of the 8th International Conference on Communities and Technologies*, 305–7. C&T '17. New York, NY, USA: ACM. https://doi.org/10.1145/3083671.3083712.

Avram, G., Hee-jeong Choi, J., De Paoli, S., Light, A., Lyle, P. and Teli, M. 2019. 'Repositioning CoDesign in the Age of Platform Capitalism: From Sharing to Caring.' *CoDesign* 15(3): 185–91. https://doi.org/10.1080/15710882.2019.1638063.

Bassetti, C., Sciannamblo, M., Lyle, P., Teli, M., De Paoli, S. and De Angeli, A. 2019 'Co-Designing for Common Values: Creating Hybrid Spaces to Nurture Autonomous Cooperation.' *CoDesign* 15(3): 256–71.

Bassetti, C., Botto, F. and Teli, M. 2018 'The Commonfare Project. Designing to Support Grassroots Welfare Initiatives'. *DIGITCULT*, 1(3). https://digitcult.lim.di.unimi.it/index.php/dc/article/view/69. DOI: https://doi.org/10.4399/97888255159095

Belk, R. 2017 'Sharing without Caring.' *Cambridge Journal of Regions, Economy and Society* 10(2): 249–61. https://doi.org/10.1093/cjres/rsw045.

Bidwell, N.J. 2016. 'Moving the centre to design social media in rural Africa'. *AI & Soc* 31, 51–77. https://doi.org/10.1007/s00146-014-0564-5

Blomberg, J. and Karasti, H. 2013 'Ethnography: Positioning ethnography within participatory design'. In *Routledge international handbook of participatory design*, edited by Jesper Simonsen and Toni Robertson, 106–136. New York: Routledge.

Blomberg, J., Giacomi, J., Mosher, A. and Swenton-Wall, P. 1993 'Ethnographic field methods and their relation to design'. In *Participatory Design: Perspectives on Systems Design*, edited by Douglas Schuler and Aki Namioka, 123–55. Hillsdale, NJ: Lawrence Erlbaum Associates.

Cabitza, F., Simone, C. and Cornetta, D. 2015 'Sensitizing Concepts for the next Community-Oriented Technologies: Shifting Focus from Social Networking to Convivial Artifacts.' *The Journal of Community Informatics* 11. http://ci-journal.net/index.php/ciej/article/view/1155.

Cibin, R., Robinson, S., Scott, K.M., Sousa, D., Žišt, P., Maye, L., Sciannamblo, M., Ashby, S., Csíkszentmihályi, C., Pantidi, N. and Teli, M. 2020 'Co-designing convivial tools to support participation in community radio'. *Radio Journal: International Studies in Broadcast & Audio Media* 18(1): 43–61.

Cibin, R., Teli, M. and Robinson, S. 2019 'Institutioning and Community Radio. A Comparative Perspective.' In *Proceedings of the 9th International Conference on Communities & Technologies-Transforming Communities*, 143–54. ACM.

Conference, R.T.D., Csíkszentmihályi, C. and Mukundane, J. 2019 'RTD2015 19 RootIO – Platform Design for Civic Media.' https://doi.org /10.6084/m9.figshare.1328001.v1.

Csíkszentmihályi, C. and Mukundane, J. 2016 'RootIO: ICT+ Telephony for Grassroots Radio.' In *2016 IST-Africa Week Conference*, 1–13. IEEE.

Di Salvo, C., Clement, A. and Pipek, V. 2012 'Communities: Participatory Design for, with and by Communities.' In *Routledge International Handbook of Participatory Design*, 202–30. Routledge.

Dombrowski, L., Harmon, E. and Fox, S. 2016 'Social Justice-Oriented Interaction Design: Outlining Key Design Strategies and Commitments.' In *Proceedings of the 2016 ACM Conference on Designing Interactive Systems*, 656–71. DIS '16. New York, NY, USA: ACM. https://doi.org /10.1145/2901790.2901861.

Dunbar-Hester, C. 2014 *Low power to the people: Pirates, protest, and politics in FM radio activism*. MIT Press.

Eurostat. 'People at Risk of Poverty or Social Exclusion – Statistics Explained.' Accessed July 31, 2019. https://ec.europa.eu/eurostat/statistics-explained /index.php/People_at_risk_of_poverty_or_social_exclusion

Fernback, J. 2007 'Beyond the Diluted Community Concept: A Symbolic Interactionist Perspective on Online Social Relations.' *New Media & Society* 9(1): 49–69. https://doi.org/10.1177/1461444807072417.

Fumagalli, A. and Lucarelli, S. 2015 'Finance, Austerity and Commonfare.' *Theory, Culture & Society* 32(7–8): 51–65.

Fumagalli, A., Serino, R., Gobetti, S., Morini, C., Allegri, G., Paes Leão, D., Willemsen, M. et al. 2017 'PIE News – Research Report.' *Deliverable D2.1 Produced for the PIE News Project*. http://pieproject.eu/wp-content /uploads/2017/03/PIE_D2.1.pdf.

Huws, U. 2015 'ICapitalism and the Cybertariat: Contradictions of the Digital Economy.' *Monthly Review* 66(8): 42.

Irani, L.C. and Silberman, M. 2013 'Turkopticon: Interrupting Worker Invisibility in Amazon Mechanical Turk.' In *Proceedings of the SIGCHI Conference on Human Factors in Computing Systems*, 611–20. ACM.

Ismail, A., Karusala, N. and Kumar, N. 2018 'Bridging Disconnected Knowledges for Community Health.' *Proc. ACM Hum.-Comput. Interact.* 2 (CSCW): 75:1–75:27. https://doi.org/10.1145/3274344.

Kuznetsov, S., Odom, W., Moulder, V., DiSalvo, C., Hirsch, T., Wakkary, R. and Paulos, E. 2011 'HCI, Politics and the City: Engaging with Urban Grassroots Movements for Reflection and Action.' In *CHI'11 Extended Abstracts on Human Factors in Computing Systems*, 2409–12. ACM.

Lave, J. and Wenger, E. 1991 *Situated Learning: Legitimate Peripheral Participation*. Cambridge university press.

Light, A. and Akama, Y. 2014 'Structuring Future Social Relations: The Politics of Care in Participatory Practice.' In *Proceedings of the 13th Participatory Design Conference: Research Papers-Volume 1*, 151–60. ACM.

Light, A. and Miskelly, C. 2019 'Platform of Platforms: Meshing Networks, Scales and Values for a Local Sustainable Sharing Economy.' https://doi.org/10.1007/s10606-019-09352-1.

Mörtberg, C., Bratteteig, T., Wagner, I., Stuedahl, D. and Morrison, A. 2010 'Methods that matter in digital design research'. In Exploring Digital Design: MultiDisciplinary Design Practices, edited by Ina Wagner, Tone Bratteteig and Dagny Stuedahl, 105–46. London: Springer-Verlag.

Puig de la Bellacasa, M. 2017 *Matters of Care. Speculative Ethics in More Than Human Worlds*. University of Minessota Press.

Robinson, S., Bidwell, N.J., Cibin, R., Linehan, C., Maye, L., McCarthy, J., Pantidi, N. and Teli, M. 2021 (in press). 'Islandness and HCI'. *Transactions on Computer-Human Interaction, Rural Islandness as a lens for (Rural) HCI*, 28(3) (in press 2021): 1–28.

Rough, D., De Paoli, S. and Botto, F. 2019 'Supporting social innovation through visualisations of community interactions'. *Proceedings of the 9th International Conference on Communities & Technologies-Transforming Communities.*

Sciannamblo, M., Cohn, M.L., Lyle, P. and Teli, M. 2021 'Caring and Commoning as Cooperative Work: A Case Study in Europe'. *Proceedings of the ACM on Human-Computer Interaction CSCW1* 5: 1–26. DOI: https://doi.org/10.1145/3449200

Sciannamblo, M., Lyle, P. and Teli, M. 2018 'Fostering Commonfare. Entanglements Between Participatory Design and Feminism.' *Proceedings of DRS Design Research Society Conference*, 2. Limerick, Ireland: University of Limerick. https://doi.org/10.21606/drs.2018.557.

Sciannamblo, M. and Teli, M. 2017 'Undoing the Ontology of the Poor: A Participatory Design Project.' 2017. http://www.4sonline.org/blog/post/undoing_the_ontology_of_the_poor_a_participatory_design_project

Suchman, L. 1987 *Plans and Situated Actions: The Problem of Human–Machine Communication*. Cambridge: Cambridge University Press.

Teli, M., Lyle, P. and Sciannamblo, M. 2018 'Institutioning the common: the case of commonfare'. *Proceedings of the 15th Participatory Design Conference: Full Papers-Volume 1.*

Tufekci, Z. 2014 'The Medium and the Movement: Digital Tools, Social Movement Politics, and the End of the Free Rider Problem.' *Policy & Internet* 6(2): 202–8. https://doi.org/10.1002/1944-2866.POI362

PART 4

Ethnographies of Spaces
for Collaborative Economies

CHAPTER 11

Ethnography of True Sharing Initiatives in Brno

Alena Rýparová
Masaryk University, Czech Republic

Abstract

The sharing economy is a topic of the current discussion. Platforms like Airbnb or Uber are often criticized for exploiting the positive connotations of the word 'sharing' to achieve financial gain. On the other hand, sharing has always been present in society, especially in families or closely related communities, where it was a fundamental form of asset redistribution. There is a third form of sharing that is often neglected. In this chapter, I focus on true sharing in the form of initiatives that are motivated by social, environmental, or other goals. I will present several sharing initiatives that operate in Brno, the second largest city in the Czech Republic. I will mainly focus on relational geography to show how communities are able to access resources and further control their flow through networks. Based on semi-structured interviews and ethnographic fieldwork, I will clarify how initiatives of true sharing manage and redistribute resources such as food, clothes, books, and houseplants. Resource management can highlight the materiality of true sharing as social practice, and also the transformational potential of this type of sharing. I place the whole theme in the broader context of a diversified and community-based economy as presented by Gibson-Graham (2006).

How to cite this book chapter:
Rýparová, A. 2022. Ethnography of True Sharing Initiatives in Brno. In: Travlou, P. and Ciolfi, L. (eds.) *Ethnographies of Collaborative Economies across Europe: Understanding Sharing and Caring.* Pp. 213–228. London: Ubiquity Press. DOI: https://doi.org /10.5334/bct.l. License: CC BY-NC-ND

The Transformational Potential of True Sharing

Sharing is common in different cultures and historical stages of human-kind (Sahlins, 1972; Belk, 2007; Hyde, 2012; Gurven and Jaeggi, 2015). People share with family and friends. They share for free, with the purpose to strengthen interpersonal ties and to help loved ones. Sharing is associated with positive connotations, relationships, and care. In recent years, sharing has been closely linked to the concept of a sharing economy. Some authors (Botsman and Rogers, 2011; Plewnia and Guenther, 2018) see the sharing economy in a positive light as efficient use of resources, new opportunities for extra income, and leaving the consumer lifestyle, where people do not need to own things but need only temporary access. However, many others (Belk, 2014a; Richardson, 2015; Martin, 2016; Murillo et al., 2017) point out that a sharing economy has nothing to do with sharing: its main goal is financial gain. The activities of a sharing economy are often problematic from a legal or social point of view and can lead to hyperconsumerism when people consume in the name of sharing (with the feeling that they are acting ecologically and economically favourably) more things and services than they normally use (Richardson, 2015).

The fundamental problem is in the ambiguous definition of the concept of sharing. In particular, the relationship between sharing and profit is problematic in defining and distinguishing between 'sharing' and the 'sharing economy'. Belk (2010) defines gifts, sharing, and market exchange based on ideal prototypes of these activities, like sharing body and milk between a mother and her child. He emphasizes the proximity of gifts and sharing and, on the other hand, shows a relatively clear line between these two types of resource distribution and market exchange. According to Belk, sharing does not include reciprocity and financial compensation. However, other authors (see Table 11.1) also include in the sharing or sharing economy activities that may contain this compensation, or it may even be crucial for the given activity.

A broad or, on the contrary, very narrow concept of sharing then creates misunderstandings in the academic discussion. Some scholars use 'sharing economy' as an umbrella term for different forms of behaviour and business models (Heinrichs, 2013; Curtis and Lehner, 2019). Following various definitions of sharing, I will use 'sharing economy' to describe profit-oriented activities (e.g. Airbnb, Uber). On the other side of the sharing axis is non-profit sharing within the family, which is of particular interest to anthropologists and sociologists. However, there is a third type of sharing: so-called true sharing (Geiger et al., 2018) combines elements from a profitable sharing economy and non-profit sharing within the family and stands between them (see Fig. 11.1). It is a sharing that takes place between people who are not connected by family

Table 11.1: Different approaches of authors to defining sharing according to profitability and non-profitability.

For-profit sharing	Non-profit sharing	Author
Pseudosharing	Sharing	Belk, 2014a, 2014b
Sharing economy		Richardson, 2015; Davies et al., 2017; Michelini et al., 2018
Economic sharing	Social sharing	Plewnia and Guenther, 2018
Sharing economy	True sharing	Geiger et al., 2018

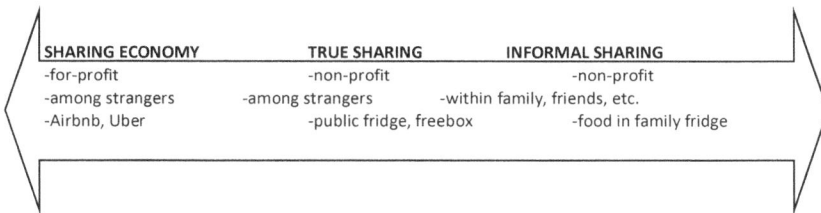

SHARING ECONOMY	TRUE SHARING	INFORMAL SHARING
-for-profit	-non-profit	-non-profit
-among strangers	-among strangers	-within family, friends, etc.
-Airbnb, Uber	-public fridge, freebox	-food in family fridge

Figure 11.1: Brief characteristics of three types of sharing.

or friendly ties, but at the same time they share not for profit but for different motivations (social, environmental, etc.).

Ede (2014) and Davies et al. (2017) point out that more important than the profitability of activities is their transformational nature. Transactional activities seek to make efficient use of resources in the current system and are often profit-oriented (but financial transactions may not always be present). On the contrary, transformational activities change the power scheme and social ties in the sharing network. Joint control and decision-making on resources within the community are strengthened. From this point of view, it is important to explore more about true sharing activities, because they have strong transformational potential. They extend the capacity of mutual care and relationships from family and friends to strangers. They use and mediate resources that would not otherwise be available to users of sharing. In terms of the Gibson-Graham (2006, 2008) concept, non-profit, and therefore true sharing, is below the level of attention of economic science, although it completes the diversity of economic activities.

I will present several true sharing initiatives that operate in Brno, the second largest city in Czechia. I will use the relational geography approach to show how communities are able to access resources and further control their flow through networks (Radil and Walther, 2019). As I showed in my previous work (Rýparová, 2020), true sharing initiatives create several types of networks, thanks to which initiatives are connected by hierarchical links to authorities, organizations or companies that support them and provide them with some resources. Furthermore, the initiatives are interconnected by friendly and collegial relations. The last type of networking is in the form of links to the local community and users of sharing. The resources that are managed in these networks show how diverse economies (Gibson-Graham, 2008) manifest themselves in practice, how they are 'made material' (Holmes, 2018), and to what extent this is a transformational activity (Ede, 2014).

Methods

During 2018, I conducted semi-structured interviews with representatives of nine initiatives, listed in Table 11.2. I selected these initiatives and their representatives based on a survey of the internet, the news media, or personal knowledge of some of the activities.

The interviews lasted an average of about an hour; I then rewrote the recordings with the consent of the communication partners and continued working with the text. A thematic and open analysis of the text was performed through the Atlas.ti program. The interviews were supplemented by knowledge gained

Table 11.2: Initiatives in this study.

Name	Name translation	Abbreviation used below
Food not Bombs Brno	Food not Bombs Brno	FNB Brno
Freebox na Fakultě Sociálních studií Masarykovy univerzity	Freebox at the Faculty of Social Studies of Masaryk University	Freebox at FSS MU
Freebox u Tří ocásků	Freebox at Tři ocásci	Freebox at Tři ocásci
Freeshop Nadačního fondu studentů Filosofické fakulty Masarykovy univerzity	Freeshop of the Endowment Fund of Students of the Faculty of Arts of Masaryk University	Freeshop EFS FA MU
Květena	Flora	Flora
Literární lavičky	Literary benches	Literary benches
Paběrkování po Brněnsku	Gleaning in the Brno region	Gleaning in the Brno region
Potravinová banka pro Brno a Jihomoravský kraj	Foodbank for Brno and South Moravian Region	Foodbank for Brno and SMR
Veřejné lednice Brno	Brno Public Fridges	Brno Public Fridges

during ethnographic research–participatory observation, which took place from January to June 2019. I joined as a volunteer the cooking and food distribution activities organized by Food not Bombs Brno. Ethnographic research was chosen because it allows a deeper understanding of how the initiative works, what people are involved in sharing and what their motivations are. The FNB group seemed to be the most suitable, as it is one of the few initiatives that allow a larger number of people to be involved in their activities on the part of the organizers. As part of handing out food, I had the opportunity to talk to several users of the initiative, i.e. recipients of food distributed. At the same time, the FNB Brno initiative is partly connected with the Freefood Brno initiative, whose activities I was able to learn more about, although I did not interview its representative. I recorded the experience and information from the research in a field diary and also as notes on a dictaphone. Due to the anonymization that some communication partners wanted, I will use pseudonyms below.

Brno was chosen for the research because it involves several activities of true sharing. It is the second largest city in Czechia. There are several universities and colleges, international companies, etc. A certain cosmopolitan and at the same time student character of the city is favourable for the establishment and development of true sharing initiatives. There is the possibility of inspiration from abroad, but also the potential for the development of local activities.

Resource Management in True Sharing Networks

I identified 17 initiatives of true sharing in Brno. However, this is a dynamic phenomenon and some of the initiatives disappeared during the research (e.g. Brno Public Wardrobe, Sharepoint). Some are open all year round, others only occasionally. Some of the initiatives have a local character (Freeshop EFS FA MU), while others follow national or even international activities (FNB Brno). Some initiatives operate as volunteer informal groups, or are sponsored by an organization (e.g. Literary Benches are organized by the Jiří Mahen Library). Some activities have well-defined rules on how people can share, while others leave the responsibility largely to the users themselves. From these few characteristics, a great variety of true sharing activities emerges. This also leads to different approaches of individual initiatives to obtaining, controlling and redistributing resources.

The resources in the case of true sharing initiatives are food, clothing, books, household equipment, flowers, seeds, etc., which their original owner would no longer use and would probably end up as waste. Thanks to sharing, these resources become reused and again valuable. Initiatives thus purposefully or unintentionally follow the current debate on the need for sustainable use of resources and the ideas of waste minimization, such as zero waste, reusing and recycling. In the following pages, we focus on the process of obtaining the resources by the initiatives, their management, logistics, and the actual sharing. We will also state to whom community resources travel and what will happen to them at the end of this process.

Obtaining resources by initiative

True sharing initiatives purposefully look for unused resources in society and give them new meaning. At the same time, true sharing creates space for other people to pass on their unnecessary things. Initiatives access resources in different ways. Most of the things subsequently shared are donated to the initiative. People, businesses, and organizations donate things because they support the idea of reducing waste, reusing things, they want to help other people, etc., or they are also motivated to do so by legislation. For example, large retail chains are required by law to pass unsold food that is safe to assisting organizations. Thanks to this, the work of the Foodbank is a bit easier, as the retail chains themselves respond to it with the offer of food. In some cases, it is necessary to involve the initiatives themselves, which they look for, where there are unused resources in their vicinity and they try to negotiate their transfer. For example, Gleaning in the Brno region negotiates with farmers so that they can harvest their crop, which does not meet the quality and aesthetic requirements of shops and would remain unused in the field. A special case is so-called dumpster diving, which is sometimes run by FNB Brno. It is about obtaining resources from garbage cans, for example at supermarkets. Their original owner did not want to share the resources obtained by dumpster diving, and this is an activity on the edge of the law. The Literary Benches, initiated by the Jiří Mahen Library, are also specific. In addition to cooperating with another organization and the users themselves, it also uses its books, which were discarded from the library and would end up in an incinerator.

> Gleaning began to negotiate with the farmers around Brno so that the vegetables could be picked up and used. And then, in cooperation with the Brno Foodbank, it was further distributed to shelters and other helping organizations, for which it is a source of food for the people they care about and which does not cost them anything, which is quite important for them. At the same time, it uses vegetables that would otherwise rot in the field. (Radek, member of FNB Brno and founding member of Gleaning in the Brno region)

> Not all the food we share, the original owner probably wanted to share, but I am a supporter of the fact that if someone throws something away, they have lost any right to it, but the law does not look at it that way. (Radek, FNB Brno)

Initiatives such as FNB Brno and Foodbank for Brno and SMR take care of the logistics themselves, collect resources from donors and transport them on. Gleaning in the Brno region also ensures the harvest of surpluses in the field or orchards. Others (e.g. freeboxes, Flora, Brno Public Fridges, Literary Benches) only create a space where people can bring their surpluses and share them with others.

> Of course, there are always some logistics associated with this, such as on Friday it is necessary to pick up the food and vegetables from various places, from which we then cook on Saturday. So basically it's like on Friday night and Saturday all day, there is always one group dedicated to it. (Radek, FNB Brno)

> We had a lot of plants and we like to pass them on to each other, as between our friends. And then we said to the girls that we would like to mediate it for other people as well … (Bětka and Monika, Flora)

The process of sharing

Some sharing activities are open to everyone (Literary Benches, Sharepoint) because they take place in a public and constantly accessible space. The accessibility of others (freeboxes, public fridges) is limited by the opening hours of, for example, cafes or universities where sharing takes place. Placement in a building can also be a barrier, and not everyone who might be interested in sharing can get to share. Café Tři ocásci works purposefully to break down this obstacle that can be caused by the commercial environment. The 'hanging coffee' offer opens up to people in financial need, who can then use the freebox more easily.

> We still promote it as books that we bring closer to people who, for example, have a barrier, don't want to come to the library, can't, or it's just better for them to take those books on the street for some reason. At the same time, it is an opportunity for people who can put their books away there. (Eliška, Literary benches)

> So it had the social dimension in the sense that they don't just give those people something they don't have and they don't pay for anything, and at the same time you see them, you meet them in the cafe where they wouldn't otherwise come because the cafe is a commercial environment, where for that type of people come … it was supported by the fact that we are in a coffeeshare system or we have this hanging coffee. (Klára, Freebox at Tři ocásci)

Some forms of sharing work all year round (Foodbank for Brno and SMR, Brno Public Fridges); some take place as weekly (FNB Brno) or occasional events (Flora, Freeshop EFS FA MU). In some cases, the time of year or the day of the month also plays a role in the interest of sharing.

> It's quite different, but it's a few dozen people every Saturday. And it depends a lot on the time of year and which weekend of the month it is. Depending on whether it is warm or cold, depending on whether those who are needed from lodging houses still receive some social support, so at the end of the month or the beginning of the month they may be waiting for the money and do not have, so they will come for food, while the support will come, so they have something to live on so far, so maybe they will not come at all because they still have something to buy the food from. (Radek, FNB Brno)

The exclusivity or, on the contrary, the inclusiveness of certain forms of sharing is also given by the form of promotion and dissemination of information. For example, FNB Brno hands out food at the same time and in the same place every weekend. They disseminate information about their activities to helping organizations that can inform their clients. They also create information leaflets. On the other hand, Freefood Brno informs about the place and time of distribution through a closed group on Facebook. Becoming a member of this Facebook group is easy, but the precondition of access to the internet already means a certain barrier, which means that the food distributed is not intended for everyone (a specific case is the joint distribution of food with FNB Brno).

> ... they [Freefood Brno] do it, I think, primarily through a Facebook group, where they announce when and where they will be. And they actually distribute food just like us, but by doing it primarily through Facebook, there is a slightly different goal, that it is not primarily about the socially needy or partly can, but it is about students and various alternative-minded people. (Radek, FNB Brno)

Initiatives allow sharing in the form of one-way and two-way resource flows. One-way flows (i.e. the user has the opportunity to play only one role – donor or recipient) predominate in food sharing, except the public fridges. Most other initiatives operate on the principle that people can be both donors and recipients of shared resources. The user is encouraged to do so, for example, by the inscriptions: 'Take what you want here. Leave here what you don't need.' (Freebox at Tři ocásci). In practice, however, even in initiatives that allow two-way flows of resources, people are usually involved in only one role.

> … We tried to spread the idea of sharing from the beginning, yeah people come, put something in there, take something, but I think that the

group here is more in the minority, that it's more the people who put it there and then there is another group of people who take it, but it's just my theory, we didn't do any research. (Táňa, Brno Public Fridges)

Most of all there were people who brought a lot of it and then took one or two things. But there were no such people that they would come to hoard up things. (Vendula, Freeshop EFS FA MU)

The volume of shared resources

In terms of the volume of things shared through the initiatives, research has not covered this topic with precise quantitative statistics. However, the statements of the communication partners show that the number varies significantly across initiatives. The largest volumes are probably reached by the Foodbank for Brno and SMR, which at the time of the research ensured the sharing of tens of tonnes of food per year. Some initiatives want to increase the volume of shared resources (e.g. Foodbank), other initiatives (e.g. Freebox at FSS MU) are afraid about whether they will manage their activities with a greater flow of things. The communication partners also mentioned that at the beginning they had doubts as to whether the interest of the people, and therefore the number of things to share, would be sufficient. In practice, however, they have found that the resources that people want to share are often more numerous than the interest of others in those things.

In a single year, it was possible to harvest several tonnes of vegetables, and that certainly not everything has been collected yet. (Radek, member of FNB Brno and founding member of Gleaning in Brno region)

So we keep statistics, and when we see each year or quarter, we look at how much food we've distributed, and as long as the chart goes up, it's good. And so far it's headed up, because every time a warehouse or a driver is added, it has to show, now is a new law. So every year we hand over more food than in previous years – last year it was 94 tonnes and this year we hope to reach 250–300 tonnes. (David, Foodbank for Brno and SMR)

There was a lot left, but it was probably because we had a terrible onslaught of those things. That there were a lot of things, a lot of things were spinning there, a lot of things were there, and if I say half, three-quarters were taken away, and even so, eight Ikea bags were still given to the Veronica Foundation. So it was really big. We didn't expect that, we thought it would be so small that we would be happy if at least someone brought something. (Vendula, Freeshop EFS FA MU)

...we were afraid that no one would come there too much, and then we were afraid that they had brought too much, and that we didn't know what we were going to do with it ... we had a lot left, and then we had to give it away. So I think that these people quite understood the concept and it was good and they brought a lot of it. (Bětka and Monika, Flora)

To whom do resources go – charity or lifestyle?

Thanks to sharing, people who are in socially and financially difficult situation also have access to resources. In a market economy, they would have a problem obtaining these resources. The focus on the people in need is most noticeable at the Foodbank for Brno and SMR, whose activities consist mainly in handing over food to helping organizations such as Caritas and asylum houses. The FNB Brno initiative is open to all people, but the food is distributed mainly to homeless people etc. Brno Public Fridges has a similar experience.

The Foodbank is an organization whose main mission is to take food where it is surplus of it and give it where it is missing. We try to save the food that we threw away and gave it where people used it, so to helping organizations and they give it to clients. (David, Foodbank for Brno and SMR)

It's a thing that has clearly visible results, a clear meaning, simply in conditions where [a] third [of] food that is produced all over the planet is thrown away, ends up in the trash, and at the same time there are people on the streets and lodging houses who can't afford food at all, otherwise they can't afford quality food and here we have the opportunity to get it at least occasionally, whether they have to pay for the food. (Radek, FNB Brno)

And then a few people who take it there are homeless people, that's the way it is. (Táňa, Brno Public Fridges)

At the same time, sharing networks involve people who think differently about things and ownership. They often more or less oppose the consumerist way of life, and the use of second-hand things instead of buying new ones is common for them as a lifestyle. It is in this case crucial that resources are shared for free. Their value lies not in the financial price but in the fact that they are environmentally friendly, help other people, etc. At the same time, the initiatives send a message to their surroundings, enabling people to think about their resource management.

Well, for me, it's definitely not necessary to keep buying things. And spending money unnecessarily when this is a thing that grows on its own, so I don't see a reason to buy it somewhere, and I find it nice when people share it with each other that it's not necessary to give everything some monetary value ... we wanted it to be free and for everyone ... (Bětka and Monika, Flora)

It is based on the concept of how we work, that we strive for some environmental attitudes and sustainability, that we do not want to buy new things, that we want to use rather old things or recycle them or use them again. And one of the ways to make it possible for people is to have the freebox. (Klára, Freebox at Tři ocásci)

But that gesture, I don't just think about the people walking around it in that hallway, but the gesture towards the people who use the freebox, which means they can think about what they want, what they don't want, and when ... just don't stick to them that much. (Marek, Freebox at FSS MU)

Subsequent life of shared resources

The resources that people gain from initiatives are immediately consumed (in the case of food), used for a longer period (clothing, dishes, books, etc.) or shared again. Whether it is a one-way or a two-way sharing activity also plays a role here. Literary benches motivate people to return the book to the bench or share it in another way after reading it. In some cases, the freeboxes work similarly. Flora teaches people to propagate flowers so that they can donate them further. The subsequent life of shared resources has not been explored in more detail, but it is worth noting that sharing within an initiative does not end the resource cycle.

I'm terribly messy and I take a lot of things out of that freebox and then I have them at home and I don't need them at all, so after a while, I'll return it with the fact that I don't need it, so I'm getting rid of the property again. (Klára, Freebox at Tři ocásci)

I would like them to work ... if, for example, the bookshelves didn't empty so quickly, so that people would learn to look at it in such a way that when something is free somewhere, it is not necessary to take it home right away, but that they could share more with others ... that's how I wish, and so I secretly hope that over time people will find out that if the books are still available there, there won't be so many people taking them away ... but I don't know. (Eliška, Literary Benches)

Discussion

True sharing initiatives are an example of the diversity of economic activities (Gibson-Graham, 2006, 2008). They show the variety of ways to obtain resources and how to manage them further. At the same time, the initiatives themselves work in different forms and modes, and the people involved in them have different motivations (Rýparová, 2020). The economic side of sharing is manifested primarily in relation to the acquisition and distribution of resources to fill the material needs of people. Through sharing networks, communities can enforce power to control resources, access resources and manage them in network flows (Radil and Walther, 2019). This shows the transformational potential of true sharing. Thanks to initiatives, a community seizes otherwise unused resources and participates in their management and redistribution. In particular, initiatives that allow two-way flows, so users can be both donors and recipients of resources, have stronger transformation potential. People have the opportunity to participate in multiple roles. They can learn that things do not just have to be bought in a store or received as a birthday present, but there are a lot of unused resources around us that can be used legally and ethically. Sharing can be a common way for them to obtain, give or manage resources.

The material side of sharing shows how diverse economies are practised while revealing the benefits and pitfalls of sharing (Holmes. 2018; Sovová, 2020). Community resource management through the true sharing initiative means that more resources are used and do not end up as waste. At the same time, these resources are mediated to people who would not otherwise have access to them. In some cases, it is the targeted low threshold of these resources. The initiative is either significantly involved in shared resources logistics or creates capacity and space for resource sharing and redistribution. In the second case, there is the potential for greater activation of people who have to be more involved in the process if they are interested in sharing.

Resources shared through initiatives are usually in the form of a donation, as they are provided free of charge and there is a permanent or at least temporary transfer of ownership. After all, gifts and sharing are very close to each other and arguably it is not possible to determine the boundaries between them as precisely as the boundary to the market exchange (Belk, 2007; Jehlička and Daněk, 2017). The amount of resources shared in this way ranges from units to thousands of shared pieces. In relation to weight, grams to tens of tonnes of things are shared. Some communication partners themselves emphasized that it was of key importance for them that sharing could exist and work at all. Thus, the volume of sharing is often not paramount for them, but the creation of space for 'others'. Here again we can find a connection with the concept of diverse economies (Gibson-Graham, 2006, 2008), where the authors show the importance of diversity in the landscape of economic practices without highlighting the activities that are most significant in terms of frequency, the volume of resources or finances, etc.

In the sharing process, it is necessary to realize that the initiatives do not stand alone but work in a network of relationships with other initiatives, organizations, authorities, etc. (Rýparová, 2020). Each link in the chain in which shared resources flow is important, but their role is different. Some provide resources for sharing, others distribute them, some provide financial support, participate in the promotion of activities, etc. True sharing thus draws on the gift economy, because the material, finances and time devoted to initiatives are a gift (Holmes, 2018). The most prominent supporters of the Brno initiatives are the Brno-Centre Municipal Authority, Masaryk University, some non-profit organizations with an environmental focus or local businesses (cafés, restaurants, etc.). Their influence is reflected in the material support for the functioning of initiatives, but also, for example, by promoting certain activities, it increases the trust of users in sharing but also the trust of people who do not participate in sharing but live or work near the place of sharing.

Bridging social exclusion and poverty can be a positive aspect of sharing as well as the sustainable use of resources (Holmes, 2018). People who join the sharing networks created by the initiatives have access to food, clothing, books, flowers and more. Holmes (2018) points out that in contact sharing when people meet face to face, intangible aspects such as emotions, advice and support are also shared. However, in some cases, initiatives can create barriers to sharing – purposefully or unintentionally. This most often is the location in the building, where not all potential users have easy access. The rules of movement in the building allow everyone to enter, but shyness or fear can play a role. The opening hours of these places can be a barrier. Also, framing sharing activities in everyday practice and academic discussion can have a major impact on how people view true sharing initiatives and how willing they are to engage in the work. A significant limitation may be the explicit focus of some initiatives on people in socially disadvantaged situations. Again, shyness, pride and other psychological factors can discourage people from using even initiatives that are open to all people. Jehlička and Daněk (2017) and Holmes (2018) suggest that non-profit sharing be interpreted as a practice that has a positive role in society, strengthens community cohesion, is environmentally sustainable and is anchored in everyday relationships and ethics. Positive and empowering framing of sharing will support its transformational potential and at the same time, people can be encouraged to use these activities.

Barriers to sharing should be the focus of attention in further research (in relation to the sharing economy, e.g., Spindeldreher et al. (2018), for non-profit sharing Holmes (2018)). It would also be useful to focus in more detail on the importance of sharing, involving and motivating users themselves. As Sovová (2020) points out, if diverse economies are made up of practices, then it is necessary to know the people who are involved in these practices and how the practices work from their point of view. Ethnographic research, which is based on participatory observation or direct autoethnography, where the researcher can be at the centre of events and have direct experience with the people involved in the activity, is an invaluable tool for a thorough understanding of true sharing.

Conclusion

This chapter focuses on true sharing initiatives that operate in Brno, Czech Republic. Given that resources are shared through these initiatives on a non-profit basis and at the same time between people without family or friendly ties, true sharing has a strong transformational potential. Based on the process of acquiring, managing, and redistributing resources, I have shown how communities apply their power over resources, as well as how these activities are practised in terms of their materiality. People can be more involved in managing the resources available in the community, but true sharing initiatives also reduce waste and promote solidarity between people and in relation to the environment.

Through the quoted statements of my communication partners from among the organizers of initiatives, we were able to look into the practice of initiatives, but also into the different types of thinking and opinions that these organizers have on sharing. Thanks to participatory observation within the FNB Brno, I also had the opportunity to talk informally with more people who are involved in sharing: organizers, other volunteers and people who receive shared food. This helped me get a broad picture of the materiality of sharing, but also of the motivations and other psychosocial aspects of sharing. As the discussion showed, it would be useful to focus the following research more on users themselves to better understand their role in sharing networks. Barriers that people have to overcome when they share, or that discourage them from sharing, are also crucial.

References

Belk, R. 2007 Why Not Share Rather Than Own? *The ANNALS of the American Academy of Political and Social Science* 611(1): 126–140. https://doi.org/10.1177/0002716206298483

Belk, R. 2010 Sharing. *Journal of Consumer Research* 36(5): 715–734. https://doi.org/10.1086/612649

Belk, R. 2014a You Are What You Can Access? Sharing and Collaborative Consumption Online. *Journal of Business Research* 67(8): 1595–1600. https://doi.org/10.1016/j.jbusres.2013.10.001

Belk, R. 2014b Sharing Versus Pseudosharing in Web 2.0. *The Anthropologist* 18(1): 7–23. https://doi.org/10.1080/09720073.2014.11891518

Botsman, R. and Rogers, R. 2011 *What's Mine Is Yours: How Collaborative Consumption is Changing the Way We Live.* London: Collins.

Curtis, S.K. and Lehner, M. 2019 Defining the Sharing Economy for Sustainability. *Sustainability* 11(3): 567. DOI: https://doi.org/10.3390/su11030567

Davies, A.R. et al. 2017 Sharing Economies: Moving Beyond Binaries in a Digital Age. *Cambridge Journal of Regions, Economy and Society* 10(2): 209–230. https://doi.org/10.1093/cjres/rsx005

Ede, S. 2014 Let's Reclaim the Sharing Economy. *Post Growth Institute* (December 2014). http://postgrowth.org/transactional-sharing-transfor mational-sharing-2/

Geiger, A. et al. 2018 'Give and Take': How Notions of Sharing and Context Determine Free Peer-to-Peer Accommodation Decisions. *Journal of Travel & Tourism Marketing* 35(1): 5–15. https://doi.org/10.1080/10548408.2016 .1231101

Gibson-Graham, J.K. 2006 *Postcapitalistic Politics*. Minnesota: University of Minnesota Press.

Gibson-Graham, J.K. 2008 Diverse economies: performative practices for 'other worlds'. *Progress in Human Geography* 32(5): 613–632. https://doi .org/10.1177/0309132508090821

Gurven, M. and Jaeggi, A.V. 2015 Food Sharing. In *Emerging Trends in the Social and Behavioral Sciences*, edited by Robert Scott and Stephan Kosslyn. John Wiley & Sons. DOI: https://doi.org/10.1002/9781118900772 .etrds0133

Heinrichs, H. 2013 Sharing economy: A Potential New Pathway to Sustainability. *GAIA – Ecological Perspectives on Science and Society* 22(4): 228–231. https://doi.org/10.14512/gaia.22.4.5

Holmes, H. 2018 New Spaces, Ordinary Practices: Circulating and Sharing within Diverse Economies of Provisioning. *Geoforum* 88: 138–147. https:// doi.org/10.1016/j.geoforum.2017.11.022

Hyde, L. 2012 *The Gift: How the Creative Spirit Transforms the World*. Edinburgh: Canongate.

Jehlička, P. and Daněk, P. 2017 Rendering the Actually Existing Sharing Economy Visible: Home-Grown Food and the Pleasure of Sharing. *Sociologia Ruralis* 57(3): 274–296. https://doi.org/10.1111/soru.12160

Martin, C.J. 2016 The Sharing Economy: A Pathway to Sustainability or a New Nightmarish Form of Neoliberalism? *Ecological Economics* 121: 149–159. https://doi.org/10.1016/j.ecolecon.2015.11.027

Michelini, L. et al. 2018 Understanding Food Sharing Models to Tackle Sustainability Challenges. *Ecological Economics* 145: 205–217. DOI: https:// doi.org/10.1016/j.ecolecon.2017.09.009

Murillo, D. et al. 2017 When the Sharing Economy Becomes Neoliberalism on Steroids: Unravelling the Controversies. *Technological Forecasting and Social Change* 125: 66–76. https://doi.org/10.1016/j.techfore.2017.05.024

Plewnia, F. and Guenther, E. 2018 Mapping the Sharing Economy for Sustainability Research. *Management Decision* 56(3): 570–583. https://doi .org/10.1108/MD-11-2016-0766

Radil, S.M. and Walther, O.J. 2019 Social Networks and Geography: A View from the Periphery. https://arxiv.org/abs/1805.04510

Richardson, L. 2015 Performing the Sharing Economy. *Geoforum* 67: 121–129. https://doi.org/10.1016/j.geoforum.2015.11.004

Rýparová, A. 2020 Sítě pravého sdílení a sociální kapitál. *Sociální studia* 17(2): 111–127. https://doi.org/10.5817/SOC2020-2-111

Sahlins, M. 1972 *Stone Age Economics*. New York: Aldine de Gruyter.

Sovová, L. 2020 *Grow, share or buy? Understanding the diverse food economies of urban gardeners*. Dissertation. Brno: Masaryk Univerzity, FSS.

Spindeldreher, K. et al. 2018 I Won't Share!: Barriers to Participation in the Sharing Economy. *Twenty-Second Pacific Asia Conference on Information Systems*, Japan.

CHAPTER 12

A Stakeholders' Analysis of Airbnb in London and Barcelona

Cristina Miguel
University of Gothenburg, Sweden
Rodrigo Perez-Vega
Kent Business School, University of Kent, UK

Abstract

Airbnb not only has transformed the hospitality industry but also has created wider economic change in adjacent industries and in society in general. Because of this, many stakeholders are now trying to proactively shape the evolution of such platforms, as reflected by numerous actions by policymakers, industry representatives, media outlets and the public across the world. This chapter reports on a city-based case study (London and Barcelona) and examines the experiences and views of relevant stakeholders in the Airbnb sphere: hosts, guests, Airbnb public policy managers, rental apartment companies, council representatives and other local authorities. The barriers and opportunities for ethical practice were also identified and reported according to the views of these stakeholders. By using in-depth interviews and focus groups, this chapter gathers perspectives from a wide range of stakeholders on the perceived impact of Airbnb in two European cities that are major tourist destinations.

How to cite this book chapter:
Miguel, C. and Perez-Vega, R. 2022. A Stakeholders' Analysis of Airbnb in London and Barcelona. In: Travlou, P. and Ciolfi, L. (eds.) *Ethnographies of Collaborative Economies across Europe: Understanding Sharing and Caring.* Pp. 229–246. London: Ubiquity Press. DOI: https://doi.org/10.5334/bct.m. License: CC BY-NC-ND

Introduction

The sharing economy business models are driving, changing, and transforming traditional business practice (Binninger, Ourahmoune & Robert, 2015). They present several opportunities to reshape the role and nature of business and society in the digital age. The sharing economy is defined by Martos-Carrión and Miguel (2022) as a global socio-economic system based on the redistribution and management of underused goods, services (e.g., accommodation), and knowledge among peers via decentralized online platforms. As a digital disruptor, the sharing economy has changed the balance of the business-society relationship and plays a key role in guaranteeing the wellbeing or otherwise of the communities where such platforms operate. In particular, peer-to-peer (P2P) accommodation implies a number of opportunities (e.g., empowerment of individuals to generate revenue with existing assets, the democratisation of tourism) and challenges (e.g., contribution to the gentrification of cities, regulatory issues) (Farmaki & Miguel, 2022). Optimistic and utopian narratives have been increasingly challenged by the discussion of problems such as a shortage of affordable long-term housing, tax avoidance and safety. Malhotra and Van Alstyne (2014) labelled these and similar issues the '*dark side of the sharing economy*'.

A number of studies evaluate actual impacts of Airbnb, such as gentrification and lower occupancy rates in hotels (e.g., Fang, Ye & Law, 2016; Zervas, Proserpio & Byers, 2017; Barron, Kung & Proserpio, 2018). However, real knowledge about *perceived impacts* of the Airbnb model in the community and the accommodation sector in Europe is limited (e.g., Jordan & Moore, 2018; Nieuwland & van Melik, 2020; Miguel et al., 2022b). This is an important issue to study since, as Nieuwland and van Melik (2020: 12) highlight, 'the perceived impact is more important than the actual, absolute impact'. We agree with this statement, since beliefs of the perceived impact of sharing economy platforms among communities shape their attitudes more than actual facts. Our study aims to cover this gap and assesses the perceived impacts of Airbnb holistically by conducting a qualitative analysis of the phenomenon in London and Barcelona.

This chapter presents an ethnographic multiple case study that examines the perceived (positive and negative) impact of Airbnb in London and Barcelona. We chose Airbnb's original business model (peer-to-peer accommodation marketplace) as the platform is often used as an example of the success and risks associated with the sharing economy. Although originally designed as a P2P accommodation service, in recent years the activity has been professionalised and extended to advertise traditional hospitality services (e.g., hostels, bed and breakfast or boutique hotels) (Načinović Braje et al., 2021; Miguel et al., 2022a).

Factors Underpinning the Growth of Airbnb as Part of the Sharing Economy and an Examination of Impact

The sharing economy is an idealised state characterised by the movement from ownership to renting, bartering or gifting (Gansky, 2010). One of the main arguments that sharing economy companies use to promote their sustainable ethos relates to the empowerment of individuals to generate revenue with existing assets. It can be argued that accessing and sharing Airbnb rental properties help deliver greater market efficiencies and innovations in service delivery. By enabling regular homeowners to lease unused space (e.g., a room or a whole house), and by providing a marketplace where consumers can easily reach this space, the company has disrupted the hospitality market and given rise to an informal tourism accommodation sector (Sans & Quaglieri, 2016). Airbnb's business model also provides several competitive advantages over traditional hospitality alternatives. The first is cost, which is one of the most important factors that consumers take into account when deciding a place to stay (Chu & Choi, 2000). Airbnb hosts are able to provide competitive pricing due to having limited additional labour costs since the platform facilitates the booking and payment process (Guttentag, 2015).

There are also non-economic factors that favour informal tourism accommodation models like Airbnb. For example, some guests value having access to traditional amenities (e.g., full kitchen, washing machines) and having a local host who is able to provide valuable information even before the guest arrives at the location (Yglesias, 2012). Along with economic motives, studies showed the strong effect of other motivations including meeting new people (Lutz & Newlands 2018; Zhu et al., 2019), a range of 'practical' benefits such as having a kitchen or a washing machine (Belarmino et al., 2019; Tran & Filimonau, 2020), and the desire to get authentic and/or so-called 'local' experience (Bucher et al., 2018; Sung, Kim & Lee, 2018). On the other hand, Pasquale (2016) posits that the neoliberal narrative of platform competition lionizes currently dominant sharing economy firms, such as Uber and Airbnb, which takes them far away from the initial sustainable ethos of the sharing economy. For instance, a negative impact of platforms like Airbnb on the hospitality industry is starting to emerge. The hotel industry claims that Airbnb has damaged their business. The study conducted by Dogru, Mody and Suess (2019) shows that hotel room revenue is negatively impacted by Airbnb.

The impact of the adoption of the Airbnb model has also had a wider effect in society. Local neighbourhoods have been transformed by the spending of increasing numbers of visitors (Sans & Quaglieri, 2016). Visitors who choose Airbnb accommodation benefit from lower prices and can spend more money in the tourism sector (Fang et al., 2016). The study conducted by Garau-Vadell, Gutiérrez-Taño and Díaz-Armas (2019) shows residents' support for Airbnb as they perceive that the presence of short-term rentals in their neighbourhoods offers positive social and cultural impacts, and especially positive economic impacts. However, on the downside, local people seeking accommodation in their own neighbourhoods encounter increasing difficulties and this impacts on delivery of local services such as schools, leisure and healthcare. There is some evidence that this is already occurring in some of the markets where platforms like Airbnb have been widely adopted (Wachsmuth & Weisler, 2018; Cocola-Gant & Lopez-Gay, 2020). Local residents who are unable to gain property in their own neighbourhoods are likely to look further afield, and this can make it more difficult and more expensive for them to access the cultural and historic assets that were once nearby. Furthermore, by removing property from the long-term rental market, Airbnb contributes to rents increasing as supply and demand diverge.

Methodology

Research Design

The case study (based in the cities of London and Barcelona) seeks to compare and analyse different stakeholders' perspectives on the workings, impact and regulation of Airbnb in these two popular touristic cities. We used qualitative methods (interviews and focus groups) to identify the different ways that diverse stakeholders perceive and understand Airbnb and its impact on the economy and society. All the researchers are or have been Airbnb hosts, guests or both. These insights were particularly useful in the first stages of the project in order to contextualize the phenomenon and design the interviews and focus group questions. A total of four focus groups were run (a focus group with guests and another focus group with hosts in each city) plus two pilot focus groups: one with hosts and one with guests. Ten interviews (six in Barcelona and four in London) were conducted with relevant stakeholders (people from the industry and policy makers) to provide richer qualitative insights. The fieldwork took place in Barcelona between January and May 2018 and in London between July 2018 and May 2019. The next section covers the process of sampling in more depth. Later the process of conducting both focus groups and interviews is analysed.

Sampling

The participants in the focus groups and the interviews were selected based on purposeful sampling, a sampling technique where participants are selected based on pre-selected criteria that take into consideration the qualities of the participants (Etikan, Musa & Alkassim, 2016). Purposeful sampling allows the researchers to choose information-rich participants who can and are willing to provide the information needed by virtue of knowledge or experience (Patton, 2005). Because our research aimed to compare the views of different stakeholders in two locations, using this type of sampling allowed us to choose stakeholders in each location, but also to try to choose participants from equivalent organizations in London and Barcelona.

The selection criteria to identify participants for the focus groups were twofold. First for the focus group with guests, the selection criterion was any individual resident in either Barcelona or London who had used the Airbnb platform to book accommodation at least once. Second, for the focus groups with hosts, the selection criterion was individuals who had used the Airbnb platform to rent either a room or an entire property in Barcelona or London. To recruit participants, we relied on several online social media platforms. Although we were aiming to attract different types of hosts that rented either their whole property or only a room, we were not successful in attracting hosts that rented their whole property. All the participants, both in Barcelona and London, rented rooms in their properties, with the exception of one participant in London who only hosted when he was on holiday since his apartment had only one bedroom. Another type of host that we were not able to recruit was participants managing different properties on Airbnb as a business. Therefore, the more professional activity of using the Airbnb platform – the majority of the listings in many cities in Europe (Gyódi, 2019) – is not documented in this study, and this constitutes a limitation.

Another challenge when recruiting participants in two national settings was to identify the relevant stakeholders to interview. We aimed to interview participants in organisations where Airbnb had an impact (i.e., hotel association representatives to represent the hotel sector, short-term accommodation associations to represent the short-term rental sector). We were also interested in interviewing those in charge of policy (e.g., city councils' housing/environment representatives to investigate the position of the local government, competition and markets authority representatives, etc.). However, equivalent organisations were not always present in both settings, and some research was needed in order to understand the type of organisations that would be similar in both places.

At the end of our project, the interviewees included six types of participants:

1. Airbnb's heads of public policy and campaign managers (Spain & Portugal and UK & Ireland).
2. City councils' representatives: Director of the Inspection Services (Urban Ecology Management – Barcelona City Council) and Housing Policy Officer from the Greater London Authority. Interestingly, in the interview with the city council representative in Barcelona, the person responsible for monitoring short-term accommodation platforms was also present and answered some of the questions.

3. Professional bodies that represent the whole sharing economy market: Sharing Spain and Sharing UK's managers.

4. Short-term rentals associations: Director of APARTUR (touristic apartments association in Spain), Chair of STAA (Short Term Accommodation Association in the UK).

5. Competition legislator: Director of the Catalan Competition Authority. In addition, a Freedom of Information Act request was sent to the Competition and Markets Authority in the UK (which briefly replied to the questions via email) since it was not possible to schedule an interview.

6. Hotel associations: Innovation and Ecommerce Manager from a Catalan hotel association, and a public policy manager of a hospitality association in the UK. This last interview could not be used since the interviewee did not want to sign the consent form. It seems they were concerned about how the answers they gave could be too positive for the position they were supposed to hold within their organisation.

Reaching some of the interviewees was challenging. We contacted most of them through professional social networking sites (e.g. LinkedIn) and then continued the conversation through email. Building a relationship with the participants after the first contact was important. Sometimes, the person in the organisation we wanted to interview changed (e.g. Airbnb's public policy manager in Spain) and we had to start over with the new contact. Interviews with Airbnb Spain and Barcelona City Council took four to five months to be scheduled. Follow-up phone calls and emails were used to arrange all the interviews. Our learning from this process was that as more participants agreed to take part in the study, a snowball effect facilitated the process of further recruitment. Once participants heard that other organisations were already taking part, it became evident that they also wanted to have a say in the discussion. In the initial contacts, mentioning that researchers were participating in the COST Action 'From Sharing to Caring: Examining Socio-Technical Aspects of the Collaborative Economy', an EU-funded research network the authors participate in, proved helpful.

Data collection techniques

Focus groups

Focus groups usually include six to 10 participants with common characteristics relating to a discussion topic (Curran, Lochrie & O'Gorman, 2014). A focus group is a carefully planned discussion to obtain perceptions of a defined interest area and it addresses research questions that require depth of understanding (Goss & Leinbach, 1996). We chose focus groups because they are a helpful instrument: they offer distinctive information as authentic interactions are introduced and the researcher is able to appreciate the participants' opinions, beliefs, attitudes and perceptions (Mann & Stewart, 2000). We scheduled a focus group with guests in London that no participant attended; also we had a focus group with hosts in Barcelona with only three participants. Therefore, we decided to use the first non-successful focus group with hosts as a pilot and run another pilot with guests. The pilot focus groups were used to adapt the questions and introduce explanations to clarify some concepts. We ran four focus groups: two with hosts and two with guests, one of each type in both Barcelona and London. The focus groups included between five and 10 participants and they lasted between one hour and more than two hours. Focus groups are guided by a facilitator (Goss & Leinbach, 1996). In this case, the authors of this chapter acted as facilitators and, in particular, we were both present in the focus group with hosts in London. This helped to create consistency in the way of running the focus groups. In both cities there was a rich discussion in the focus groups.

Interviews

Elite in-depth interviews were conducted with 10 stakeholders in Barcelona (six) and London (four) ('elite' indicates that those members hold a significant amount of power within a group (Harvey, 2011). Because of the role and power that elite members hold in society or in an organization, interviewing them poses several methodological challenges for social researchers in terms of access, expectations during the interviews, and the design of the data collection method (Ostrander, 1993). In order to address these challenges, we used several of the strategies recommended by Harvey (2011), which include building strong relationships with elite members over time, being transparent, and adapting the interview style to the style of the elite member. For us it was very important to interview elite members due to the nature of this research, which aims to identify the perspective and perceived impact of Airbnb.

Interviews lasted between 45 minutes and two hours. Half of the interviews were conducted face to face and the other half through Skype. Interviewees received information sheets and consent forms before interviews. Some participants asked questions in relation to anonymity and it was explained to them that, except for when specified otherwise, the information would be anonymized and no real names or any information that could lead to identifying them would be disclosed in follow-up publications. Despite this, we encountered some resistance from some elite interviewees to taking part in this research. For example, the representative from one hospitality association decided to withdraw from the study after answering several questions. This illustrates the degree of sensitivity that sharing economy platforms like Airbnb have in certain industry circles.

Data analysis

Thematic analysis was used to analyse the data gathered through focus groups and interviews. Thematic analysis is a method that aims to identify, analyse and report patterns or themes within the data (Braun and Clarke, 2006). We followed Braun and Clark's (2006) six phases approach for thematic analysis. First, we familiarised ourselves with the data, and this was particularly important since data collection and data transcription were not always conducted by the same researcher. The second step involved coding the entire data set. Then codes were combined into broader patterns where the themes started to emerge. We used Nvivo for the coding and analysis processes. Two people (one of the researchers and a research assistant) looked at two different focus groups' dataset (the pilot with guests and one focus group with hosts) and coded them in order to ensure more consistency. Having two researchers involved in the coding also helped with consistency and to refine the themes. Finally, the information collected from focus groups and elite interviews was combined and compared. The primary purpose of using triangulation in qualitative research is to reduce biases and increase the consistency and reliability of the analysis (Jonsen & Jehn, 2009). This triangulation refers to 'the combination of methodologies in the study of the same phenomenon' (Denzin, 1978: 294).

Stakeholder Perspectives

This section provides an analysis of the stakeholders identified in our data. Stakeholder analysis is a common analysis method used by policy makers, regulators, governmental and non-governmental organizations, businesses and the media (Friedman & Miles, 2006). Stakeholder analysis (1) allows us to define aspects of a social and natural phenomenon affected by a decision or action; (2) allows us to identify individuals, groups and organizations who are affected by or can affect those parts of the phenomenon; and (3) helps prioritize these individuals and groups for involvement in the decision-making process (Reed et al., 2009).

Guests

The guests expressed that some of the advantages of P2P accommodations are that they augment their experience when visiting a new place, this mainly being driven by the recommendations that they receive from their host in a direct manner or by the information provided by hosts in the locations being let. For instance, Participant 3 (a guest from Barcelona) expressed how their host went out of their way to provide additional recommendations of places to visit, and the host was perceived as almost taking on the role of a tourist guide:

She (the host) was always very considerate. She wrote a list with recommended things … Places to visit … I do not know, like if she was
a tourist guide. She was very helpful (P3, Focus Group (FG) Guests,
Barcelona).

Furthermore, a positive impact also relates to the feeling of authenticity that
guests have when living 'like a local' (Lalicic and Weismayer, 2017). It is common for P2P accommodation to be located in areas where other locals live,
and not necessarily in the central areas where hotel facilities are usually found
(Benner, 2016). This was also expressed by Participant 1 from the focus groups
in London, placing additional value on the fact that living in a room in a P2P
accommodation would enable them to have that local feeling.

Another aspect that was considered a positive outcome of P2P accommodation is price. There is the sense that this type of accommodation can be considerably more affordable than more traditional hospitality options. For example:

So last time we were in an Airbnb we were almost 10 friends. Yeah, we
as a group booked a house in Marrakech near the old town. The house
had a swimming pool and it was very cheap, you can't find that price in
a hotel (P1, FG Guests, London).

In addition to price, there was perceived added value from using P2P accommodation platforms in terms of privacy and calmness:

This is a little bit more private, at least to me. From my point of view, if
both would have the same price and I would have to choose I would take
Airbnb. Because of that, because I do not want to be with 20,000 tourists from I do not know where … very noisy … and the huge swimming
pool and everything … all the atmosphere that you find in these mega
hotels (P1, FG Guests, Barcelona).

For some guests, staying in a house brings additional benefits, such as having
the facilities that one would normally expect in one's own home. Airbnb guests
valued the fact that a P2P accommodation would enable them to cook their
own food or use the washing machine and utilities.

Despite the advantages mentioned by the guests, there were aspects of P2P
accommodations that were perceived more negatively. The first related to information asymmetry, which happens when one party in a relationship has more
or better information than the other party (Bergh et al., 2019). In this case
several guests perceived the existence of information asymmetry as it was not
possible to assess from the outset how much a room would cost:

To get the final price in the first step, because it shows the price per night
but then you see that it is 100€ per night for two persons, and then you

realize that for 4 nights it is 500€ because of the fee, plus cleaning fee, and so … (P4, FG Guests, Barcelona).

Another perceived drawback from P2P accommodation was the perception that it leads to gentrification. Gentrification happens when a lower-income population is replaced by one of a higher status (Jover & Diaz-Parra, 2020). There is a perception that as the number of P2P accommodations increases, it is displacing people from lower income brackets from certain areas:

> Like in the suburbs, for sure. The city centres are already, I guess, expensive enough in London and West London. Since people are going to be looking at like Airbnbs further out from the city centre because they think it's cheaper, then more will spring up, and then it can make the rents higher everywhere (P4, FG Guests, London).

Nevertheless, guests showed double standards since they consider that hosts contribute to gentrification in their own city but they do not consider that they contribute to the gentrification of the cities they visit when using Airbnb.

There was also the perception that safety standards in P2P accommodation were not the same as in a hotel. The fact that hotels tend to have several security mechanisms (e.g. 24/7 security, electronic keys) led to the impression that the security mechanisms in P2P accommodation were below those standards:

> The point is that it is not a hotel, you assume that risk. If you take an Airbnb instead of a hotel is because it is cheaper, then the security is not going to be the same (P2, FG Guests, Barcelona).

Hosts

It was notable that the level of support that the platforms provide to their hosts was highlighted by several of them as a positive. The level of support has also been linked to the creation of a trusting relationship between the hosts and the platforms:

> When we have had a problem, we have called Airbnb and they have done well so we could solve the problem (P3, FG Hosts, Barcelona).

> The support you get from the platform side is great and that gives you a lot of trust (P1, FG Hosts, Barcelona).

Hosts perceived the platform to be trustworthy, and this trustworthiness appears to be related to the brand recognition of the platforms used. Trust between the host and the guest, but also on the platform (institutional trust) are important elements that have been found in the literature to drive usage of P2P accommodation platforms among guests (Reinhold & Dolnicar, 2017) and hosts (Park & Tussyadiah, 2020). One host from London was confident that the trust mechanisms set on the platform (e.g. ID verification, insurance) were sufficient for them to offer to host strangers. However, there was some scepticism in relation to the legal aspects of the reparation if something went wrong in terms of the host guarantee.

There is also the perception that P2P accommodation platforms offer a great level of flexibility to hosts. Some evidence has found that hosts perceived less flexibility about how the property is marketed (Farmaki, Christou & Saveriades, 2020). However, hosts perceived a high level of flexibility when deciding when the property is made available:

> You control the calendar you know you can you make the availability as it suits you so therefore you're going on holiday you shut that calendar for that time. Weekends, whatever you know if you want to do something you can close the calendar (P2, FG Hosts, London).

In terms of disadvantages, similarly to the case of guests, gentrification appeared to be a concern among hosts. There was a perception among hosts that foreign investors with greater purchasing power were driving the prices up:

> When rental prices go up because people are investing, let's think where the money comes from, it is from local people? Or is it from any other country? A foreigner who comes with money and pay for this. We need to ask ourselves about it, what is the origin of the fact that prices increase? People that come with a lot of money, they buy many flats in order to invest. They are free to do it but it is not our fault (P6, FG Hosts, Barcelona).

There is also the perception that P2P platforms like Airbnb have driven smaller hotels out of business, leading to price increases in chain hotels. This perception of unfair competition has been found not only in the hospitality sector but also in restaurants, transport and appliances (Frenken and Schor, 2019). In our study, a clear manifestation of this perceived unfairness is described by Participant 1:

> The big counter argument against Airbnb is that they're a new competitor that decreases revenues for hotels, traditional hospitality industry, so to speak. And that might be one of the reasons why they become even more expensive because the small hotels, they can't exist anymore, because of Airbnb, I don't know the exact figures how big is Airbnb but it's huge, it's global (P1, FG Hosts, London).

Furthermore, among hosts there was awareness of some levels of unfairness between hotels and people offering rooms or property through P2P accommodation platforms, namely, the regulations in terms of licensing and other guidelines. This view was particularly strong for hosts in London.

There were also safety concerns among hosts regarding the security mechanisms that Airbnb has set in its platform:

> They're supposed to take identities from the guest sometimes they only give a phone number and email which I think is wrong ... we've done it as a host but we find that some guests who haven't used it before no photograph and they've been given a phone number which could be anything and an email address neither of which is secure (P3, FG Hosts, London).

The STAA chair claimed that she did not consider it necessary to create a policy to enforce the registration of guests. In her opinion, it is a commercial choice of the host whether to requests passport details: 'Every homeowner makes those choices when they choose who they want to work with, and how they want to work' (STAA Chair, UK). She referred to working with intermediaries, like UnderTheDoorMat, where passport verification is mandatory, or including ID verification as a prerequisite before booking the property via Airbnb, an option that already exists.

Policy makers

One of the advantages that policy makers expressed was how sharing economy platforms like Airbnb helped redistribute the economic benefits of tourism, even in cases where the owners of these properties were companies rather than individuals:

> We see those two benefits; the empowerment of the peers and the redistribution of the wealth in local commerce that normally do not get tourist clients, small shops or supermarkets ... so tourists go to zones which a priori are not touristic, so it allows other zones to get some benefit from tourism (Sharing Spain, Chair).

Another benefit that policy makers identified in the context of London related to how platforms like Airbnb provided the city with more flexible options to accommodate a transient workforce.

> There are people who want to come and stay in London again on an internship or for a project or whatever and they can't sign a six month lease or a 12 month lease which is a standard so Airbnb allows people to

find housing accommodation for short periods which didn't exist before and that's amazing so from a housing point of view, Airbnb actually helps to solve some housing challenges and that's great (STAA chair, UK).

In terms of health and safety, both STAA and Sharing Economy UK (SEUK) pointed out that P2P accommodation activity is helping to raise the health and safety standards of residences since intermediaries and platforms inform the hosts about good practices:

A platform like Airbnb actually does a lot of proactive steps to help things and mitigating health and safety risks for example they have partnerships with the Fire Chief Council and they produce a lot of guidance for the hosts (SEUK Chair, UK).

The theme of a distortion in competition for the hospitality industry also emerged among policy makers. The hospitality industry often makes claims about the unfair playing field, especially in terms of health and safety, since hotels must comply with strict measures (Frenken and Schor, 2019). Likewise, the Innovation and Ecommerce Manager from a Catalan Hotel Association complained about this issue:

If I want to open a hotel I have to wait two years ... emergency stairs ... everything protected from fire ... that absolutely means unfair competition.

SEUK and STAA agreed that the regulation should be proportionate to the type of accommodation, as is already the case for the regulation of different types of accommodation in the traditional hospitality industry (e.g., B&B is different to hotels). For example:

You cannot expect a home where someone lives in all year around to have the same standards as a hotel, where there are hundreds of guests staying in the same location at the same time, because it doesn't make sense. And the same way that a B&B doesn't have the same standards as a hotel (STAA Chair, UK).

Furthermore, there were some issues related to illegal premises being advertised on these platforms, which can raise some safety concerns for users. For instance, the Director of the Inspection Services at Urban Ecology Management, Barcelona City Council mentioned that illegal apartments are an issue in terms of public safety because terrorists and thieves may use them for accommodation.

In terms of regulatory issues, taxation emerged as one of the key aspects that raises important challenges for policy makers, in particular in relation to possible loopholes that may exist and that both platform and hosts take advantage of (Guttentag, 2015). Industry reports highlight that the loss in tax revenue could be an estimated €800 million annually in Spain (Salces, 2016). This has several implications for how the matter of taxation is perceived by different stakeholders. The hospitality industry considers this aspect a crucial regulatory challenge. There are also challenges in relation to enforcing the law. For instance, in order to comply with the requirements of the 2015 Deregulation Act, Airbnb agreed to cap the listings once they arrived at 90 nights of occupation (Airbnb, 2019a). Nevertheless, hosts still can advertise their properties on other paid P2P accommodation platforms such as Booking.com or Homeaway. The Mayor's office (London Mayor, 2019) called for a 'registration system to enforce short term letting law'.

Conclusion

This chapter concludes by reflecting on some of the main challenges when conducting ethnographic studies with multiple stakeholders that include participants that are difficult to reach (e.g., certain types of hosts, and elite participants) in an international context where different languages and institutions exist. Finding participants for the focus group was one challenge that we faced when doing this study, because we aimed to gather very specific types of participants based on their involvement with the platform. To overcome this challenge, rewards had to be introduced to foster participation. Another challenge was interviewing high-profile elite participants in key Government positions, industry associations and platforms. Building relationships with those stakeholders was central to enabling the interviews to happen, and even then, the time scales to organise them were more difficult than with other types of interviews. In addition, identifying the different bodies that were affected by Airbnb in the two settings required some familiarisation with the local environment before an approach could be made.

The tension between stakeholders around the sharing economy in the hospitality sector continues to be driven by the impact that different stakeholders have. Our study has found that guests, hosts and policy makers acknowledge economic and social benefits of the growth of these platforms in both London and Barcelona. Nevertheless, concerns around safety, unfair competition and regulatory challenges continue to be in the minds of these stakeholders. Our study identified those positives and negatives in the context of two European cities that are highly affected by this phenomenon, but have taken different regulatory approaches when managing the continuous growth of these platforms. Including multiple stakeholders' perspectives also illustrated the complexity that users of these platforms (e.g., guest and hosts) and those looking to regulate them need to consider when looking to make improvement to the impacts that they are having in the contexts where they operate.

Acknowledgments

This study was funded by Leeds Beckett University and the University of Reading.

References

Airbnb Citizen. (n.d) *Airbnb Policy Tool Chest.* Retrieved from https://www .airbnbcitizen.com/airbnb-policy-tool-chest.

Barron, K., Kung, E. and Proserpio, D. 2018 The effect of home-sharing on house prices and rents: Evidence from Airbnb. Retrieved from https://ssrn .com/abstract=3006832 or http://dx.doi.org/10.2139/ssrn.3006832.

Belarmino, A., Whalen, E., Koh, Y. and Bowen, J.T. 2019 Comparing guests' key attributes of peer-to-peer accommodations and hotels: Mixed-methods approach. *Current Issues in Tourism*, 22(1): 1–7.

Benner, K. 2016 Airbnb wants travelers to 'live like a local' with its app [website]. Retrieved from https://www.nytimes.com/2016/04/20/technology /airbnb-wants-travelers-to-live-like-a-local-with-its-app.html

Bergh, D.D., Ketchen Jr, D.J., Orlandi, I., Heugens, P.P. and Boyd, B.K. 2019 Information asymmetry in management research: Past accomplishments and future opportunities. *Journal of Management*, 45(1): 122–158.

Binninger, A.S., Ourahmoune, N. and Robert, I. 2015, Collaborative consumption and sustainability: a discursive analysis of consumer representations and collaborative website narratives. *Journal of Applied Business Research*, 31(3): 969–986.

Braun, V. and Clarke, V. 2006 Using thematic analysis in psychology. *Qualitative Research in Psychology*, 3(2): 77–101.

Bucher, E., Fieseler, C., Fleck, M. and Lutz, C. 2018 Authenticity and the sharing economy. *Academy of Management Discoveries*, 4(3): 294–313.

Chu, R.K. and Choi, T. 2000 An importance–performance analysis of hotel selection factors in the Hong Kong hotel industry: a comparison of business and leisure travellers. *Tourism Management*, 21(4): 363–377.

Cocola-Gant, A. and Lopez-Gay, A. 2020 Transnational gentrification, tourism and the formation of 'foreign only' enclaves in Barcelona. *Urban Studies*, 57(15): 3025–3043.

Curran, R., Lochrie, S. and O'Gorman, K. 2014 Gathering qualitative data. In K. O'Gorman & R. MacIntosh (Eds.), *Research methods for business & management*. Oxford: Goodfellow.

Dogru, T., Mody, M. and Suess, C. 2019 Adding evidence to the debate: Quantifying Airbnb's disruptive impact on ten key hotel markets. *Tourism Management*, 72: 27–38.

Etikan, I., Musa, S.A. and Alkassim, R.S. 2016 Comparison of convenience sampling and purposive sampling. *American Journal of Theoretical and Applied Statistics*, 5(1): 1–4.

Fang, B., Ye, Q. and Law, R. 2016 Effect of sharing economy on tourism industry employment. *Annals of Tourism Research*, 57(C): 264–267.

Farmaki, A. and Miguel, C. 2022 Peer-to-peer Accommodation in Europe: Trends, Challenges, and Opportunities, in Česnuitytė, V., Klimczuk, A., Miguel, C., and Avram, G. (Eds.) *The Sharing Economy in Europe: Developments, practices, and contradictions*. London: Palgrave Macmillan, 115–136.

Farmaki, A., Christou, P. and Saveriades, A. 2020 A Lefebvrian analysis of Airbnb space. *Annals of Tourism Research*, 80: 102806.

Frenken, K. and Schor, J. 2019 Putting the sharing economy into perspective. In O. Mont (Ed.), *A research agenda for sustainable consumption governance*. Cheltenham: Edward Elgar Publishing.

Gansky, L. (2010) *The mesh: Why the future of business is sharing*. New York: Penguin.

Garau-Vadell, J.B., Gutiérrez-Taño, D. and Díaz-Armas, R. 2019 Residents' support for P2P accommodation in mass tourism destinations. *Journal of Travel Research*, 58(4): 549–565.

Goss, J.D. and Leinbach, T.R. 1996 Focus groups as alternative research practice: Experience with transmigrants in Indonesia. *Area*, 28(2): 115–123.

Guttentag, D. 2015 Airbnb: Disruptive innovation and the rise of an informal tourism accommodation sector. *Current Issues in Tourism*, 18(12): 1192–1217.

Gyódi, K. 2019 Airbnb in European cities: Business as usual or true sharing economy? *Journal of Cleaner Production*, 221: 536–551.

Harvey, W.S. 2011 Strategies for conducting elite interviews. *Qualitative Research*, 11(4): 431–441.

Jonsen, K. and Jehn, K.A. 2009 Using triangulation to validate themes in qualitative studies. *Qualitative Research in Organizations and Management*, 4(2): 123–150.

Jordan, E.J. and Moore, J. 2018 An in-depth exploration of residents' perceived impacts of transient vacation rentals. *Journal of Travel & Tourism Marketing*, 35(1): 90–101.

Jover, J. and Díaz-Parra, I. 2020 Gentrification, transnational gentrification and touristification in Seville, Spain. *Urban Studies*, 57(15): 3044–3059.

Khoo, M., Rozaklis, L. and Hall, C. 2012 A survey of the use of ethnographic methods in the study of libraries and library users. *Library & Information Science Research*, 34(2): 82–91.

Lalicic, L. and Weismayer, C. 2017 The role of authenticity in Airbnb experiences. In R. Schegg & B. Stangl (Eds), *Information and communication technologies in tourism 2017* (pp. 781–794). Cham: Springer.

Lutz, C. and Newlands, G. 2018 Consumer segmentation within the sharing economy: The case of Airbnb. *Journal of Business Research*, 88: 187–196.

Malhotra, A. and Van Alstyne, M. 2014 The dark side of the sharing economy … and how to lighten it. *Communications of the ACM*, 57: 24–27.

Mann, C. and Stewart, F. 2000 *Internet communication and qualitative research: a handbook for researching online.* London: Sage.

Martos-Carrión, E. and Miguel, C. 2021 Sharing economy: History, definitions and related concepts, in B. Taheri, R. Rahimi & D. Buhalis (Eds.), *The sharing economy: Perspectives, opportunities and challenges.* Oxford: Goodfellow Publishers.

Miguel, C., Pechurina, A., Kirkulak-Uludag, B., Drotarova, M., Dumančić, K., Načinović Braje, I. and Giglio, C. 2022a Short-term rental market crisis management during the COVID-19 pandemic: Stakeholders' perspectives. International Journal of Hospitality Management, 102, 103147, https://doi .org/10.1016/j.ijhm.2022.103147.

Miguel, C., Lutz, C., Alonso-Almeida, M.M., Jones, B., Majetić, F. and Perez-Vega, R. 2022b. Perceived impact of short-term rentals in the community in the UK, in Farmaki, A., Bogazici, S.K., and Ioannides, D. (eds.) Peer-to-Peer Accommodation and Community Resilience: Implications for Sustainable Development. Wallingford: CABI, pp. 55–67.

Načinović Braje, I., Pechurina, A., Bicakcioglu-Peynirci, N., Miguel, C., Alonso-Almeida, M. and Giglio, C. 2021 The changing determinants of tourists' repurchase intention: The case of short-term rentals during pandemic. International Journal of Contemporary Hospitality Management, 34(1): 159–183, DOI: https://doi.org/10.1108/IJCHM-04-2021-0438

Nieuwland, S. and van Melik, R. 2020 Regulating Airbnb: How cities deal with perceived negative externalities of short-term rentals. *Current Issues in Tourism*, 23(7): 811–825.

Oskam, J. and Boswijk, A. 2016 Airbnb: the future of networked hospitality businesses, *Journal of Tourism Futures*, 2(1): 22–42.

Ostrander, S.A. 1993 Surely you're not in this just to be helpful: Access, rapport, and interviews in three studies of elites. *Journal of Contemporary Ethnography*, 22(1): 7–27.

Park, S. and Tussyadiah, I.P. (2020) How guests develop trust in hosts: An investigation of trust formation in P2P accommodation. *Journal of Travel Research*, 59(8): 1402–1412.

Pasquale, F. 2016 Two narratives of platform capitalism, *Yale Law & Policy Review*, 35: 309.

Patton, M.Q. 2005 *Qualitative research.* Encyclopedia of statistics in behavioral science. *Qualitative Research in Psychology*, 3(2): 77–101.

Pearce, L.D. 2002 Integrating survey and ethnographic methods for systematic anomalous case analysis. *Sociological Methodology*, 32(1): 103–132.

Reed, M.S., Graves, A., Dandy, N., Posthumus, H., Hubacek, K., Morris, J., Prell, C., Quinn, C.H. and Stringer, L.C. 2009 Who's in and why? A typology of stakeholder analysis methods for natural resource management. *Journal of Environmental Management*, 90(5): 1933–1949.

Reinhold, S. and Dolnicar, S. 2017 The sharing economy, in S. Dolnicar (Ed.), P2P accommodation platforms: Pushing the boundaries (pp. 15–26). Oxford: Goodfellow Publishers.

Robertson, D., Oliver, C. and Nost, E. 2020 Short-term rentals as digitally-mediated tourism gentrification: Impacts on housing in New Orleans. *Tourism Geographies*, DOI: https://doi.org/10.1080/14616688.2020.1765011.

Sans, A.A. and Quaglieri, A. 2016 Unravelling Airbnb: Urban perspectives from Barcelona. *Reinventing the local in tourism: Producing, consuming and negotiating place*. Buffalo, NY: Channel View Publications.

Sung, E., Kim, H. and Lee, D. 2018 Why do people consume and provide sharing economy accommodation? A sustainability perspective. *Sustainability*, 10(6): 2072.

Tran, T.H. and Filimonau, V. 2020 The (de)motivation factors in choosing Airbnb amongst Vietnamese consumers. *Journal of Hospitality and Tourism Management*, 42: 130–140.

Wachsmuth, D. and Weisler, A. 2018 Airbnb and the rent gap: Gentrification through the sharing economy. *Environment and Planning A: Economy and Space*, 50(6): 1147–1170.

Watts, J. 2006 'The outsider within': Dilemmas of qualitative feminist research within a culture of resistance. *Qualitative Research*, 6(3): 385–402.

Yglesias, M. 2012 Legalize Airbnb! *Slate*, 5 June. Retrieved from http://www.slate.com/articles/business/moneybox/2012/06/is_airbnb_illegal_why_hotels_are_so_upset_about_you_renting_a_bedroom_to_a_stranger_.html

Zervas, G., Proserpio, D. and Byers, J.W. 2017 The rise of the sharing economy: Estimating the impact of Airbnb on the hotel industry. *Journal of Marketing Research*, 54(5): 687–705.

Zhu, Y., Cheng, M., Wang, J., Ma, L. and Jiang, R. 2019 The construction of home feeling by Airbnb guests in the sharing economy: a semantics perspective. *Annals of Tourism Research*, 75: 308–321.

CHAPTER 13

Tensions around Housing in the Collaborative Economy: Resisting against Platform Capitalism in Athens

Dimitris Pettas

Marie Skłodowska-Curie Postdoctoral Fellow, Institute of Urban
and Regional Planning, Technical University of Berlin

Penny Travlou

Edinburgh College of Art, University of Edinburgh

Abstract

In this chapter, we explore how different sets of practices that have been framed as 'sharing' and 'collaborative', coexist in the central Athenian district of Exarcheia. We mainly focus on issues related to housing and touristification and the ways the 'platform capitalism' side of sharing economy (through digitally mediated short-term rentals) operates in tension with grassroots, anti-gentrification initiatives that rely upon the rich political landscape of the district and involve the sharing of materials, knowledge and experiences, while evolving around the notion of caring for the most vulnerable parts of local population that are facing direct and indirect displacement. More specifically, we look into the sharing praxis itself: what is shared, by whom and how, while further elaborating on the labour and gendered dimensions of sharing.

How to cite this book chapter:
Pettas, D. and Travlou, P. 2022. Tensions around housing in the collaborative economy: Resisting against platform capitalism in Athens. In: Travlou, P. and Ciolfi, L. (eds.) *Ethnographies of Collaborative Economies across Europe: Understanding Sharing and Caring.* Pp. 247–264. London: Ubiquity Press. DOI: https://doi.org/10.5334/bct.n. License: CC BY-NC-ND

We argue that, despite their common framing as parts of the sharing (and/ or collaborative economy), 'platform capitalism' and grassroots collaborative practices constitute the materialization of different, often contrasting, broader visions concerning the organization of production, consumption and social reproduction, providing engaged actors with different capacities and possibilities of empowerment.

Introduction

Sharing and collaboration have long been common societal practices, especially among groups and communities whose rights (i.e., access to housing, education, work, health) are constantly under attack (Schor, 2014). Since the 1970s, feminist scholars (e.g., Dalla Costa and James, 1975; Federici and Linebaugh, 2018; Fraser, 1992, 2009; Gibson-Graham, 1996) have introduced in academic debates the multiplicity of practices and modes of sharing, collaboration and care involved in everyday social reproduction that were largely neglected in both mainstream and critical strands of scholarship. Such theorizations shed light upon the role of alternative modes of labour, and non-monetary transactions emerge and operate in parallel – and often in tension – with capitalist socio-economic ones. Recently, a series of insightful works renewed the interest in transformative sharing and collaborative practices, focusing on their development through grassroots initiatives and networks. Within this body of literature, topics of interest include the production, as well as the collective management and sharing, of resources (Gorenflo, 2015; Santala and McGuirk, 2019; Scholz, 2016), the provision of healthcare and educational services (Bagayogo et al., 2016; Grove and Fischer, 2006), modes of collaborative consumption (Rowe, 2017), environmental innovations (Smith and Stirling, 2018), the social reproduction of the commons (Chatterton and Pusey, 2019), and social and solidarity economy networks (Daskalaki et al., 2019).

However, during the past decade, the notions of sharing and collaboration re-emerged as popular buzzwords in public discourse. In this context, market actors have partly re-coded these terms, after dissociating them from the aforementioned transformative practices. More specifically, for-profit, particularly large corporate actors in the gig economy (e.g., Airbnb, Uber, Deliveroo) exploit notions of sharing and collaboration while accounting for the commodification of social practices that have been traditionally considered to develop beyond the reach of the market (i.e., hospitality, transport, delivery services). Relevant activities, often regarded as 'platform capitalism', account for a series of negative externalities related to the deterioration of working conditions for engaged actors (Drahokoupil and Jespen, 2017; Walker, 2015) and the deepening of racial and gender discrimination (Edelman et al., 2015; Cansoy and Schor, 2017; Shade, 2018). At the same time, their negative impacts on urban settings may also be substantial. For instance, digitally mediated short-term rentals

(STRs) account for the creation of rent-gaps, and play a pivotal role in processes of touristification and displacement (Brousseau et al., 2015; Lee, 2016; Pettas et al., 2021; Wachsmuth and Weisler, 2018). However, the employment of sharing- and collaboration-related terms and narratives on behalf of large corporations has been highly controversial. Considering that these terms are also employed by corporate actors, the question arises as to what extent sharing and collaboration are notions compatible with profit-oriented goals and capital-intensive practices. Belk (2007) and Martin (2016) argue that sharing practices, by definition, cannot include monetary exchanges, while Kalamar (2013) came up with the term 'sharewashing' to argue that the exploitation of the positive associations of the notion of sharing have been largely deployed to hide self-interested activities. Morozov (2013) described platform economy as 'neo-liberalism on steroids', arguing that related practices commercialize aspects of life and social activities that were beyond the reach of the market. Moreover, according to Frenken and Schor (2017), similar practices undermine social cohesion through the commodification of previously non-monetized modes of sharing.

In this chapter, we explore how different sets of practices that have been framed as 'sharing' and 'collaborative' coexist in the central Athenian district of Exarcheia. We mainly focus on issues related to housing and touristification and the ways in which the 'platform capitalism' side of the sharing economy (through digitally mediated STRs) operates in tension with grassroots, anti-gentrification initiatives that rely upon the rich political landscape of the district and involve the sharing of materials, knowledge and experiences, while evolving around the notion of caring for the most vulnerable parts of the local population that are facing direct and indirect displacement. More specifically, we look into the sharing praxis itself: what is shared, by whom and how, while elaborating on the labour and gendered dimensions of sharing. We argue that, despite their common framing as parts of the sharing (and/or collaborative) economy, relevant practices constitute the materialization of different, often contrasting, broader visions concerning the organization of production, consumption and social reproduction, providing engaged actors with different capacities and possibilities of empowerment.

Methodologically, this chapter is based on qualitative research that the two authors carried out independently. The first author carried out 22 semi-structured interviews with actors engaged in the everyday social reproduction of STRs through various roles (hosts that are either also the dwellings' owners or hired for that role, cleaners, photographers and architects) while the second author carried out ethnographic fieldwork with an activist grassroots initiative against gentrification and touristification in Exarcheia. The two research projects were conducted between January 2019 and June 2021. More specifically, the first author conducted his interviews from January to June 2021 while the second author's ongoing ethnographic fieldwork started in early 2019. It is also worth mentioning that both authors have been residents of the neighbourhood for several years.

The remainder of the chapter is structured as follows: we first delineate the implications of the 2008 austerity crisis for the Athenian housing landscape, placing emphasis on the central district of Exarcheia; then we explore two contrasting sets of practices that developed and coexist in tension in the aforementioned district, namely digitally mediated STRs and anti-gentrification and solidarity networks that attempt to reverse the unfolding gentrification processes and also operated as infrastructures of care during the recent pandemic outbreak; finally, we discuss the multiple framings of sharing and collaborative practices and their implications for the urban environment and urban actors in Athens.

The housing context of Athens

During the past decade, Greece has experienced the harsh implications of a multi-level crisis, including the shrinking of the welfare state, anti-labour institutional change, substantial cuts in salaries and pensions, high levels of unemployment (especially among young people) and a deepening of inequalities (European Data Journalism Network, 2021; Hadjimichalis, 2013; Statista, 2021). Housing was one of the sectors worst affected by the austerity crisis through processes that disrupted the – up to then – widespread access to affordable housing, enabled by the high rates of homeownership and the diffusion and segmentation of land property, despite the lack of either housing policies that protect the rights of tenants by regulating the rental market or a provision of social housing for low-income households. Since the 1950s, as the country was rebuilding after WWII and the Civil War, and the people were migrating en masse from the countryside to the urban centres, housing has been one of the key economic drivers, and home ownership has been widespread across social classes.

Recently, however, and particularly during the austerity crisis, there has also been a growing number of people renting properties in the centre of Athens. These people are mainly younger and low-paid, and thus unable to afford to buy property: migrants, young families, etc. At the same time Athens has also experienced a massive touristification of its centre and the gentrification of many of its central neighbourhoods. Between 2015 and 2019, Athens became one of the top tourist destinations in Europe – a development in which the recurrent presence of Athens in the global media narrative about the austerity and refugee crises and their discontents probably had a role. In 2018, the city received over 5 million tourists as it transformed into a year-round tourist destination (Travlou, 2021). Athens is now considered an 'affordable' tourist destination, one of the most affordable European capitals to visit, with a world-branded history and a vibrant city life.

During its time in office (2015–2019), the left-wing Syriza government saw tourism as the economic sector that could possibly ameliorate the country's austerity crisis; it thus encouraged further investment in tourism-related businesses. Airbnb and similar short-let accommodation platforms offered homeowners the opportunity to boost their finances and secure some extra profit. At the same time, foreign property investment was encouraged through initiatives such as the Golden Visa scheme, with Greece offering the lowest rate EU-wide (€250,000) to non-EU investors. This made Athens an attractive location for individual investors, property developers and international investment funds. Within a very short time, the socioeconomic demographics of Athens' central neighbourhoods changed dramatically: many local residents were forced to move out of rented homes as owners sold these homes to overseas investors or converted them into short-let accommodation. The number of evictions also increased, as existing tenants could not afford to pay the skyrocketing rent and utility bills. These changes in the housing market, along with gentrification, have had a direct impact on central neighbourhoods such as Exarcheia, where many local residents have been displaced. Airbnb short-lets and new cafes, bars and restaurants have turned these neighbourhoods into night economy hubs and made it impossible for many of their earlier local residents to afford to live there. Exarcheia was particularly affected by this touristification and incipient gentrification. Its 'bohemian' reputation and nightlife, and the presence of many social spaces and self-organized initiatives, together with its central location, made it appealing to many, mainly young, foreign visitors (Pettas et al., 2021; Travlou 2021).

Sharing, caring and collaboration in Exarcheia:
From platform capitalism to solidarity

Digitally mediated STRs expanded rapidly in Athens, especially from the mid-2010s to the COVID-19 pandemic outbreak, initially as a spontaneous, bottom-up, individual activity. On the demand side, a series of conditions and trends contributed to the transformation of Athens from a one-day-stop destination to a year-round, city break destination: the framing of Athens in international media as the city that made it through the crisis through means of grassroots solidarity practices (Henley, 2015; Kitsantonis, 2017) and as the new arts capital of Europe (Da Silva and Dickson, 2017; Sooke, 2017), the expansion of low-cost flights that increased Athens' connectivity, the political instability in 'antagonistic' destinations and policies designed and implemented by the Municipality of Athens and the Greek Ministry of Tourism that explicitly aimed in rebranding Athens as a vibrant urban landscape that could meet the demand for 'authentic' experiences. On the supply side, contrary to the housing landscape of other European capitals, the high levels of home ownership enabled even lower-middle- and middle-class populations to engage in STRs, largely as a survival strategy during the crisis. The emergence of STRs as a large-scale touristic accommodation infrastructure was further supported by a wide range of professionals who were experiencing high levels of unemployment and precarity during that time. Beyond the owners, mostly young professionals and unskilled workers participated in the everyday social reproduction of STRs through various roles: hosts, cleaners, architects, interior designers and photographers are among the occupations that supported the STR infrastructure. Gradually, large companies, funds and investors got more involved in the STR market (Balampanidis et al., 2019) and, through the creation of scale economies and the increased professionalization of STR-related practices created an environment in which small owners were unable to compete. Within this frame, precarity, exploitation and self-exploitation defined labour conditions in cases of owners with limited numbers of dwellings and – and providers of 'peripheral' activities.

We initially focus on small-scale STR networks (involving owners with one or two housing units) and build on informants' narratives: the vast majority of engaged actors entered the STR market out of necessity, as they were facing unemployment or labour precarity in their professional lives. 'Small' home-owners experienced the transformation of home-ownership from an advantage to a burden (due to increased property taxation and inability to respond to housing costs) and, in this environment, STRs constituted their exclusive or major source of income. The same applies to people operating as hosts (e.g., undertaking the overall management of the listings, including online posting and communication, reception of visitors, cleaning or coordinating cleaning activities, etc.), professionals (architects, engineers, interior designers, photographers) and cleaners. However, although this provided an alternative within a harsh socio-economic environment, the conditions of exploitation that prevailed in most economic sectors in Greece during the crisis were also reflected in the STR market. First, labour relations within STR-related activities develop within the shadow economy, leading to an overall condition of precarity due to the lack of contracts, social and health security, etc. As a result, informants were also concerned about the impact of this unofficial engagement in their future work opportunities, due to their inability to prove their work experience. Second, concerning labour exploitation, despite the unofficial status of their engagement and the consequent evasion of taxation for 'employers', the jobs offered to 'peripheral' actors were largely underpaid, especially those of unskilled workers. On many occasions, cleaners mentioned that they were paid €1.5–2 per hour or €500 per month for a six-day working week. Even for small owners who undertake large parts of STRs' everyday operation themselves, self-exploitation is widespread. Informants mentioned that unstable and extended working hours and multitasking (communication with visitors, cleaning, shopping, etc.) created stressful working conditions that rarely were combined with high earnings. The harsh labour landscape in the STR market is confirmed by the fact that most informants chose another professional path when they came across alternatives. Finally, the informal and precarious labour relations posed disproportionate challenges to female participants, who often faced wage discrimination and, in some cases, aggressive behaviours that they perceived as gender-based.

Within this context, practices of sharing and collaboration were nowhere to be found in the landscape of STRs in Athens. 87.8% of the total Airbnb listings in Athens concern renting out whole apartments, constituting a departure from the initial logic of apartment-sharing facilitated through platforms such as Couchsurfing and Airbnb during their first steps. More importantly, the resources and goods (house, furniture, electronic equipment, etc.) as well as the labour (cleaning, communication, etc.) involved come exclusively – through either personal labour or outsourcing – from the provider's end, who bears the cost of their purchase and maintenance as well as the risk that is inherent in their commercial exploitation of dwellings. Then, a special form of sharing is developed between the provider and the platform, as they jointly exploit the resources, goods and/or labour of the former, while what is offered by the platform is the 'networking' i.e., the provider's access to a large pool of possible users. At the same time, the possibilities for developing relationships beyond those contained in the formal framework of the provider–user relationship are minimal, due to both the very nature of this relationship and the impact that certain features of the platform (such as the rating system and reviews) have on the 'attractiveness' of and future demand for the product provided. Based on the above, the activities included in the 'platform capitalism' side of the sharing economy not only are detached from sharing but are produced and reproduced through individualized and fully commercialized practices that constitute aggregated versions of the mainstream capitalist economy.

The above discussion raises further scepticism towards the sharing economy, its links to platform capitalism, and its impact on the local economy and communities in Athens. Airbnb and similar short-let accommodation platforms have been considered as partly responsible for the worsening of the local housing crisis (Skopeliti, 2018; Balampanidis et al., 2021). Since the early 2010s and during the austerity crisis, housing became one of the core causes that local social movements focused their actions upon, resisting neoliberal politics on the issue and actions such as evictions, repossessions and auctions. Inspired by Henri Lefebvre's (1996) 'right to the city', they called for 'the right to housing', opposing any legislation and/or state politics that endanger this fundamental right of citizens. Resisting the state meant that the tactics of mobilization for housing activist groups were mostly focusing on direct actions – such as street demonstrations – to acquire visibility for their cause. It became apparent by the mid-2010s, though, that the housing crisis was getting worse and more complex as the touristification and gentrification of central neighbourhoods intensified. Housing activists had to confront not only the state but a complex system of private investors, international real estate funds and sharing economy digital platforms such as Airbnb. The last of these has been the most problematic and difficult to fight against, as it is regarded as a digital service provider rather than an individual online business. For this reason only, Airbnb has so far avoided onerous national regulations across Europe, with very few exceptions (such as Barcelona and Berlin), as it has been recognized as 'an information society service, a status that comes with the right to operate freely across the EU' (Boffey, 2019). Arguably, it is the first time that housing activists, neighbourhood groups and local social movements have an opponent that is beyond their territory and outside national borders. Traditional forms of resistance such as those described earlier cannot be effective anymore. The question to pose here is how to resist a global phenomenon and a stateless (digital) enterprise with unprecedented impact on local communities.

In January 2019, Action Against Regeneration and Gentrification (AARG), an activist collective, assembled in Exarcheia to resist the touristification and gentrification of the neighbourhood, and the rise of property values and displacement of less affluent residents (see https://www.facebook.com/aargathens). AARG is a group of anti-authoritarian activists, residents and scholars who came together to study and understand the transformation of Exarcheia in recent years and find ways to mitigate and resist it. Until the Covid-19 outbreak in early 2020, AARG's core cohort of around 10 members met in weekly open assemblies in the free social space 'Nosotros' in Exarcheia; afterwards they continued to hold regular open assemblies online. Since its formation, AARG has organized a series of public events (roundtables with international and local academics and activists, film screenings, etc.), neighbourhood mapping activities and anti-gentrification demonstrations alongside similar grassroots initiatives in Athens. Its activism has also included campaigns against Airbnb and anti-eviction actions (see Figure 13.1).

From its inception, AARG positioned itself as a platform for resistance at the intersection of the long-term austerity crisis and the housing crisis that it drove. The connection between these two crises is not simple and straightforward; however, AARG members and other housing activists in Greece could clearly see that the unprecedented economic recession resulting from the implementation of the EU-dictated austerity measures had a dire impact on many people's livelihoods. As the country's economy collapsed in the early 2010s, the state became increasingly unable and/or unwilling to provide organized relief, while many people lost their employment, income and homes and/or became excluded from the formal economy.

In these conditions, many turned to each other for help in building infrastructures of care. From the onset of the austerity crisis, local activists from different factions of the left and the anarchist/anti-authoritarian movement mobilized to build self-organized networks that provided medical, housing, and other support to those affected the most by the economic recession (Rakopoulos, 2014; Cabot, 2016; Arampatzi, 2017). The emergence of numerous solidarity economy initiatives across the country (from time banks and agricultural cooperatives to urban free markets, collective kitchens and social clinics) exemplifies practices of solidarity and socio-economic alternatives based on non-monetary and/or non-capitalist economic models (Margariti and Travlou, 2018; Travlou

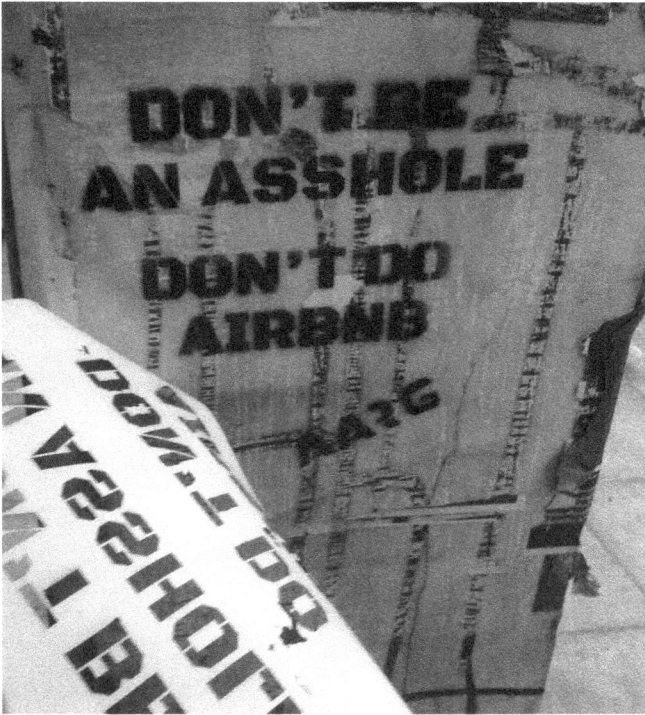

Figure 13.1: AARG anti-Airbnb campaign with stencil in Exarcheia. Copyright permission: AARG/Penny Travlou.

and Bernat, 2022). By matching the use and exchange value of goods and balancing pressures of offer and demand, these projects strengthened community relations. The vibrant grassroots movement that emerged in austerity-ridden Greece in the early 2010s planted the seeds of informal, solidarity economy infrastructures that would play a crucial role during the subsequent arrival of large numbers of migrants and refugees in the country (from 2015 onwards). It is worth noting that, by early 2015, the grassroots solidarity movement was internationalized as activists from abroad came to Greece to experience first-hand the sociopolitical change that the newly elected government, headed by the radical left Syriza party, had promised to foster, and the response of the anarchist/antiauthoritarian movement to these changes.

Although AARG's original scope was anti-gentrification actions, it soon focused on the impact of short-let accommodation in Exarcheia. One of its key actions was to map the Airbnb apartments in the area as a tool for understanding how the platform reshapes the housing market, produces a shortage of available and affordable rental properties and, thus, affects local residents. The research carried out by AARG members revealed the close correlation between the increase in the number of Airbnb flats and evictions. A case that illustrates this was that of an elderly tenant who had rented a flat in Exarcheia for more than 20 years. The tenant was asked by the new landlord – an international real estate company – to vacate the place within 15 days as they were planning to renovate it and convert it to short-let accommodation. To prevent the tenant's eviction, AARG organized an anti-eviction campaign and offered legal support. The campaign attracted local and foreign media coverage. As a result, the new landlord, apprehensive of further negative publicity, permitted the tenant to remain in the property for a longer period. Cases like this, nonetheless, where local residents are forced to leave their homes with only a short notice, have become more common in Exarcheia and other neighbourhoods in Athens recently. The lack of a housing bill that protects the rights of tenants has obviously contributed to this situation (see Figure 13.2).

To make matters worse, during the Covid-19 pandemic, rents in a number of Athens' central neighbourhoods increased despite the measures announced by the conservative government to mitigate hardship. In response to this, AARG joined the Rent Strike 2020 campaign organized by the International Tenant Solidarity Network (from the US, UK, Spain, Italy, Portugal, Germany, Netherlands) and the local Initiative for Housing Action and Solidarity to resist the housing crisis during the pandemic (Travlou, 2021). The network had online assemblies to first plan an international day of action on social media and then discuss actions at local level to demand a rent freeze. 'Through these assemblies, we became aware of how national lockdowns and neoliberal policies were conflated into a catastrophic housing crisis worldwide' (Travlou, 2021: 71). Although the campaign was successful in a number of cities in the US (about two million rents and mortgages paused in San Francisco and New York in 2020) and in the UK (the Scottish Government banned all evictions following the Living Rent

Figure 13.2: An anti-gentrification campaign organized by AARG. Slogan on banner: 'Our neighbourhoods are not a commodity for your profit. STOP gentrification and Airbnb.' Copyright permission: author/Penny Travlou.

campaign), in Greece it did not manage to achieve a wider resonance beyond the network of housing activists. As part of this campaign, AARG demanded the suspension of all evictions and house repossessions, the immediate closure of refugee camps, the decriminalization of housing squats and the expropriation of hotels and Airbnb flats to house homeless and those in need of housing during the pandemic. By the end of the second lockdown in May 2021, Nosotros Free Social Space – the venue hosting AARG's assemblies and events – was embroiled in a dispute with the building's owners, who wanted an increase in rent. At the end of the summer, Nosotros closed down amid rumours that the owners wanted to sell the property to real estate investors. Nosotros and AARG members were concerned that this building – a landmark for Athens' anti-authoritarian movement – would be converted to a boutique hotel or short-let accommodation.

The ethnographic work with AARG identified the issue – common with activist groups – of resource shortage and dependence on relational infrastructures. It is very difficult to respond promptly to the changes that happen at a neighbourhood level, especially when this response places AARG against aterritorial digital platforms such as Airbnb. Yet, in the two years of its operation, AARG has organized a number of events and actions at the local level that brought together local residents, activists and academics. AARG's organization is based on regular open assemblies. These alone require a level of infrastructure and planning that can slow down AARG's activity. An additional challenge that AARG as a self-organized activist group has to overcome is the use of communication technologies. The different levels of digital literacy within the group made communication and the organization of specific actions and events (e.g. hybrid roundtables with invited speakers from abroad participating via digital platforms) difficult. These challenges were accentuated during the Covid-19 lockdown, when the assemblies had to move entirely online.

These issues made it difficult for AARG to keep pace with the aggressive changes in Exarcheia, where the housing crisis has deepened even further for all the aforementioned reasons and resulted in what the group considers 'displacement' of local residents. Stemming from an anti-authoritarian political discourse and praxis, AARG also rejects the authority of the state and hence is not pursuing change in the legal framework that could regulate housing. For the group, the solution lies in direct action at neighbourhood level and in dialogue with the local communities.

Recognizing the unprecedented health crisis and its impact on the most vulnerable, AARG together with members of Nosotros Free Social Space set up Kropotkin-19, a mutual aid initiative based on solidarity economy and relational infrastructures. 'As a (local) network of care and solidarity', Kropotkin-19 provided food, essential goods and legal advice to those most in need (i.e. refugees and migrants including mothers with toddlers, unemployed, elderly) (Travlou, 2021: 75). On the one hand, AARG was faced with the challenge of fighting an uneven struggle against Airbnb; on the other hand, it successfully mobilized to provide assistance fast and efficiently to those in need across the city (see Figure 13.3).

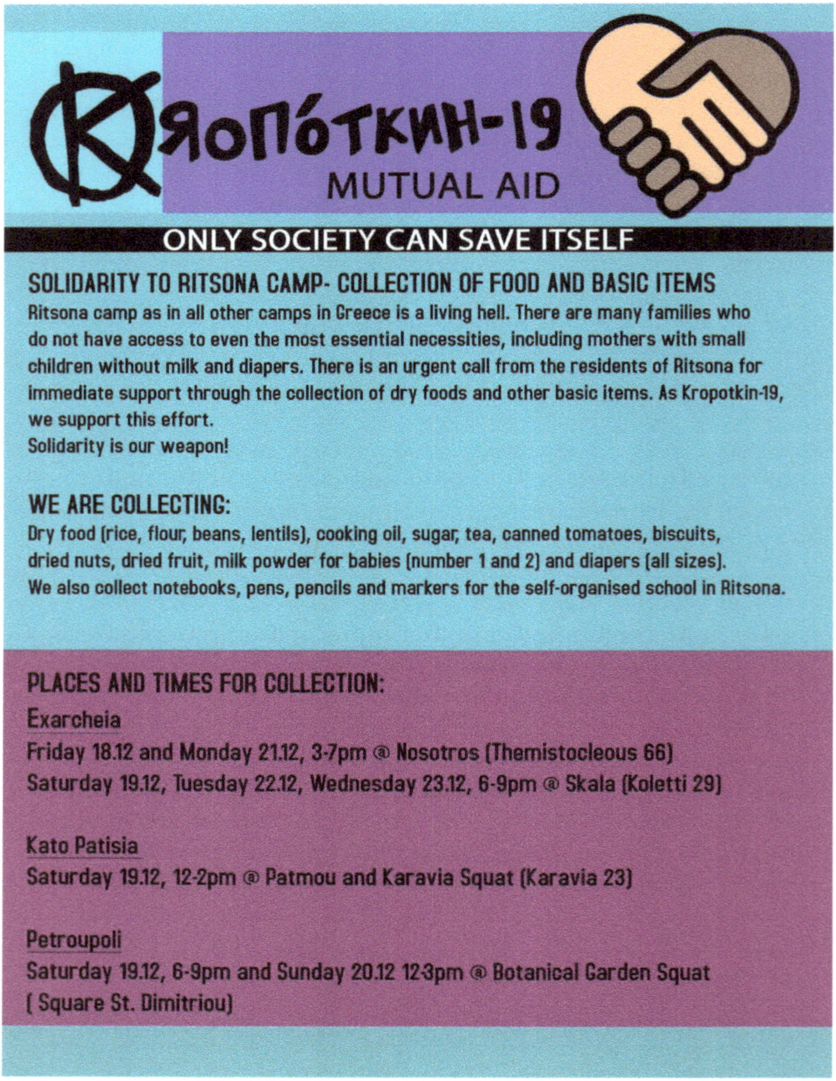

Figure 13.3: Kropotkin-19 Mutual Aid Group: Collection of food and other basic necessities for a refugee camp near Athens. Copyright permission: Kropotkin-19/Penny Travlou.

Discussion

In Athens, as in many metropolitan areas around the globe, the two 'extreme' and contrasting sides of the sharing/collaborative economy coexist, each enabling processes that involve competing sets of actors, networks, political and economic visions and goals, while leading to differentiated effects on the urban environment and creating diversified socio-economic, political and cultural ecosystems. The case of Exarcheia and the emergence of, on the one hand and through digitally mediated STRs, exploitative relations that reproduce and aggravate capitalist conditions of production and consumption without involving gestures of sharing and collaboration and, on the other hand, networks of solidarity, care and support that involve the sharing of goods, resources, physical spaces and infrastructure while being on the borderline of mainstream socio-economic practices, renders this gap evident.

In this frame, the question arises as to which actors and networks are ultimately entitled to be considered agents that foster meaningful and socially beneficial transformations in the fields of production, consumption and social reproduction in contemporary urban contexts through practices of sharing and collaboration. In both academic and policy debates, small but impactful initiatives and networks that are proposing and realizing alternative ways of reorganizing labour, welfare provision, production and consumption channels and, more broadly, social reproduction and everyday life remain largely neglected, while large, for-profit companies are solely 'entitled' to be considered as agents of collaboration (as well as innovation and entrepreneurship). Given the fact that most activities that fall within the description of sharing/collaborative economy are in a state of limbo between these two extremes, as they are often rooted in social movements while at the same time interacting with circuits of the market, it is crucial that meaningful and socially transformative sharing/collaborative practices are further explored and also supported through both formal and informal institutionalizations and relevant policy frameworks.

Additional crucial issues within the current sharing/collaborative economy debates concern the response of social movements to spatially diffused processes facilitated by platform capitalism, which have severe impacts on specific local settings, as well as the capacities and potentials of social and workers' movements to reappropriate digital tools and infrastructure towards their empowerment. Concerning the former issue, it becomes more and more evident that 'traditional' actions of protest on the neighbourhood level cannot solely create the conditions for the subversion of the direct and indirect implications of platform capitalism for various fields (e.g. housing, labour), given the global topologies of relevant networks. Instead, further actions will create new spaces for asserting claims concerning the strengthening, adaptation and extension of relevant regulations to activities that develop in the frame of the platform economy. Concerning the latter, relevant initiatives are already taking place in the form of platform cooperatives, hackerspaces, digital commons and other grassroots initiatives and networks that operate in the digital realm. Further attempts and experimentations that promote alternative, bottom-up reconfigurations of labour, production and consumption can operate as paradigm shifts on the antipodes of platform capitalism. Moreover, within the recent pandemic outbreak and, as mobility restrictions applied in most cities around the globe, solidarity movements rapidly incorporated digital means and tools towards establishing communication channels among participants, promoting and disseminating their actions, and acquiring resources and finance. Thus, the ways in which more 'traditional' grassroots initiatives and networks enrich and expand their digital and virtual components are of great interest for future research within the debates of bottom-up sharing and collaborative networks.

Conclusion

In this chapter, by combining their distinct ethnographic research projects in Athens, the two authors have provided a multifaceted view of collaborative economy: from sharing to caring practices. As presented earlier in the chapter, digitally mediated short-rentals such as those listed on the Airbnb platform offered at first new opportunities for small-scale entrepreneurship and economic stability to people affected by the financial crisis during the first part of the 2010s. By the mid-2010s, larger companies, funds and investors had entered the STR market, where neoliberal state policies on housing made it easier for them to invest in local properties, pushing out of any profit-making the smaller businesses and individual short-let accommodation owners. At the same time, the prices of renting and/or buying property have increased to such a level that low-income tenants couldn't afford to live in a number of central neighbourhoods that have turned into gentrified tourist enclaves. Apparently, while tourism is recognized (by both the former and current governments) as one of the key sectors of the economy to help the country out of the financial crisis, it has been linked to a number of other issues such as those presented in this chapter and specifically the housing crisis in the centre of Athens. The latter has been addressed as a counter-argument within local activist circles, suggesting that economic prosperity through tourism is a fallacy and its real consequences are shown in local neighbourhoods via mass touristification, aggressive gentrification, and airbnbization resulting to residents' displacement (i.e. a rise in the number of housing evictions, auctions and repossessions). The fundamental question to raise here is twofold: what the real impact of digital platforms such as Airbnb is on local communities, and who shares within this model of sharing economy that by now is mostly associated with platform capitalism.

Solidarity and the care economy lie on the opposite side of the spectrum of collaborative economy. This has been manifested in various forms in Athens since the early 2010s, responding to the various crises that impacted the city (and the country at large). The ethnographic study of the anti-gentrification activist group AARG in Athens has revealed how the solidarity networks that emerged within the austerity crisis have quickly responded to later crises such as the refugee, housing and recently health crises. Solidarity, self-organization and affective (relational) infrastructures as manifested within the local activist social movements offered alternative ways of doing through commoning and caring practices. AARG responded to the unprecedented housing crisis as experienced in the central neighbourhood of Exarcheia. As activists with close links to Exarcheia, AARG's members saw the changes in their neighbourhood that came with gentrification and touristification. Their struggle against aterritorial digital platforms (i.e., Airbnb), real estate funds and investors has been uneven: it has proved too difficult to fight against a transglobal business. On the other hand, they successfully organized, at a local level, mutual aid initiatives to help those in need during the pandemic and anti-eviction campaigns to support their neighbours from losing their homes. These actions are representative of a much wider understanding of an economy of care. Building on the case of Exarcheia, and as digital mediations are rapidly incorporated in most aspects of cities' economic, social and political life, tensions among practices that are currently commonly framed as part of the 'sharing economy' notion are expected to escalate, bringing out the contradictory visions of engaged individual and collective actors.

Acknowledgements

Dimitris Pettas has received funding from the European Union's Horizon 2020 research and innovation program under the Marie Skłodowska-Curie grant agreement No 895305.

Penny Travlou would like to thank the members of the activist group AARG for their input on the issues of gentrification and touristification in the neighbourhood of Exarcheia.

References

Arampatzi, A. 2017 The spatiality of counter-austerity politics in Athens, Greece: Emergent 'urban solidarity spaces'. *Urban Studies*, Vol. 54(9): 2155–2171.

Bagayogo, F.F., Lepage, A., Denis, J.L., Lamothe, L., Lapointe, L. and Vedel, I. 2016 Grassroots inter-professional networks: The case of organizing care for older cancer patients. *Journal of Health Organization and Management*, Vol. 30(6), 971–984.

Balampanidis, D., Maloutas, T., Papatzani, E. and Pettas, D. 2021 Informal urban regeneration as a way out of the crisis? Airbnb in Athens and its effects on space and society. *Urban Research & Practice*, Vol. 14(3): 223–242.

Belk, R. 2007 Why not share rather than own? *Annals of the American Academy of Political and Social Science*, Vol. 611(1), 126–140.

Boffey, D. 2019 Airbnb should be seen as a digital service provider, ECJ advised. *The Guardian*, 30 April 2019. Available at https://www.theguardian.com /technology/2019/apr/30/airbnb-should-be-seen-as-a-digital-service -provider-ecj-advised

Brousseau, F., Metcalf, J. and Yu, M. 2015 *Analysis of the impacts of short term rentals on housing.* San Francisco, CA: City and County of San Francisco.

Cabot, H. 2016 'Contagious' solidarity: Reconfiguring care and citizenship in Greece's social clinics. *Social Anthropology*, Vol. 24(2): 152–166.

Cansoy, M. and Schor, J.B. 2017 *Who gets to share in the sharing economy: Racial discrimination on Airbnb.* Working paper, Boston College.

Chatterton, P. and Pusey, A. 2019 Beyond capitalist enclosure, commodification and alienation: Postcapitalist praxis as commons, social production and useful doing. *Progress in Human Geography*. DOI: https://doi.org /10.1177/0309132518821173.

Dalla Costa, M. and James, S. 1975 *The power of women and the subversion of the community.* London: Butler and Tanner.

Da Silva, C. and Dickson, J. 2017 Graffiti city: The rise of street art in Athens. *The Independent*, 15 September. https://www.independent.co.uk/arts-enter tainment/photography/athens-greece-graffiti-city-street-art-financial-crisis -a7947506.html

Daskalaki, M., Fotaki, M. and Sotiropoulou, I. 2019 Performing values practices and grassroots organizing: The case of solidarity economy initiatives in Greece. *Organizational Studies*, Vol. 40(11), 1741–1765.

Drahokoupil, J. and Jespen, M. 2017 The digital economy and its implications for labour. 1. The platform economy. *Transfer*, Vol. 23(2), 103–119.

Edelman, B.G., Luca, M. and Svirsky, D. 2015 Racial discrimination in the sharing economy: Evidence from a field experiment. *American Economic Journal: Applied Economics.* http://www.benedelman.org/publications/airbnb -guest-discrimination-2016-09-16.pdf

European Data Journalism Network. (2021, 8 September). Ten graphs to understand the Greek crisis. https://www.europeandatajournalism.eu/eng/News /Data-news/Ten-graphs-to-understand-the-Greek-crisis.

Federici, S. and Linebaugh, P. 2018 *Re-enchanting the world: Feminism and the politics of the commons.* Oakland, CA: PM Press.

Fraser, N. 1992 Rethinking the public sphere: A contribution to the critique of actually existing democracy. In C. Calhoun (Ed.), *Habermas and the public sphere.* Cambridge, MA: MIT Press, 109–141.

Fraser, N. 2009 Feminism, capitalism and the cunning of history. *New Left Review*, Vol. 56, 97–117.

Frenken, K. and Schor, J. 2017 Putting the sharing economy into perspective. *Environmental Innovation and Societal Transitions*, Vol. 23, 3–10.

Gibson-Graham, J.K. 1996 *The end of capitalism (as we knew it): A feminist critique of political economy*. Oxford: Blackwell Publishers.

Gorenflo, N. 2015 How platform coops can beat death stars like Uber to create a real sharing economy. http://www.shareable.net/blog/how-platform -coops-can-beatdeath-stars-like-uber-to-create-a-real-sharingeconomy.

Grove, K. and Fischer, D. 2006 'Doing collaboration': The process of constructing an educational community in an urban elementary school. *Ethnography and Education*, Vol. 1(1), 53–66.

Hadjimichalis, C. 2013 From streets and squares to radical political emancipation? Resistance lessons from Athens during the Crisis. *Human Geography*, Vol. 6(2), 116–136.

Henley, J. 2015 Greece's solidarity movement: 'It's a whole new model – and it's working'. *The Guardian*, 23 January. https://www.theguardian.com/world /2015/jan/23/greece-solidarity-movement-cooperatives-syriza

Kalamar, A. 2013 Sharewashing is the new greenwashing. OpEdNews, 13 May. https://www.opednews.com/articles/Sharewashing-is-the-New-Gr-by -Anthony-Kalamar-130513-834.html

Kitsantonis, N. 2017 Anarchists fill services void left by faltering Greek governance. *The New York Times*, 22 May. https://www.nytimes.com/2017/05/22 /world/europe/greece-athens-anarchy-austerity.html

Lee, D. 2016 How Airbnb short-term rentals exacerbate Los Angeles's affordable housing crisis: Analysis and policy recommendations. *Harvard Law & Policy Review*, Vol. 10(1), 229–254.

Lefebvre, H. 1996 *Writings on cities*. Cambridge, MA: Wiley-Blackwell.

Margariti, E. and Travlou, P. 2018 Sharing within a city in crisis: Two ICTs-supported P2P economic networks in Thessaloniki, Northern Greece. *International Journal of Electronic Governance*, Vol. 10(2): 196–217.

Martin, C.J. 2016 The sharing economy: A pathway to sustainability or a nightmarish form of neoliberal capitalism? *Ecological Economics*, Vol. 121, 149–159.

Morozov, E. 2013 *The 'sharing economy' undermines workers' rights*. http:// evgenymorozov.tumblr.com/post/64038831400/the-sharing-economyun dermines-workers-rights.

Pettas, D., Avdikos, V., Iliopoulou, E. and Karavasili, I. 2021 'Insurrection is not a spectacle': Experiencing and contesting touristification in Exarcheia, Athens. *Urban Geography*. DOI: https://doi.org/10.1080/02723638.2021.1888521.

Rakopoulos, T. 2014 Resonance of solidarity: Meanings of a local concept in anti-austerity Greece. *Journal of Modern Greek Studies*, Vol. 32: 95–119.

Rowe, P.C. 2017 Beyond Uber and Airbnb: The social economy of collaborative consumption. *Social Media + Society*. DOI: https://doi.org/10.1177/205630 5117706784journals.sagepub.com/home/sms.

Santala, I. and McGuirk P. 2019 Sharing cities: Creating space and practice for new urban agency, capacities and subjectivities. *Community Development*, Vol. 50(4), 440–459.

Scholz, T. 2016 *Platform cooperativism: Challenging the corporate sharing economy*. New York: Rosa Luxemburg Stiftung.

Schor, J. 2014 *Debating the sharing economy*. Great Transition Initiative. http://greattransition.org/publication/debating-the-sharing-economy.

Shade, L.R. 2018 Hop to it in the gig economy: The sharing economy and neo-liberal feminism. *International Journal of Media & Cultural Politics*, Vol. 14(1), 35–54.

Skopeliti, C. 2018 How Airbnb is changing the face of Athens, arguably for the worse. *Shout Out UK*, 16 October. https://www.shoutoutuk.org/2018/10/16/how-airbnb-is-changing-the-face-of-athens-arguably-for-the-worse/

Smith, A. and Stirling, A. 2018 Innovation, sustainability and democracy: An analysis of grassroots contributions. *Journal of Self-Governance and Management Economics*. DOI: https://doi.org/10.22381/JSME6120183.

Sooke, A. 2017 Can Athens become Europe's new arts capital? *BBC*, 9 May. https://www.bbc.com/culture/article/20170509-can-athens-become-europes-new-arts-capital

Statista, D. 2021 *Greece: Youth unemployment rate from 1999 to 2019*. https://www.statista.com/statistics/812053/youth-unemployment-rate-in-greece/.

Travlou, P. 2021 Kropotkin-19: A mutual aid response to COVID-19 in Athens. *Design and Culture*, Vol. 13(1): 65–78.

Travlou, P. and Bernat, A. 2022 Solidarity and care economy in times of 'crisis': A view from Greece and Hungary between 2015 and 2020. In V. Česnuitytė, A. Klimczuk, C. Miguel and G. Avram (eds), *The sharing economy in Europe: developments, practices, and contradictions*. London: Palgrave Macmillan (forthcoming).

Wachsmuth, D. and Weisler, A. 2018 Airbnb and the rent gap: Gentrification through the sharing economy. *Environment and Planning A: Economy and Space*. DOI: https://doi.org/10.1177/0308518X18778038.

Walker, E.T. 2015 Beyond the rhetoric of the 'sharing economy'. *Contexts*, Vol. 14(1), 15–17.